William Holmes, John Warner Barber

Religious Emblems

Being a Series of Emblematic Engravings, with Written Explanations, Miscellaneous Observations and Religious Reflections, Designed to Illustrate Divine Truth

William Holmes, John Warner Barber

Religious Emblems
Being a Series of Emblematic Engravings, with Written Explanations, Miscellaneous Observations and Religious Reflections, Designed to Illustrate Divine Truth

ISBN/EAN: 9783337259082

Printed in Europe, USA, Canada, Australia, Japan

Cover: Foto ©Andreas Hilbeck / pixelio.de

More available books at **www.hansebooks.com**

RELIGIOUS EMBLEMS:

BEING A SERIES OF

EMBLEMATIC ENGRAVINGS,

WITH

WRITTEN EXPLANATIONS, MISCELLANEOUS OBSERVATIONS,

AND

RELIGIOUS REFLECTIONS,

DESIGNED TO ILLUSTRATE

DIVINE TRUTH,

IN ACCORDANCE WITH THE CARDINAL PRINCIPLES OF

CHRISTIANITY.

I have used similitudes. Hosea, 12 chap., 10 v.

BY WILLIAM HOLMES,
MINISTER OF THE GOSPEL; AND
JOHN W. BARBER,
AUTHOR OF "THE ELEMENTS OF GENERAL HISTORY," ETC.

NEW YORK:
GEO. F. TUTTLE, PUBLISHER,
No. 147 FULTON STREET.
1860.

ENTERED
ACCORDING TO THE ACT OF CONGRESS, IN THE YEAR 1848,
BY JOHN W. BARBER,
IN THE OFFICE OF THE CLERK OF THE DISTRICT COURT OF
CONNECTICUT.

PREFACE.

The art of communicating truth to the mind by emblems, parables, and other similitudes, is of the remotest antiquity. It is, in fact, a mode which the Divine Being often uses to convey instruction to his creatures. Of course it must be admitted to be a legitimate method of communicating instruction sanctioned by the highest possible authority.

The object of the authors of this work is to give to the public a book of emblems, with suitable explanations, observations, and reflections, the tone or standard of which shall be in accordance with the great cardinal principles of the Christian religion. Works of a somewhat similar kind have occasionally appeared, some of which, though valuable, yet the standard of morality which they apparently set forth, is too vague and ill-defined, or too far below what ought to be the standard of those professing Christianity. It has been our aim in the drawing of the cuts, to avoid all the monstrosity connected with heathen mythology, or any thing overstrained or uncouth in appearance. We have also endeavored to produce a work, the tone or morality of which shall be in accordance with Christian principles.

Many portions of divine truth are forcibly illustrated by similitudes. The Prodigal Son, the Parable of the Sower, the Good Samaritan, the Good Shepherd, and many other parables recorded in sacred writ are beautiful demonstrations of this truth. These illustrations are, in reality, pictures to the mind, as the pictorial representations in this work are to the eye. They therefore have a double advantage over mere precept, speaking not only to the mind, but also to the eye, in an ocular language, singularly emphatic and universally intelligible.

A work of this kind was suggested upwards of twenty years since, and a few preliminary steps in its preparation were at that time taken; but no favorable opportunity has since appeared to bring it into a form proper for publication, till the assistance of the Rev. William Holmes was procured. The drawings, and the engraving of the cuts, were for the most part executed by the writer of the preface; the work itself is written by Mr. Holmes.

J. W. Barber.

New Haven, Con., Dec. 1845.

It is with a degree of diffidence that the writer of the following pages presents them to the public. This arises from the responsibility assumed by every one who attempts to convey divine truth to his fellow-beings about him, either orally or by the press. The method of communicating instruction adopted in this publication, is somewhat different from the usual form, consequently more caution is necessary, lest imperfect or erroneous impressions be given.

Some of the most important subjects that can command the attention of mankind, have passed in review before the writer. The short space allotted to each, would allow only of a few brief observations thereon. In these he has aimed to adhere to the truth, as it is in Jesus. With regard to the propriety of employing pictorial representations for the purpose of conveying instruction, it is presumed that there is but one opinion, as the eye sends impressions home to the soul more readily, more forcibly, and more permanently, than any other of the senses.

W. Holmes.

New Haven, Dec., 1845.

CONTENTS.

	Page		Page
True and False Principles,	7	The Threefold Demon, or Envy, Hatred, and Malice,	82
Truth,	10	Christian Faith, or Religion,	85
Symbols of Faith,	13	Hope,	88
The Way of Holiness,	16	Brotherly Kindness,	91
The Weight of God's Word,	19	Divine Love and Justice,	94
The Christian Race,	22	Reconciliation,	97
Salvation,	25	Adoption,	100
The Christian Soldier,	28	Spiritual Pride,	103
The Strait or Narrow Gate,	31	Hypocrisy,	106
Double-mindedness,	34	Slander and Backbiting,	109
The House founded on a Rock,	37	The Tree of Evil,	112
Self-Confidence,	40	Anger, or Madness,	115
The Sun of Truth,	43	Repentance,	118
Light in Darkness,	46	Fearless and Fearful,	121
The Worldling,	49	The Two Worldlings,	124
The Cross-Bearer,	52	Faith and Works,	127
Worldly Honor,	55	Precipitation,	130
Heavenly Desire,	58	Vain Pursuits,	133
The Fatal Current,	61	Danger of Greatness,	136
Salvation by Faith,	64	Guilt,	139
Simplicity, or Want of Understanding,	67	Patience and Long-suffering,	142
The Persecuted Christian,	70	Temptation,	145
The Soul in Bondage,	73	Prudence and Foresight,	148
The Danger of Self-Indulgence,	76	Fortitude and Constancy,	151
		The Fast-anchored Ship,	154
Carnal Security,	79	Unanimity,	157

But the word of the Lord endureth forever. 1 Pet. i. 25. ——— *Heaven and earth shall pass away, but my words shall not pass away.* Matt. xxiv. 35.

TRUE AND FALSE PRINCIPLES.

Tis thus amid the arctic regions, rise,
The Iceberg's turrets glittering in the skies,
Like some cathedral Gothic built, it rides,
Borne by the winds, and ever-shifting tides:
All shapes fantastic soon the phantom wears,
A palace now, and now a ship appears:
At length it drifts towards some southern shore,
When lo! 'tis vanish'd, and is seen no more.
  Not so the Rock that rears its ancient head,
Its deep foundation's laid in ocean's bed;
All change resists, unalter'd is its form
Amid the sunshine, and amid the storm,
Unmoved it stands, and still 'twill stand secure,
Long as the moon, and as the sun endure.

The Iceberg lifts its towering summit to the clouds, sparkling and dazzling, like a group of temples overlaid with silver. Its crystalline magnicence is bewildering; it forms one of the most splendid objects that the mariner meets with in the northern seas, and at the same time one of the most dangerous. It is a floating mass without foundation; winds, waves, and currents bear it along in all directions. It assumes the most fantastic shapes imaginable: sometimes it looks like mountains piled on mountains; then temples, palaces, and ships are seen by turns; then again, cathedrals of every order of architecture appear to the eye of the wondering beholder. After awhile it drifts out of the high latitudes into milder climes. It is carried towards the southern shores, the sun pours its burning rays upon the mammoth temple, turret after turret, spire after spire disappear, until the whole has dissolved. Its glory has departed.

How very different is the nature and destiny of the Rock that is seen lifting its time-worn head above the surrounding waves! It is probably as old as time itself; it retains its ancient position; its foundations take hold of the world; it is marked in the charts, men always know where to find it, and are therefore not endangered by it. Changing the form of the element that surrounds it, itself unchanged, the summer's sun and winter's storm alike pass harmlessly by it. It is one of the everlasting hills, it must abide forever.

The engraving is an emblem of True and False Principles. False principles are represented by the Iceberg. Like the iceberg, they are without a foundation; however specious, brilliant, and fascinating their appearance, they have no solidity. Like it, too, they are ever-changing: their form receives its various impression from the ever-fluctuating speculations of mankind, and from the power and influence of the times. Like it, they are cold and cheerless to the soul, nipping all its budding prospects, cramping all its mighty powers. Like the iceberg, also, false principles will melt away before the burning sun of truth, and pass into oblivion. *It will not do to trust in them.* Who would make a dwelling-house of the transitory iceberg?

It is not so with true principles; although they may appear somewhat homely at first sight, yet the more they are contemplated the more they will be admired. Like the Rock, their foundations are laid broad and deep. The principles of truth rest on the throne of God, they are as ancient as eternity. Like the Rock, they may always be found. Are they not written in the *Holy Bible?* Like their Author, they are without variableness or shadow of turning, for,

"Firm as a Rock, God's Truth must stand,
When rolling years shall cease to move."

Semper idem—"Always the same"—is their motto. Like the Rock of Ages, true principles live when time shall be no more. As are the principles, so are all who trust in them, for "the righteous shall be had in everlasting remembrance."

Lord, who shall abide in thy tabernacle? He that speaketh truth in his heart. Ps. lv. 23. *Thy word is Truth.* John xvii. 17.

TRUTH.

Truth, glorious truth, of heavenly birth, and fair,
In simple majesty array'd, is there;
Her right hand holds the faithful mirror clear,
Where all things open as the light appear:
Her left, upon the sacred page reclines,
Where unadulterate truth resplendent shines;
The world's false mask she tramples down with scorn,
Adorn'd the most when she would least adorn.
As her own temple on the margin seen,
Stands forth reflected in the silvery stream;
So what by her is thought, or said, or done,
Appears conspicuous as the noonday sun;
Truth is the image of our God above,
That shines reflected in his sea of love.
All hail, bless'd Truth! thou daughter of the skies,
Reign thou on earth, and bid earth's sons arise;
Bid Virtue lead, and Justice hold the scale,
For thou art mighty, and wilt soon prevail.

TRUTH is represented in the drawing above in the person of an artless female. She is attired with simplicity. In her right hand she holds a mirror. As the mirror reflects objects that pass before it as they are, without addition, alteration, or diminution, so Truth presents every thing just as it is. The left hand rests on the Holy Bible. This is to show that it is from thence she derives the principles which regulate her conduct, the source of unadulterated truth to mankind. She is seen trampling a mask beneath her feet. It is the mask of hypocrisy, which she rejects with scorn, as being utterly at variance with her principles and feelings. In the background stands the Temple of Truth, the image of which is plainly reflected by the clear, placid stream that glides before it.

Truth, in an evangelical sense, is all-important. It alone will give character to an individual, more than all other qualities put together. It is of itself a rich inheritance, of more worth than mines of silver and gold. It is more ennobling than the highest titles conferred by princes. Everybody loves to be respected, but an individual to be loved and respected must be *known*. He only can be *known* who speaks the truth from his heart, and acts the truth in his life. We may guess at others, but as we do not know we cannot respect them, for like pirates they oftentimes sail under false colors.

"Nothing is beautiful except Truth," is a maxim of the French, although it has been most deplorably neglected. Nevertheless, the sentiment is correct. Truth is glorious wherever found; Jesus, who is "*the truth*," is the altogether lovely, and the fairest among ten thousand. Truth is the glory of youth, and the diadem of the aged. But Truth is *essential* to happiness, both in this world and also in the next. For "what man is he that desireth life, and loveth many days that he may see good? Keep thy *tongue* from evil, and thy lips from speaking guile." Lord, who shall dwell in thy holy hill? He that "speaketh the truth." It is related of Cyrus, that, when asked what was the first thing he learned, he replied, "*To tell the truth.*" Cyrus must have been very fortunate in having such good instructors. Lord Chesterfield would have instructed him differently.

In the days of Daniel, (as the tradition says,) the wise men were ordered by the king to declare what was the strongest thing on earth. Each man brought in his answers; one said *wine* was the strongest, another mentioned *women;* Daniel declared that TRUTH was the most powerful, which answer pleased the king, and the palm of victory was decreed to Daniel.

"Seize, then, on truth where'er 'tis found,
 Among your friends, among your foes;
On Christian or on heathen ground,
 The plant's divine where'er it grows."

Let not mercy and truth forsake thee; bind them about thy neck; write them upon the table of thine heart: so shalt thou find favor and good understanding in the sight of God and man. *Prov.* iii. 3.

The lip of truth shall be established forever: but a lying tongue is but for a moment. *Prov.* xii. 19.

Buy the truth and sell it not. *Prov.* xxii. 23. Lie not against the truth. *James* iii. 11. Speak ye every man the truth to his neighbor; execute the judgment of truth. *Zech.* viii. 16.

Lying lips are an abomination to the Lord; but they that deal truly are his delight. *Prov.* xii. 23.

Till we all come in the unity of the Faith. Ephes. iv. 13.

SYMBOLS OF CHRISTIAN FAITH.

See on the right, all glorious *Hope* doth stand,
And gives to heavenly *Truth* the plighted hand:
With Seraph's wings out-spread, *Love* stands between:
And binds their hearts with his celestial chain.
These are *Faith's* emblems;—These its Parents three:
To produce Faith, *Hope, Truth,* and *Love* agree.

CHRISTIAN Faith is represented above, by a union of Truth, Hope, and Love. The hope of heaven is represented by the apostle Paul as the anchor of the soul, consequently Hope is usually depicted leaning on an anchor. She holds Truth by the hand, showing that they must be in close alliance. Truth holds in her hand the Holy Bible as a mirror, whereby sinful men can see the deformity of their hearts. With her right hand, she receives the overtures of Hope; she tramples under her feet the *mask* of Hypocrisy; simple and unadorned, she rejects the cloak of dissimulation, and casts aside all concealment. Love holds the middle place, and strengthens the union subsisting between Hope and Truth. Divine Love is drawn with wings to represent her heavenly origin.

Faith is both created and preserved by Hope, Truth, and Love. This Triad constitutes its efficient cause. Truth is indeed the mother of Faith. Hope assists in its creation, by its expectations and desires; Love nourishes and reconciles, and thus contributes to lay a foundation for Faith.

True faith, as represented in the Scriptures, is always connected with a "good hope through grace." The truths of God's word form the only proper objects for its exercise. Without Love, there can be no good works; and "without works faith is dead." Christian Faith, as described above, is distinguished from the faith of devils, who are said to "believe and tremble" because they have no *hope;* and from the faith of wicked men, who "*love* not the Lord Jesus Christ," and who are consequently "accursed;" and from the faith of the carnal professor, who has sold the *truth* and has pleasure in unrighteousness.

The proper use of faith is to bring us to God, to enable us to obtain the promises contained in the word or truth of God. If Christ had not been moved by *love,* he would not have suffered; if he had not suffered, we should have had no promise of pardon; if we had no promises, we should have no *hope;* if we have no hope, we shall have no saving *faith* in the mercy of God. Christ is set forth a refuge for sinners, he saves all who flee for refuge to the *hope* set before them; but those only who believe in him, flee to him. Faith then is an instrument of salvation; "by grace are ye saved through Faith."

The sinner hears, and gives credence to the Faith of God: the terrors of the Almighty take fast hold upon him; his sins weigh him down to the dust: but hark! the voice of heavenly love is heard proclaiming: "Come unto me all ye that are weary and heavy laden, and I will give you rest." He looks upward, Hope springs up, he ventures on the Redeemer, "who justifies the ungodly;" his faith has saved him. It is counted to him for righteousness, and being justified by it, he has peace with God, through our Lord Jesus Christ.

A celebrated divine once gave his little child an illustration of the nature of Faith in the following manner. The child had a beautiful string of beads, with which she was much delighted. Her father spoke to her, saying, "Come, my child, throw those beautiful beads into the fire, and I will, in the course of a few days, give you something far more beautiful and valuable." The child looked up into the face of her father with astonishment: after looking for a time, and seeing he was in earnest, she cast her beautiful toys into the fire, and then burst into tears!—Here was Faith. The child believed her father spoke the *truth;* she expected, or had a *hope,* he would fulfil his promises; and confiding in his *Love,* she was willing to obey him though it cost her tears.

And an highway shall be there, and a way, and it shall be called The way of holiness; the unclean shall not pass over it. Isa. xxxv. 8.

THE WAY OF HOLINESS.

There is a place, a Holy place above,
Where Angels holy dwell in light and love:
There is a God, a Holy God who reigns,
And holy empire over all maintains;
There is a way, a holy way, whose road
The holy Pilgrim brings to heaven and God:
See! on that way the holy Pilgrim hies,
Nor doubts at last 'twill lead him to the skies.
With robes entire, and garments clean and white,
He walks with joy along the plains of light.
See! one has left the holy way divine,
His clothes are soiled, he wallows now with swine;
Alone, the Pilgrim on his pathway speeds,
And leaves th' apostate to his worldly deeds.

SEE where the way of Holiness stands cast up. It is strongly built and conspicuous to all beholders; a pilgrim is seen walking thereon triumphantly and secure; his garments are unsullied, and untorn. Down off the way is one wallowing in the mire, see how he grubs up the filthy lucre. His garments are rent, and soiled; the beastly swine are his chosen companions.

This is an emblem of Holiness, and of its professors. The upright conduct of the pious, is called, a "way," a "highway," and "*The way of Holiness.*" It is a way of safety, "No lion shall be there," and "the wayfaring man, though a fool, [illiterate] shall not err therein." The Pilgrim pursuing his journey, with his garments unsullied and untorn, denotes the Christian ' walking in all the commandments and ordinances of the Lord blameless." "The fine linen, clean and white, is the righteousness of the saints." The man among the swine, signifies an Apostate from God and Holiness; he has "left off to do good;" the love of the world has again taken possession of him; "he has turned as the dog to his vomit again, and as the sow that was washed to her wallowing in the mire."

Holiness in man consists in obedience to the divine commands—in loving God supremely—in loving our neighbor as ourselves. Man, by nature and by practice, is sinful, and sin is superlatively selfish. A selfishness pervades the heart, which is enmity against God. It is not subject to the law of God, neither indeed can be, consequently the love of God dwelleth not in the selfish heart.

Selfishness is the prolific source of every vice; giving birth to oppression, falsehood, injustice, and covetousness; producing outbreaks of the basest passions, such as, envy, wrath, malice, pride, revenge, which end in crimes of deepest guilt.

On the other hand, Holiness is boundlessly benevolent; it embraces God, it embraces the world. It gives to God the sincere worship of an undivided heart

It gives to man the generous activities of a useful life. The man of holiness is the almoner of a world. The Law of Jehovah is the proper standard of holiness; the Almighty himself the only proper model for study and imitation; therefore, of the man of Holiness it is said, "The law of God is in his heart, none of his steps shall slide." And hence it is written, "Be ye holy, for I am holy." Hence we may learn that the subject is one of great importance, since whatever we may possess beside, without holiness, no one shall see the Lord; it is the wedding garment which renders the guest welcome at the marriage-supper of the Lamb; it is the fine linen, clean and white, which is the righteousness of the saints. Thus it signifies a preparation for eternal glory.

Holiness and happiness are divine sisters; twins, always seen together. God has stamped the seal of his approbation on every thing approaching to innocence and purity; it is seen in nature—the roar of the lion, the fierce howling of the wolf is the language of disquietude and of blood, striking terror into the boldest heart; while the cooing of the turtle dove, the bleating of the fleecy lamb, speak the language of innocence and peace. We may visit the mansions of the rich, the castles of the powerful, or the palaces of kings, yet if holiness be wanting, in vain do we search for happiness. It is not there.

We may visit the abodes of the poor, the cottage of the afflicted, the hovel of the dying. If we find the inmates in possession of holiness, there also we find happiness; poverty does not expel her, affliction does not drive her away, death even cannot pronounce a divorce; united are they in life, undivided in death, inseparable to all eternity.

We have also a more sure word of prophecy. 2 Pet. I. 9.

THE WEIGHT OF GOD'S WORD

Look where the impartial balance hangs on high,
The Almighty's word against weak man's to try;
Huge folios rare, and many a bulky bale,
Are brought, and laid upon the even scale:
Of "Council's" records many a tome is sent,
From the great Nicean, down to that of Trent;
"Creeds," "'isms," creatures of the human thought,
Ancient and modern, are together brought;
And "Fathers" numerous, a learned line
From Pseudo-Barnabas to Augustine;
The Bible now, of Protestants the pride,
Is placed alone upon the other side:
Creeds, Councils, Fathers, 'isms, twenty ream,
Fly up like chaff, and straightway kick the beam.

THE above engraving represents a pair of scales of equal balance, one side of which is loaded with books, packages, and parchments. Here are the minutes of eighteen general councils, beginning with that held in Nice, in the year of our Lord 325, and ending with that of Trent, which began in the year 1545, and closed in 1563, with many others. There are also the writings of the "Fathers," from those ascribed to Barnabas, but considered spurious, downward. Then there are Creeds without number, both of ancient and modern date; next follow the various isms of the day, that set themselves up against the word of God. These are all placed on one scale; the Bible is now brought and placed on the other, when lo! "Creeds, Councils, Fathers, and 'isms" are but as the dust of the balance. Lighter than vanity, they fly up and kick the beam; one Bible outweighs them all.

This emblem is designed to show the authority of the Bible over the doctrines and commandments of men. When the lion roars, the beasts of the forests keep silence; when Jehovah speaks, the inhabitants of the world ought to stand in awe. During the space of fifteen hundred years, God uttered His voice in the ears of the children of men. He has declared his will, and sanctioned such revelation by the repeated manifestations of his almighty power. He employed holy men as the authorized recorders of his laws; and closed the whole with the denouncement of a curse against all who should add to, or diminish therefrom.

Notwithstanding this, there have been men in all ages who have set up their will against that of the great Jehovah. They have made a record of the same, forbidding what God has commanded, and ordaining what God has prohibited. Thus, by their traditions, they make void the laws of the Eternal. What folly is this! what blasphemy! what rebellion! The words of the Lord are tried, pure, and everlasting; those of man are short weight, corrupt, and are passing away. By the laws of God, not by the opinions of men, we shall be judged at the last day.

Terribly has the curse fallen upon those who have established human opinions in opposition to the Word of God; witness the Jews, who, since the fatal overthrow of their city, have been vagabonds over all the face of the earth. Witness the poverty ignorance, and misery of those parts of the world where human creeds prevail, and where the Bible is rejected; yea, witness in the case of every man who substitutes his will for God's. To the law and to the testimony, if they speak not according to this word, it is because there is no light in them.

All scripture is given by inspiration of God, and is profitable for doctrine, for reproof, for correction, for instruction in righteousness. *2 Tim.* iii. 16.

Search the Scriptures. *Matt.* xxii. 29.

We thank God without ceasing, because when ye received the word of God which ye heard of us, ye received it not as the word of men, but as it is of truth, the word of God. 1 *Thess.* ii. 13.

Ye shall not add unto the word which I command you, neither shall ye diminish aught from it. *Deut.* iv. 2.

If any man shall add unto these things, God shall add unto him the plagues that are written in this book. *Rev.* xxi. 18.

So run that ye may obtain. 1 Cor. ix, 24.

THE CHRISTIAN RACE.

Behold! the race-course here before us lies;
See! many running for the glorious prize;
Some sweat and toil, and maugre all their pains,
Small is their progress, smaller still their gains.
With weights oppress'd, of sordid gold and care,
They run awhile, then give up in despair.
But one is seen whose speed outstrips the wind,
The laggers all he quickly leaves behind;
Conform'd to rule, he casts all burdens down,
And presses forward to receive the crown.

IN his exhortations to Christians, the great apostle of the Gentiles very often alludes to the Olympic games. These games were celebrated in different parts of Greece, particularly on the isthmus which joined the Morea to the main land; hence called the Isthmian exercises. They were held on the banks of the river Alpheus, near Olympia, a city of Elis. They were considered of so much importance, that from the period of their first regular establishment a new era of reckoning time was constituted, just as we reckon from the birth of Jesus Christ. Each Olympiad consisted of four years; hence they dated events from the first, second, third, or fourth year of any particular Olympiad. The first Olympiad commenced 776 years before the Christian era. These exercises consisted of five different kinds, viz: boxing, wrestling, leaping the quoit, and racing. We confine ourselves to the illustration of the latter. The celebration of the running match excited great interest. Hence, the preparation for these festivals was very great. No man could become a candidate for the prize unless he bore a good character, and regularly exercised himself ten months previously, according to the rules prescribed.

The rules were very severe: a strict regimen had to be observed—unpalatable food to be eaten—abstinence from all luxuries—exercises were to be continued through all weathers, and we know not what besides. And now the grand day has arrived; the judge is appointed, having been previously sworn to deal impartially—the race-course is cleared—the place of starting fixed—the judge takes his seat at the goal, or end of the race-ground, and holds in his hand the crown of olive, or of laurel, destined to grace the victor's brow; officers are appointed to keep order. The city is emptied of its inhabitants—all the principal men are there. The candidates make their appearance; every eye is fixed upon them; every heart is in motion. Divested of all needless clothing, sometimes naked they await the signal;—'tis given—off they start. Not a whisper is heard among all that multitude; with intense interest they watch the runners as they pass along. A shout is heard. The victor returns, like a triumphant conqueror, drawn in a chariot of four, wearing the crown of victory, and is everywhere greeted with the acclamations of the people.

Religion is compared to a race; the *stadium*, or race-ground, is the path of piety leading through this world to the next; the runners are those who profess religion; the officers appointed to keep order, the ministers of the gospel; the spectators, men and angels; the judge, the Lord Jesus Christ; the reward, a crown of righteousness.

Let us imagine a company of young persons just commencing the Christian race. They set off together; the directions are given to all, they are four in number: 1. *Be sure to lay aside every weight;* 2. *Relinquish the besetting sin;* 3. *Exercise patience;* 4. *Look to Jesus.* They go along pretty well for awhile. Soon one is seen lagging behind. What is the matter? He has too much weight about him. Another drops off; his besetting sin has prevailed. A third is missing; what ails him? O, he is out of patience—with God, himself, and everybody besides. Some follow the directions—persevere to the end, and obtain the prize. But mark: of those who run in the Grecian games, *one* only could receive the prize. In the Christian race, all may run so as to obtain. The judge there was sometimes partial; the Christian's Umpire is the "*Righteous Judge.*" The successful candidate, after all his labors, obtained only a garland of withering flowers; the Christian receives a glorious "crown of righteousness that fadeth not away."

RELIGIOUS EMBLEMS.

In God is my salvation and my glory. the rock of my strength, and my refuge, is in God. Ps. lxii 7

SALVATION.

Lo! where amid appalling dangers dread,
The rock undaunted lifts its welcome head;
The ship of commerce gayly sail'd along,
All hands were merry with their evening song;
When lo! they scud before a sudden blast,
The sails are shiver'd, broken is the mast;
The ship is wreck'd, the storm rolls wildly round,
The sinking sailors have no footing found.
In drowning plight, stunn'd by the wave's rude shock,
The lightning kindly points them to the rock;
The Rock they grasp, and raise themselves on high,
In conscious safety bid the storm pass by.
 So when mankind were wreck'd on Eden's shore,
Loud was the tempest, loud the thunder's roar,
Earth, sea, and skies affrighted were, and toss'd,
Tumultuous all. Shall man be saved, or lost?
In that wild ocean of despair and dread,
The ROCK OF AGES lifts his lofty head;
The sinner, sinking, stunn'd by Sinai's shock,
By Sinai's lightning, now beholds the Rock;

With glad surprise, more clear his moral sight,
He sees besides, a cross of heavenly light;
The Rock he clambers to the cross he clings,
And saved from danger, of *Salvation* sings.

A SHORT time since, and that vessel was sailing calmly and securely over the soft, blue wave. The voice of song arose and mingled its melodies with the light air around. Home, sweet home, was the theme which gladdened every heart. But ah! thou treacherous sea. Thou deceitful wind! How changed the scene! The voice of song is departed, joy and gladness are no more. Instead of the music of soft symphonies, are heard the clamors of despair, the thunder's mighty roar—old ocean's harsh sounds, and the howling of the storm. The ship is driven fiercely before the gale, sails are rent, one of the masts is gone by the board, ruin steers the ill-fated ship; she strikes upon a reef, the billows roll over her, the crew are washed overboard. Night thickens around with his stormy horrors; manfully the drowning wretches buffet the waves; the lightning flings its lurid glare around, and shows them their awful condition; again it lightens, and they descry a rock, lifting its head above the billows, and promising a place of safety. Hope revives—they swim for the rock, soon "they make it." See! they have got upon it. Now they are safe!

The vessel, sailing joyfully and securely before the gale began, may represent the safe and happy condition of our first parents before they were assailed by the storms of temptation; the drowning mariners denote the deplorable state of mankind since the fall, who are sinking amidst the waves of guilt and wo; the tempest overhead denotes the storm that howls over the head of every sinner, in consequence of the violation of Jehovah's law. Sinai thunders forth its curses, and flashes its lightnings around the sinner's path, in order to show him his weakness, his guilt, and his danger. As the lightning points the drowning sailor to the rock, so the law directs or opens the way to Christ, that the sinner might be justified by faith in the atonement.

The rock, rising in the troubled ocean, affording a shelter from the shipwreck represents Christ, the Rock of Ages, who has borne all the fury of the storm for man, and who, by his cross, giveth life and light to a dying world. The penitent sinner, feeling himself sinking in the mighty waters, and tremblingly alive to the dangers of the tempest above, and to the more fearful dangers of the rolling waves beneath, escapes to the Rock, embraces the cross, and is safe, i. e., he believes in the Lord Jesus Christ, and is saved.

<blockquote>
Jesus, lover of my soul,
Let me to thy bosom fly,
While the nearer waters roll,
While the tempest still is high.
Hide me, O my Saviour, hide,
Till the storm of life is past,
Safe to the haven guide,
O receive my soul at last.
</blockquote>

And having done all, to stand. Ephes. vi. 13.

THE CHRISTIAN SOLDIER.

The Christian hero here has made his stand,
Obedient to his Captain's great command;
In panoply divine, equipped complete,
No danger dreads, no foe he fears to meet:
Truth wove the girdle that his loins adorn,
This bears him scathless through the battle's storm
A sense of pardon guards each vital part,
And forms the Breastplate that defends his heart.
For brazen Greaves, obedience he takes,
Through thorny paths, his onward progress makes.
" Hope of Salvation" is his helmet fair ;
Though oft perplexed, it saves him from despair.
He wields, and not in vain, a trusty sword,
A right good blade it is, Jehovah's word ;
The Spirit's weapon, 'twill each knot untie,
Each foe disarm, and make Apollyon fly :
O'er all the rest he grasps Faith's mighty shield,
And onward rushes to the battle-field.

As soon as one enlists himself as a soldier of Jesus Christ, that moment the world becomes his enemy. It happens to him as it fell out to the Gibeonites; when they made peace with Joshua, the neighboring nations were highly offended, and said to one another, "Come, let us unite our forces that we may smite Gibeon, *for it hath made peace with Joshua and with the children of Israel.*"

But there are other foes more mighty and fearful, against whom he has to contend. Satan, after 6000 years practice in the art of destroying souls, is a powerful opponent. "He goeth about as a roaring lion, seeking whom he may devour," for we wrestle not against flesh and blood—merely—but "against principalities, against powers, against the rulers of the darkness of the world, against spiritual wickedness in high places." "Wherefore," on this account, "take unto you the whole armor of God, that ye may be able to withstand in the evil day, and having done all, to stand."

There are two kinds of armor, offensive and defensive; one to attack the foe, the other to protect ourselves. It is remarkable, that but one weapon is mentioned by the Apostle as belonging to the *offensive* kind, viz., the sword; all the rest are defensive. Among the Grecian warriors there were at least nine different weapons with which they assailed their enemies, yet the Apostle thinks that for the Christian this is enough.

The Captain of our salvation has provided us with all that is necessary for the Christian warfare. Is our head exposed to the assaults of the devil, he has furnished us with a "helmet" to guard it; this is called in another place, the *hope of Salvation.* This good hope prepares the soldier for the warfare, upholds him in it, and brings him off a conqueror. Is the heart liable to be pierced, there is a breastplate provided to protect it, it is the *breastplate of Righte-*

ousness; this is a consciousness not only of his own sincerity, but also of his favorable acceptance with God. He feels that he is honest in his profession of attachment to the Saviour, and that Christ, his Captain, acknowledges him for a true soldier.

The feet being exposed to injuries, a pair of brass boots are given to protect them. It would not have answered any good purpose to protect the head, oftentimes, unless the feet likewise were provided for. If the feet were wounded, the soldier could not stand to fight the foe, neither could he pursue him if conquered. The greaves simply prompt obedience to the Captain's commands; with this, rough places become as plain, and the crooked as straight.

The girdle is given to keep the rest of the armor in its place, and to strengthen the loins. "*Truth*" accomplishes this for the Christian soldier. By this he discovers *who* are his enemies, their mode of attack, and the best way to resist them. A shield also is provided; it is called the *shield of faith*, by which he is able to quench all the fiery darts of the evil one. Finally, a sword is put into his hands; with this he is to inflict deadly wounds on all his foes; it is called the *Sword of the Spirit*, because the word of God was inspired by the Holy Spirit. "Wherewithal shall a young man cleanse his way but by taking heed thereto according to thy word?" By the clear instruction, by the powerful motives and by the glorious encouragement of the word of God, the Christian soldier puts all his foes to flight

RELIGIOUS EMBLEMS. 31

Strait is the gate, and narrow is the way, which leadeth unto life, and few there be that find it. Matt. vii. 14.

THE STRAIT AND NARROW GATE.

The gate contracted, here is brought to view,
And narrow path that runs directly through.
One there is seen, who strives with all his might
To pass the gate that leads to heavenly light;
Strong drink, the deadly dram, is cast away,
And on his knees, devout, begins to pray.
Self-righteousness to enter next proceeds,
Alas for him! how heavily he treads!
His weary back a monstrous burden bears
Of legal deeds, and unavailing prayers.
He cannot enter, for the gate is small,
He must unload him, or not pass at all.
Dives has fallen, gone quite off the track,
And on the wicket gate has turned his back.
Another, heedless of Jehovah's laws,
Dreams he can enter with the world's applause:
Honor and glory, pomp of things below,
Can never through the straitened passage go.
Thus sinners all—to sensual pleasures given—
Remain excluded from the gate of Heaven.

THE first object presented in the group is, a reformed drunkard. See! he has thrown away strong drinks; he is determined to agonize—to enter in at the strait gate. Many tipplers seek to gain admission, but it will not do; over the gate is written in characters of living light, "No drunkard shall inherit the kingdom of God."

The next figure shows a man professedly in the strait and narrow way, but he has such a large mass, or bundle of self-righteousness on his back, it will be seen at the first glance that it is impossible for him to get through the gate or passage. "All our righteousnesses," which we may bring with us when seeking salvation, "are as filthy rags;" and the more we have of them, the more impossible it will be for us to enter the strait gate. Man, in order to be saved, must feel himself to be a sinner; he must feel his poverty, and like the man seen in the engraving, must get down on his knees, in order to enter into the gate of life.

St. Paul, when a Pharisee, had a large load of self-righteousness, but when he became a Christian he discarded it; he desired to be found in Christ, saying, "not having mine own righteousness, which is of the law, but that which is through the faith of Christ, the righteousness which is of God by faith."

Partly in the background is one who has fallen from the narrow way. This represents a lover of money; one who has committed "guilts, great blunder," and who is now a laughing-stock for devils. They that will be rich fall into temptations and a snare, which drown men in perdition. O that men were wise! O that they would attend to the words of Christ: "Ye cannot serve God and mammon; verily it is easier for a camel to go through the eye of a needle, than for a rich man to enter the kingdom of God."

The last depicted is one who is carrying worldly honor and glory; who foolishly thinks he can love God and the world together. No man can serve two masters of opposite interest. "How," said Jesus, "can ye be saved who seek honor one of another, and not the honor which cometh from God only."

Perhaps it was on one of those beautiful evening of surpassing loveliness, seen only in the Holy Land, that the Blessed Redeemer delivered his unexampled lessons of benevolence and wisdom from the mount made sacred by his presence. Then Jesus opened his mouth and taught them, saying, "Enter ye in at the strait gate; strait is the gate, and narrow is the way that leadeth unto life, and few there be that find it." By which words the Saviour would have us to understand the nature and requirements of Religion. Its nature—that it consists in a change of heart. Its requirements—that we do justly, love mercy, and walk humbly with the Lord.

Hence, by the "strait gate" we may learn that compliance with the first table of the Law is intended, viz.: Thou shalt love the Lord thy God with all thy heart, with all thy soul, with all thy mind, and with all thy strength. By the "narrow way," obedience to the demands of the second table is enjoined, viz.: Thou shalt love thy neighbor as thyself; or, as it is expressed by the Saviour, more copiously—"Therefore, all things whatsoever ye would that men should do unto you, do ye even so to them." As no man can love God, as required, without a change of heart, so neither can any one—Do unto others as he would they should do unto him—unless he first love God, for "he that loveth not his brother abideth in death."

Ye cannot serve God and mammon. Matt. vi. 24.———*A double-minded man is unstable in all his ways.* James i. 8.

DOUBLE-MINDEDNESS

See the professor laboring, but in vain,
The world and cross together to sustain;
The globe is in his right hand dexterous found,
His left the cross drags sluggish on the ground;
In vain for him appears the narrow way,
The world has led him from the path astray:
In vain for him shines forth the heavenly light,
The world has risen and obscured his sight;
Two minds he has, both he may call his own,
Sometimes they lead him up, and sometimes down;
Like doubtful birds, that hop from spray to spray,
His will is never at one certain stay:
Too late he learns, with deep regret and pain,
He loses both who more than one would gain.

HERE is seen a man staggering under two heavy burdens: a globe, which represents the world, and a cross, that represents the Christian religion. His knees totter and tremble beneath the cumbrous load. The cross is the badge of his profession, which he holds, or rather drags along, with his left hand; this shows that religion is only a secondary concern with him.

In his *right* hand he carries the globe. The right hand being the most dexterous, shows that the practical part of his life is employed in securing the world, notwithstanding his profession. He has succeeded so well that the globe has got uppermost. It monopolizes his attention, and controls his movements. It has turned his feet from the narrow way; it has hid from his view the glorious light of the heavenly city. In going down hill, the cross slips out of his left hand, he stumbles over it, and falls, the globe falls upon him, and grinds him to powder.

This emblem needs but little illustration. It shows the folly and end of a double-minded man. The fabled Atlas, who carried the world on his shoulders, attempted nothing, accomplished nothing, compared with the man who labors to secure both this world and the next; he has two souls, or minds, which govern him by turns; but in the end, the worldly principle prevails. His folly consists in trying to do what is in itself absolutely impossible—what no man ever did or ever can do. God himself has separated the world from the cross; what God hath separated, no man may bring together; the nature of the gospel forbids such union. Its influences, doctrines, precepts, objects, tendencies, and final issues are all opposed, and contrary to the principles, maxims, practices, and interests of this world.

In the gospel, provision is made to renew the heart, and to enable man to set his affections on things above, not on things on the earth. The cross is as much as any man can carry, let him have as much grace as he will. If any doubt remains, Christ, the great Umpire of all disputed claims of this kind, has pronounced the decision: "*No man can serve two masters*"—"*Ye cannot serve God and mammon.*"

The double-minded man is unstable in all his ways; sometimes he is seen among the disciples of Christ, then again he appears following the course of this world. He takes no comfort in religion, and none in the world. Every thing connected with him is double; a double curse rests upon him wherever he goes. True Christians are ashamed of him; the ungodly despise him; he is a laughing-stock for devils; his own conscience reproaches him; his own family upbraids him; and a double punishment will be the portion of his cup forever.

The mad prophet Balaam is a remarkable instance of double-mindedness. In profession, he would be a prophet of Jehovah; in practice, he followed and "loved the wages of unrighteousness." Despised by the people of God, to whom he was a stumbling-block; despised and reproached by Balak for his indecision, he died under the weight of a double curse, and left his name a proverb of reproach and shame.

Choose you this day whom ye will serve. *Joshua* xxiv. 15.

How long halt ye between two opinions? If the Lord be God, follow him: but if Baal, then follow him. 1 *Kings* xviii. 21.

I know thy works, that thou art neither cold nor hot: I would thou wert cold or hot. So then, because thou art lukewarm, and neither cold nor hot, I will spue thee out of my mouth. *Rev.* iii. 15, 16.

And the rain descended, and the floods came, and beat upon that house, and it fell not: for it was founded upon a rock. Matt. vii. 25.

THE HOUSE FOUNDED ON A ROCK.

High on a rock, the wise man marks his plan,
Its deep foundations, closely he would scan;
Though gentle zephyrs breathe through summer skies,
He knows that storms wide wasting may arise;
On solid base his building rises fair,
And points its turrets through the ambient air.
With tranquil joy, his eyes delighted, greet
The beauteous fabric furnished and complete;
In conscious safety makes it his abode,
His duty done, he leaves the rest with God.
But soon dark clouds o'erspread the troubled sky,
And soon is heard the voice of tempest high;
Deep rolls the thunder, rains in torrents pour,
And floods tumultuous beat with deafening roar.
Floods, rain, nor thunder, nor rude tempest's shock,
Can harm the house—'tis founded on a Rock.
  Not so the simpleton who built on sand,
And wrought his labor with penurious hand;
'Midst howling tempests, and loud thunder's roar,
His house—it vanish'd, and was seen no more.

A WISE man, desiring to build a house for himself and family, sees many very pleasant and romantic lots: he is tempted to choose a delightful situation, but he remembers that the country is often visited with violent storms, that hurricanes are frequent, and that the rivers frequently overflow their banks, and sweep away bridges, houses, cattle, and inhabitants, all together. This makes him cautious. He sacrifices what is merely ornamental for what is useful and essential. He fixes upon a rock for the site of his mansion. He builds in such a manner that his house looks like a part of the rock itself, it is so imbedded within its shelvings. When all is snug and complete, he enters his new dwelling, thankful that he has been enabled to finish it. In a little while, one of those storms come on so common to the country; the rains descend, the winds blow, the floods beat against the house, but it stands unmoved. All night the tempest lasts; at length morning comes; the son of wisdom opens the door and goes forth, like Noah when he left the ark after the waters of the deluge had abated. He looks around: all is desolation except his own house. At a little distance from him he discovers some of the fragments of his neighbor's house. The foolish man had studied only ease and present convenience; he chose a showy place, but the foundation was sandy. The hurricane swept them all away together.

The house on the rock, and its builder, is an emblem of the man who hears the word of God and keeps it. He makes the word of God a ladder by which he climbs to heaven. Beginning at repentance, he goes on to faith in our Lord Jesus Christ, then to holiness; thus he mounts from faith to faith, till finally he reaches glory.

Observe, it is not the person who hears, or understands, or remembers, or believes, merely, the word of God; but the DOER, that is, the prudent or wise man. He fastens on the Rock of Ages: Christ is his foundation, where, in obedience to the word, he has fled for refuge; hence, he is protected against all the storms of earth and hell.

"To *obey* is better than sacrifice, to hearken than the fat of rams." The word of God is compared to seed, which, if received in good ground, beareth much fruit. As the seed requires that the ground should be prepared, watered, weeded, etc.; so the word requires that it should be received with attention and nourished by meditation, much prayer, and faith. No one can enter the kingdom of heaven unless he is a disciple of Christ; but he is not a disciple unless he bringeth much fruit. He, and he alone, that *doeth* the will of God shall abide forever.

A person having just returned from church, was met with the following exclamation: "What, is it all done?" "No, by no means," was the prompt reply. "It is all *said*, but not all *done*."

For not the hearers of the law are just before God, but the doers of the law shall be justified. *Rom.* ii. 13.

But be ye doers of the word, and not hearers only . . . . . a doer of the work, this man shall be blessed in his deed. *James* i. 22, 25.

If ye know these things, happy are ye if ye do them. *John* xiii. 17.

Seest thou a man wise in his own conceit? There is more hope of a fool than of him. Prov. xxvi. 12.

SELF-CONFIDENCE.

See how Self-confidence his friend doth treat,
Nor heeds the danger from beneath his feet:
With head erect, he proudly stalks along,
The warning voice is but an idle song;
As to the precipice he draws more nigh,
His friend yet louder lifts his voice on high,
But deaf and blind, he neither sees nor hears,
From friends or foes he nothing wants, or fears;
He "knows, and that's enough—all right," when lo!
At once he falls into the gulf below:
Adown the rocks he tumbles o'er and o'er,
And sinks in darkness, to arise no more.

THE engraving shows a traveller in the greatest peril. He is on the brink of an awful precipice: he knows it not. But this is not the worst of his case: he is confident in his knowledge, and that he is fully prepared for every emergency, although he has not examined any book of roads, or any charts, or maps, nor has he made inquiries of others who have travelled these parts before him. A friend is seen who endeavors to apprize him of his danger; he calls to him, but he turns a deaf ear to his remonstrances, and still proceeds. As he draws near the fatal brink, his friend, knowing his danger, exerts himself to the utmost to have him stop—to listen —but for one moment; but no, he has no need of advice—on he goes. The ground, which is hollow, gives way beneath his feet, he falls, and is instantly lashed to pieces. The name of the man is "*Self-confidence.*"

The moral of this is, that dangers stand thick all through the path of human life; dangers such as the lust of the flesh, the lust of the eye, and the pride of life, with their numerous attendants. False doctrines also, the tendency of which is to destroy the happiness of mankind, prevail. They are covered with a flimsy garb, which deceives superficial observers.

Moreover, youth is presumptuous, self-willed, and self-confident. They are too much inclined to follow the light which their own vanity has kindled. But their self-confidence does not remove the dangers from their path, nor render them invulnerable. But man is ignorant—how shall he know? Helpless—what shall he do? If any man lack wisdom, let him ask of God. " Do" ponder well the paths of thy feet. Lean not to thine own understanding. He that trusts to his own heart is a fool. In all thy ways acknowledge God; he will direct thy paths. Here, then, is the conclusion of the whole matter; imminent perils surround the youth, but the greatest of all perils is the danger of trusting to his own heart. Lean upon God, and all will be well. Though weak and ignorant, yet God is wise and strong, able to guide and preserve all those who trust in him.

The mariner who should put to sea without chart or compass, trusting to his own knowledge, would, without doubt, on the first stormy night, repent heartily of his folly. O how much greater is the folly of those who, trusting to self, neglect to use the lamp of God's truth, or to seek the enlightening influences of his Holy Spirit, or to follow the advice of the wise and good.

The case of Pharaoh, the Egyptian monarch, affords a striking example of self-confidence. When the children of Israel had left the house of bondage, and were well on their journey towards the land of promise, the king, confiding in his strength, exclaimed: "I will pursue, I will overtake," and presumptuously set forth for that purpose. Each recently received plague remonstrated, and forbade the rashness of the monarch; but all in vain. On he rushed, even to the division of waters. In his self-confidence he engaged in battle with Jehovah, God of Armies. The conflict was of short duration; the arm of the Lord prevailed; Pharaoh and his men of war were swept away with the waters of destruction.

Thy word is a lamp unto my feet, and a light unto my path. Ps. cxix. 105. *The Lord God is a sun and shield.* Ps. lxxxiv. 11.

THE SUN OF TRUTH.

Lo! on a path that through the mountains sweeps,
And climbs their summits, and descends their deeps,
The Sun pours wide his bright diffusive rays,
And shows two travellers on their different ways;
His shade behind, his pathway always bright,
One travels forward with increasing light,
Till equatorial o'er his head it burns,
And all of shadow into day it turns;
The other turns upon the sun his back,
His lengthening shadow darkens all his track;
Which now not seen, he turns him from the right,
And ends his journey in the realms of night.

SEE where, among the mountain heights, a long straight path stretches itself till it is lost in the distance beyond. The sun pours wide his rays of living light, illuminating the path, and shedding lustre all around. Two travellers are pursuing their different routes. One advances toward the sun; his shadow is behind, his path is bright before him. As he proceeds his shadow diminishes, while his path grows brighter and brighter, until, directly overhead, the sun pours the full tide of its glory upon him, and the whole of the shadow disappears.

The other has turned his back upon the orb of day. See, he follows his own shadow. It darkens his pathway before him. Now he leaves the track; his shadow lengthens more and more; he wanders into sunken labyrinths, and finally loses himself amidst the darkness of night.

This emblem represents the moral world. The sun designates the Sun of Truth. The travellers denote, first, those who follow the light: their path shines brighter and brighter unto the perfect day; their souls become enlightened, vivified, and purified; darkness disappears, and heavenly light shines on their souls forever. Secondly, it signifies those who turn their backs on the light, and who, as they journey, wander farther and farther from his bright beams; their path becomes darker and darker; their shadow lengthens as they proceed, until, having forsaken altogether the way of truth, they lose themselves among the wilds of error, and perish in the darkness of everlasting night.

Where shines the Sun of Truth? In the Holy Bible. The Scriptures are a "light" to the weary traveller, illuminating all his goings, pointing out his proper path, and showing where the mountains of error lift up their desolating heads. This Sun of Truth shines on the traveller himself. It discovers his ignorance, guilt, danger, helplessness, and, at the same time, his immortality. Again it shines, and he beholds Calvary, with all its weeping tragedies. It reveals to him now his "wisdom, justification, sanctification, and redemption." Where shines the Sun of

Truth? In the person of Jesus Christ. He who wisely uses the light of the Scriptures, will be led to contemplate Him who is the "Light of the world," "the Sun of Righteousness," "the Splendid Glory of Jehovah," "the Way, the Life, and the *Truth*."

The Christian, following the light of the glorious Sun of Truth, discovers ever-opening mines of richest knowledge. Fountains of living waters roll their treasures at his feet. Trees of Life overhang his pathway, and drop into his lap their golden stores, till at length he beholds the opening gates of the New Jerusalem,

> Where Light and Truth their mystic powers combine,
> And o'er the realms of Love forever shine.

The infidel, turning his back upon the light, walks in the vain shadow of his own opinions. Darker, and yet more dark, the shadow grows; he waxes worse and worse; one truth after another is given up—one lie after another is embraced; farther and farther he wanders from God and bliss, and finally he takes his fearful "leap in the dark," and finds himself, contrary to his expectations, in outer darkness, where there is weeping, and wailing, and wo.

Unto the upright there ariseth light in the darkness. Ps. cxii. 4.——
Yea, though I walk through the valley of the shadow of death, I will fear no evil, for thou art with me. Ps. xxiii. 4.

LIGHT IN DARKNESS.

The faithful Christian walks in darkest gloom,
As though enclosed in some monastic tomb;
And clouds of darkest night surround his head;
A Pall, like that which canopies the dead;
His path lies through the palpable obscure,
Nor can he yet discern an open door;
Yet he's resolved to penetrate his way,
Nor doubts but darkness will be turned to day:
To Christ he prays, the light of mortals here;
And Christ, the light of mortals, shines out clear,
Full on his path, pours down the heavenly light,
And on he goes, with vigor and delight.

THE engraving represents a Christian walking through a dark and shadowy vale, wherein is no light; the mantle of darkness encircles him, the pall of the grave has enfolded itself around him. Nevertheless, his path runs directly through it; he knows not what dangers may lie in the midst; he knows not when, or where the end may be. No chink, outlet, or open door presents itself to him, yet he is determined to persevere; it is the path of duty.

Addressing himself to his work, he addresses himself also to his Master; he calls on Christ, whose he is, and whom he serves; the Saviour shows his bright and glorious countenance; the light of his glory falls full upon the traveller; the reflection irradiates his pathway, all is light. He goes on his way rejoicing in the Lord.

Every Christian must at times pass through the valley of tribulation. Mental anxiety, sickness, loss of friends, poverty, persecution, death—with many other things—make the materials of the valley of tribulation. The Blessed Saviour has said that all who live godly must pass through this valley. And again, through much tribulation ye must enter into the kingdom of God. And John the beloved, looking with wonder at the glory of some who were seen before the throne of God, was informed by the angel, that they were those who had come out of great tribulation.

But Christ is the light of the world, the *Sun* of Righteousness, the source from which all intellectual and spiritual light is derived. Wherefore God our heavenly Father says to us, Awake thou that sleepest, arouse from the dead thou that dwellest among the tombs, and Christ shall give thee light. But to the Christian passing through the dark valley of trouble, he says, Arise, shine, *thy* light is come, and the glory of the Lord is risen on thee. To the disciple of Jesus this light indeed belongs, and much he needs it in his pilgrimage. To him it is given by promise. To the upright there ariseth light in darkness; light is sown for the righteous, and gladness for the upright in heart. The light of knowledge, the light of consolation, the light of holiness, and the light of eternal glory, are the Christian's inheritance, in and through Christ Jesus. Without Christ all is darkness, wretchedness, and death. With Him all is Light, Life, Love, and Peace.

Stephen was a good man, yet he had to pass through the valley of tribulation. Perhaps he was more highly favored than any other man in similar circumstances; probably this was on account of his being the first Christian martyr—the model for all succeeding martyrs. He looked up through the clouds of persecution that surrounded him, and saw "*the glory of God and Jesus;*" he could not keep silent; "Behold," he cried, "I see the heavens opened, and the Son of man standing at the right hand of God." The glorious light shone in him, and through him, and around him; he looked as an angel of the Lord.

> In darkest shades, if he appear,
>   My dawning is begun!
> He is my soul's sweet morning star,
>   And he my rising sun.
>
> The opening heavens around me shine
>   With beams of sacred bliss,
> While Jesus shows his heart is mine,
>   And whispers, *I am his!*
>
> My soul would leave this heavy clay,
>   At that transporting word,
> Run up with joy the shining way,
>   To embrace my dearest Lord.   *Watts.*

RELIGIOUS EMBLEMS.

He heapeth up riches, and knoweth not who shall gather them. Psa. xxxix. 6.——*A rich man shall hardly enter into the kingdom of heaven.* u. xix. 23.

THE WORLDLING.

And now, the worldling, with his gathering rake,
Performs his task, the glittering dust to take;
Devoted man! with many cares oppressed,
Gold he collects, to ease his aching breast
The fool's insignia he most truly bears,
He but increases what he mostly fears:
As dropsied patients, who with thirst are faint,
Drink and are dry, and strengthen their complaint.
While in this grovelling, melancholy plight,
Religion comes, a messenger of light;
Mercy's blest Angel has from heaven come down,
She meets the worldling and presents her crown;
"Behold," she cries, "the diadem I bear,
Enriched with gems such as bright Angels wear,
Yield then to me, first lay thy muck-rake down,
Bear thy brow upward, and receive my crown."
The worldling, stupid, toils and rakes away;
Still looking down, he rakes from day to day;
Himself his foe he lives, and greatly poor;
And dies remembered as a fool—no more.

The engraving represents a man hard at work; he holds a rake in his hand, with which he gathers dust and rubbish together. The yellow shining dust is called gold; he is altogether absorbed, lost, as it were, in his employment. He kneels down to his work; this shows his devotion to the object of his affections. For this grovelling work he has forsaken all intellectual and religious pleasures; all social and domestic happiness. He is a poor man, although he has a great deal of that hard shining dust you see lying there; he is craving after more; he is in want, therefore he is poor; he is a *miser*, therefore he is *miserable*. The poor man is altogether beside himself.

The bright lovely one bearing a starry crown is *Religion*, daughter of the skies; she has many attendants, who are concealed at present; she has come a long way to meet the poor man; she looks upon him with compassion; she sees his miserable condition, she knows his great folly. Addressing him, she says: "Poor soul, why labor you for the dust which perisheth? Why do you spend your strength for naught? Hearken unto me and I will give you riches, more abundantly than earth can give, and lasting as eternity. Look up, poor man, behold this crown, beautiful and glorious; it contains the riches of a million of such worlds as this, and the happiness of ages upon ages; throw by your rake and be happy." Worldling, for that is the name of the infatuated mortal, takes no notice whatever. He still continues at his task; there is no voice nor any that regard. And Religion, after waiting a long time, departs and leaves him to his folly.

They that *will be rich*—though by means ever so fair—fall into temptation and a snare, which drown men in *perdition*. Youth, beware! when men neglect to employ the talent of wealth according to the will of God, he gives them up to the *love* of it, and they become fools, intoxicated with the alcohol of mammon. The worldling lives in the world as though he was never to quit it. Bound for eternity, he makes no preparation for the voyage—going to the Judgment, and before a holy God—and continues unrepentant and polluted. He is treasuring up, what?—gold; what else? wrath against the day of wrath. The love of money, an evil disease, has taken hold upon him; the more he adds, the more he feeds the disease; like persons with the dropsy, who drink and are still dry. When Garrick, the actor, showed Dr. Johnson an estate he had lately purchased, Johnson remarked: "Ah! it is these things that make death dreadful." But the love of money makes life miserable. The Roman citizen, Apicius, after spending some 800,000 pounds, and finding he was worth only about 83,000, fearing want, ended his life by poison.

But the worldling heapeth up riches, and knows not *who* will gather them. Cupidus, with great labor, accumulated a great estate, and dying, left his wealth to his two sons, Stultus and Effusio. Stultus had in a little time to be placed under guardians, who spent his money for their own pleasures. Effusio squandered his patrimony in riotous living, and died in a lunatic asylum.

If any man will come after me, let him deny himself, and take up his cross and follow me. Matt. xvi. 24.

THE CROSS-BEARER.

Dear reader, o'er this sacred emblem pause,
And view the Christian bearing up his cross;
Nor steep ascent, nor roughness of the way,
E'er makes him halt, or turns his feet astray:
Should he in weakness think to lay it down,
His strength increases when he sees the crown;
His soul enkindles at the glorious sight,
His yoke's more easy, and his cross more light.
The Cross all hallowed, is the Christian's boast—
His WATCHWORD, fighting at his arduous post—
His true *insignia* as he glides along,
Conspicuous, through the pleasure-loving throng;
His *royal passport*, sanctioned by the skies,
By which he triumphs, and secures the prize.

BEHOLD here the Christian bearing up manfully under his cross. It is a glorious sight. You see him going with his cross up the difficult mountain passes, as well as along the smooth and flowery plain. View the crown! It is seen in the distance. Sometimes the clouds gather around it; in general, however, to the *cross-bearer* the sky is clear; he can discover the crown glittering in its beauty.

The young Christian will know what this means spiritually. It is not of the Saviour's cross, but of the Christian's own proper cross that we now speak. What is it to bear the cross? To bear the cross always, is to do right always. It is no less than to fulfil the high commands of the Saviour, under all circumstances. It is to deny, control, and conquer self. It is to watch, pray, and by divine meditation have constant hold upon Christ. It is to glorify God before men by a holy walk and conversation; forgiving enemies, loving all men, aiming to do them good bodily and spiritually—in a word, it is to follow Christ as far as the disciple can follow his Lord, in piety toward God, in benevolence toward man. When Peter exclaimed, "I know not the man," he laid down his cross. When Paul declared, "I am ready, not to be bound only, but also to die at Jerusalem for the name of the Lord Jesus," he expressed his willingness to take up his cross, and his delight therein.

The Christian's proper work is to bear the cross. This is his calling, his trade, or profession. It is the business of a watchmaker to make watches; it is the business of the Christian to bear the cross as above, at home, abroad, in the shop, in the store, in the market-place, or in the field. By reason of corruption within, of opposition without, of the malice of the wicked one, the burden is sometimes a heavy one, but strength will increase by practice. He has many discouragements, many solicitations to lay it aside. It sometimes presses heavily upon him, but the sight of the crown inspires him with fresh vigor, he glows, and bounds along the heavenly road. By the cross, i. e., by his conduct, the Christian is distinguished from the lover of the world. While he bears the cross, the cross will bear him. It will guide him through labyrinths of darkness. As a shield, it will protect him in dangerous conflicts.

Among the Romans, criminals about to be crucified were compelled to bear their own cross to the place of execution; but the Christian bears his to the place of triumph. If it should prove at any time so heavy as to crush him down to death, as did Stephen's, like him he beholds the heavens opened, the King in his beauty, and the crown of celestial glory. He comes off more than a conqueror.

"O may I triumph so, when all my conflict's past,
And dying, find my latest foe under my feet at last."

Who suffer with our Master here,
We shall before his face appear,
  And by his side sit down;
To patient faith the prize is sure;
And all that to the end endure
  The cross, shall wear the crown.

In hope of that ecstatic pause,
Jesus, we now sustain the cross,
  And at thy footstool fall;
Till thou our hidden life reveal,
Till thou our ravish'd spirits fill,
  And God is All in All.

.... *the pride of life, is not of the Father, but is of the world.* — *The world passeth away, and the lust thereof.* John ii. 16. — *Man being in honor abideth not: he is like the beasts that perish.* Ps. xlix. 12.

WORLDLY HONOR.

Lo! here are honors, floating in the breeze,
That wafts them changeful o'er the land and seas:
The air-inflated bubbles pass along,
Attract the gaze, and fascinate the throng;
Away they go, pursuing and pursued,
O'erleap all bounds, the legal and the good;
Through fields of fire, and seas of blood and wo,
Through broken hearts, and blasted hopes they go.
On others' carcass, see! they strive to rise,
And grasp the phantom that before them flies;
In blood-red garb, the butchering knife one bears,
Nor friend, nor foe, if in his way, he spares.
All this for what? For what this vast outlay?
This sum infinite, squandered every day?
Of those thus fool'd, some answer in despair,
"*We clasp'd the phantoms, and we found them air.*"
Not so the honors that from God descend,
Substantial, pure, and lasting without end.

This emblem is a representation of the vain pursuits of mankind. Honors, titles, and fame, are borne upon the wings of the wind, which is ever changing, as are the sources from whence worldly honors are derived. Numbers are seen pressing after them with all their mind and strength, and in their haste to possess them, they sacrifice all that is good and holy, all that is benevolent and divine.

One, with his tongue, assails the character of the pious and the wise; another, with his pen dipped in gall, attacks the reputation of a suspected rival; others, as seen in the emblem, hew down with the sword those who stand in their path, and, trampling on the bleeding body of the victim, strive to obtain the object of their desires; while the shrieks of the wounded, the groans of the dying, the tears of the widow, and the sobs of orphans, seem only to add wings to the speed of ambition.

It often costs them much to enable them to accomplish their ends. They expend peace of conscience, ease, and often life itself. Nay, the soul's salvation—the favor of God, eternal life, immortality in heaven, are exchanged for this empty nothing. The peace and happiness of others, of millions, with their lives, fortunes, and destinies, are thrown away for the same worthless object.

Perhaps the reader will say, "Surely, a thing that costs so much must be valuable?" True wisdom condemns such things as valueless, and true wisdom is justified of all her children. The little boy who left his satchel and his school to run after the rainbow, expecting to catch it, was a philosopher compared to the idiots in the picture.

Alexander, called the "Great," bought the title of "Son of Jupiter" for the consideration of many lives of his followers, and enduring much fatigue while passing through burning and distant climes. After conquering mighty kings and warriors, he attained the pinnacle of honor and fame, and adding to his own dominions the rest of the earth, he became master of the world, and then——he wept, because there were no more worlds to conquer; and, at the age of 32, died in a drunken fit, and was laid in a drunkard's grave. He left his extensive empire a legacy of desolation to mankind.

How different the honors which come from above! The Almighty Saviour, Jesus, hath ascended up on high; he hath received gifts for men—honors, titles, fame—in abundance. The saints, who are the excellent of the earth, God delighteth to *honor*. Angels are their body-guard, the Saviour is their friend. He confers on them the *title* of "Sons of God," of "Kings and Priests," who shall possess a kingdom that shall endure forever. Their *fame* is immortal: the righteous shall be had in everlasting remembrance.

The honors of earth come from inconstant mortals; the honors which are spiritual flow from the unchangeable Jehovah. The honors of earth are sought by trampling on the rights of others; the honors of God are sought by the increase of human happiness. Earthly honors are unsatisfactory when obtained; the honors of God fill the soul with bliss. Earthly honors are transitory, like the source from whence they spring; the honors of heaven are abiding like their Divine Author.

For I am in a strait betwixt two, having a desire to depart, and to be with Christ; which is far better. Phil. i. 23.

HEAVENLY DESIRE.

Behold the Christian where he doubtful stands,
Fast bound to Friends by blooming roseate bands;
He feels the touch of love on earth below,
And yet to heaven straightway would gladly go;
For them, more needful longer here to stay,
For him, far better thus to soar away;
As when safe-anchored in some foreign bay,
The ship of merchandise may proudly lay;
The Captain's cleared, with passport, to set sail,
He longs for home, and courts the coming gale.
The general interests of the firm demand,
His longer service in that far-off land;
He fain would weigh, and homeward point his prow,
Yet to his duty would submissive bow;
This done, he'll trip, and loose the flowing sail,
And homeward scud before the sounding gale.

The engraving represents an affectionate Father who, though standing on the world, and bound with the strong corde of affection, yet looks upward, erneatly longing to depart and be with Christ, which, as the Apostle says, is far better. Though he may feel this, yet oftentimes he feels strongly bound with the cords of love to remain with the objects of his affection here on the earth, to whom his stay at present seems needful. He, however, does not consider this world as his abiding-place; he has it beneath his feet, he is looking upward, and waiting for his translation to one above.

Thus the Christian stands ready prepared, and longs to depart and be with Christ; but the interests of earth exercise an influence over him and bind him down with the golden bands of affectionate love. When a sinner becomes a saint, his relations become changed, "old things have passed away. Behold all things have become new." A "new heart" is given, filled with love to God and man. A new world is presented full of glorious realities, substantial and eternal. A new God is given, Jehovah is His name. He formerly worshipped the gods of this world. A new Saviour is embraced, who is the "altogether lovely." New companions, the noblest, the wisest, and the best. He is the subject of another King, one Jesus,—the citizen of another city which is out of sight, whose Builder and Maker is God,—the heir of an inheritance, which is incorruptible, undefiled and which fadeth not away.

No wonder, then, if he should oftentimes desire to depart in order to possess all this happiness. Wandering on earth, "here he has no abiding city;" a stranger and pilgrim as all his fathers were. Nevertheless, he has interests, affections, and duties of an earthly kind; these have a weighty claim upon him, they are connected with God and eternity. The religion of the Bible, while it strengthens the powers of the intellect, and sanctifies the soul, does also increase the power of natural affection, and makes us capable of the most lively emotions.

The true minister of the Gospel, like the great Apostle, would cheerfully lay down his work and away to Jesus, but the interests of his master demand that he should stay, and build up the waste places of Jerusalem; therefore he says, "All the days of my appointed time will I wait till my change come."

The pious parent, when visited by sickness, would fain regard it as a call to heaven, but the dear pledges of love are weeping round the bedside, and their youthful state demands a faithful guardian. He can only say, "I am in a strait betwixt two, having a desire to depart and be with Christ, which is far better. Nevertheless, to abide in the flesh is more needful for you; the will of the Lord be done."

> "How happy is the pilgrim's lot!
> How free from every grovelling thought,
> From worldly hope and fear!
> Confined to neither court nor cell,
> His soul disdains on earth to dwell,
> He only sojourns here.
>
> "Nothing on earth I call my own:
> A stranger to the world, unknown,
> I all their wealth despise;
> I trample on their whole delight,
> And seek a country out of sight,
> A country in the skies."   *Wesley.*

RELIGIOUS EMBLEMS.   61

Escape for thy life. Gen. xix. 17.——*The course of this world*
Ephes. ii. 2.

THE FATAL CURRENT.

See! where the fatal current, broad and deep,
Rolls its swift waters down the awful steep;
While from below the steaming clouds arise,
And spread and mingle with the distant skies;
Two men, behold! near the tremendous verge,
A moment sinks them 'neath the boiling surge,
One rows for life, he pulls with all his strength,
And from the danger well escapes at length:
The other stops, lays in his oars to drink,
While nearer drawing to the dreadful brink;
His jeers and taunts he still persists to throw,
And sinks unaided down the gulf below.

THE engraving shows the fatal current hurrying on its rolling waters to the dread abyss; see where the boiling cataract sends forth its cloudy vapors; like volumes of thick smoke they rise and mingle with the surrounding atmosphere. On the stream, and near the fatal gulf, two men are seen in their frail barks. The one on the left hand, knowing his danger, pulls with all his might. Life is at stake; he stems the current. By dint of mighty, persevering effort, he escapes the vortex, and gets beyond the reach of danger.

The one on the right, careless and unconcerned, suffers his little boat to glide down the stream; h dreams not of danger. See! he has laid in his oars he is drowning thought by drinking the intoxicating draught. He points the finger of scorn at his more thoughtful and laborious companion. Notwithstanding his unconcern, the stream bears him onward; nearer and nearer he draws toward the awful brink, on, and on he drifts, till all at once, over he goes; and sinks into the roaring, boiling gulf below.

The above is an emblem of what follows: The gulf, with its rising curling vapors, may represent the regions of the damned, where the smoke of their torment ascendeth up forever and ever.

The fatal current signifies the "course of this world" leading thereinto—the streams of sin that eventually lead to the gates of death. The man on the left, rowing against tide, represents those who stem the torrents of sin, who oppose themselves to the course of this world, "no longer fulfilling the lusts of the flesh, nor of the mind." Eternal life is at stake; they agonize that they may prevail; they endure to the end, and are saved.

The other, on the right, represents one who is indifferent about salvation, who indulges in sin and folly, and who even ridicules others who are striving to serve God. He endeavors to drown his conscience by drinking larger draughts of sin, and by plunging deeper into crime; till, carried onward by the ruling powers of evil, he approaches the horrible gulf, into which he falls, and is lost forever.

Dead fish may frequently be seen floating down

with the tide. The live fish alone stem the torrent, and swim against the stream. So those dead in trespasses and in sins, follow the course of this world; they are borne unresistingly down the fatal stream. But those who are alive spiritually, those whom God hath quickened, oppose the torrent, make headway against it, and, by divine assistance, work out their own salvation, full, and forever.

The patriarch Noah had, in his day, to swim against the stream. The floodgates of sin were opened; the turgid waters rolled down with fearful violence; truth and justice were well-nigh swept from the face of the earth. Manfully did he resist the descending torrent. Like a rock, he remained immoveable, and opposed the overflowings of ungodliness. He was preserved.

God himself bore testimony to his righteousness. He was crowned with Divine approbation, and permitted to see the Bow of Promise. At the same time, the multitude, neglecting to stem the tide, were borne away by the waves thereof, "down to the gulf of black despair."

>When wildly on rolls sin's broad tide
> To caverns of despair,
>May I be found on virtue's side,
> And meet it without fear.

Let not the water-flood overflow me, neither let the deep swallow me up. Ps. lxix. 15.——— He sent from above, he took me, he drew me out of many waters. Ps. xviii. 16.

SALVATION BY FAITH.

The pleasures of a summer's day prevail,
And tempt the youth to hoist the flowing sail:
The river, placid, rolls its waves along,
He glides exulting, like the notes of song;
But soon a cloud, dark, brooding, mounts on high,
A tempest threatens, soon it fills the sky,
He strikes his sail, and plies the lab'ring oar,
If haply he may reach the wished-for shore:
Now booming thunders shake the solid ground,
And angry lightnings fitful flame around:
The rains, descending, now begin to lave,
The winds come dancing o'er the rippling wave,
The stream still bears him from the distant shore,
Appalled he hears the cataract's dreadful roar,—
To stay on board is death—he leaps. The wave
Still bears him onward to the yawning grave.
Just as he reaches the terrific brink,
O'er which, if plunged, he must forever sink,
The king from his fair palace hastens down—
A king who wears far more than regal crown—

He saw his plight, nor feared the thunders' roar,
He threw the ROPE AND DREW him safe on shore

A YOUNG man, tempted by the delightful stillness of a summer's day, launches his little boat, and spreads his sail. The light winds spring up, and bear him some distance from the land; but he regards it not; the scenery is lovely, the banks of the river are clad in the beautiful robes of the season; all conspire to make him enjoy his sail. But his pleasure is short-lived: a storm arises—he strikes sail, and attempts to make the shore by rowing, but he cannot succeed. The eddying winds keep him in the middle of the stream; he drifts down to the place where there is a tremendous cataract; he hears the dreadful roaring thereof; his heart sinks within him. What shall he do? To stay in the boat is death; he cannot swim if he leaps out, yet he thinks it is the best course. He jumps overboard; still he continues to drift toward the awful gulf. But just as he is going over, one comes to the rescue. The king, who had been watching him from his palace on the hill, hastens through the pelting storm down to the river-side, and, throwing him a rope, draws him safe to land.

This emblem sets forth the glorious doctrine of Salvation by Faith. The drowning man represents the sinner in his sins. The fearful tempest—the anguish of his soul, occasioned by the terrors of God's violated Law. The forsaken boat—his self-righteousness. The King who flies to his help—the Lord Jesus Christ. Laying hold of the rope—Faith. His arrival on shore—Salvation. And as the individual rescued would most assuredly ascribe the merit of his deliverance to the prince upon the bank, and by no means to himself for seizing the rope, so every sinner saved by Faith will, despising self, give the glory of his salvation to Christ. As the rope connected the man dying in the waters with the man living on the land, so Faith unites the sinner to Christ. The *power* or ability to believe is the gift of God, but man is responsible for the use of the power. *He must lay hold of the rope.* God does not repent for man, neither does *He* believe for him, yet man has nothing whereof to glory. By grace he is saved through Faith, and that not of himself. God worketh in him both to will and to do.

> "With pitying eyes the Prince of Peace
> Beheld our helpless grief;
> He saw, and O, amazing love!
> He ran to our relief.
>
> "Down from the shining seats above,
> With joyful haste he fled,
> Enter'd the grave in mortal flesh,
> And dwelt among the dead.
>
> "O, for this love, let rocks and hills
> Their lasting silence break,
> And all harmonious human tongues
> The Saviour's praises speak.
>
> 'Angels, assist our mighty joys,
> Strike loud your harps of gold:
> But when you raise your highest notes,
> His love can ne'er be told."

Be not children in understanding. 1 Cor. xiv. 20.

SIMPLICITY, OR WANT OF UNDERSTANDING.

Deep in a meadow of rich verdure green,
A simple child of beauteous form is seen;
Pleased with the serpent's fascinating charms,
She fondly takes it to her circling arms;
Nor of the brilliant snake thinks aught of fear,
Though death among its charms lies lurking there.
But when the cricket's harmless form appears,
She's much affrighted, and bursts forth in tears;
Although its merry chirp no dangers bring,
Nor in its homely shape e'er wears a sting.
Just so the youth, deceived by beauty's form,
Nor knows that roses always bear a thorn.
Choose then for mates alone the good and wise,
And learn the homely never to despise.

The engraving shows a little child, all alone in a field. In its simplicity it fondles a deadly serpent; attracted by its brilliant and shining colors, the artless child takes hold of it without fear. She is about to take it to her bosom, when the cricket's merry chirp is heard; she is startled. In a moment the lively insect, with one spring, stands before her. Now she cries out for fear; she is greatly terrified. Thus, in her simplicity, she courts death, and embraces it; while she is frightened at homeliness, accompanied by innocence and song.

This is an emblem of the young and inexperienced. The term simple or simplicity, has a twofold meaning in Scripture. There are "the simple" whom "the Lord preserveth," and "the simple" who "pass on and are punished." In the first instance, it signifies *sincerity*, innocence; in the second, folly, or want of understanding. It may therefore be applied to the young, and the inconsiderate of all ages, who, for want of knowledge and experience, act without considering the consequences of their actions.

The youth knows not how to judge of objects that present themselves before him. Inexperienced, he knows not how to choose aright. He is in constant danger of putting evil for good, and good for evil, bitter for sweet, and sweet for bitter. Hence, he needs the instruction of God's Holy Word to enable him to discern the things that are excellent; to prove all things, and hold fast that which is good. Above all, he needs the enlightening influences of the Holy Spirit to "give him understanding," and guide him into all truth.

This want of understanding, moreover, displays itself in the wrong choice that is often made of companions; while the homely person, who may have much of wisdom and goodness, is rejected, the accomplished villain is selected as a bosom friend. The youth, deceived by his showy exterior and smooth tongue, unbosoms himself to him without reserve. The villain laughs at his simplicity, betrays his confidence, and leads him into ruin irreparable

Hence, how necessary it is that the inexperienced youth should seek the counsel of the aged and the wise, and follow the godly admonitions of parents and guardians. This would save them many a false step, and much misery in after life.

Appearances are deceitful. The ignis-fatuus looks like a friendly light, but it betrays the unwary traveller down to the secret chambers of death. Poisoned berries sometimes look like tempting grapes; ice, though it may seem firm, oftentimes breaks in, and plunges the rash youth into a watery grave; wine, when it giveth its color in the cup, at the last it biteth like a serpent, and stingeth like an adder. It was when Eve saw that the tree was pleasant to the eyes, that she took of the fruit thereof, by which act she lost Eden, and brought death into our world, and all our wo.

If, then, an act seem to be right, be sure it is so before you do it. If any thing appears to be good, be sure it is so before you touch it. If any of your acquaintance seem to be virtuous, be sure they are so ere you take them for bosom friends. "The simple pass on and are punished; but he that trusteth in the Lord shall be delivered."

"Ye simple souls that stray
  Far from the paths of peace,
That lonely, unfrequented way
  To life and happiness;
Why will ye folly love,
  And throng the downward road,
And hate the wisdom from above,
  And mock the sons of God?"

My soul is among lions. Ps. lvii. 4.——*O that I had wings like a dove! or then I would fly away and be at rest.* Ps. lv. 6.

THE PERSECUTED CHRISTIAN.

Lo! where the Christian walks in sore distress,
While various evils round about him press;
Fierce persecution as a wild bull found,
With rage he roars and tears the solid ground;
The mean backbiter, like a snarling cur,
Assails behind, his character to slur;
Slander, grown bold, in form of wolf appears,
Ravening for prey, the innocent he tears:
The adder envy lies along his path,
And works in secret with its sting of death;
Fraud, like the crocodile, now lays his snares,
To catch the unsuspecting unawares;
Oppression, outrage, is the lion mad,
When naught but blood his cruel heart can glad;
For dove-like wings the Christian prays, oppress'd,
To fly to mansions of eternal rest.

The engraving shows a poor man in great distress. Far from home, and apparently unprotected, he is beset with enemies on every side. He knows not which way to turn. Behind, he fears the bellowing of the furious bull, maddened with rage, threatening to overtake and destroy him; while the dastard cur yelps after him, close at his heels. Before him is the ferocious lion, gloating himself with the blood of its innocent victim; while the adder coils itself about his path, ready to pierce him with its deadly sting. On one hand is seen the hungry wolf ravening for prey; on the other, the insidious crocodile waiting to seize upon him, and drag him down to his den of rushes. In this hopeless condition, he longs for the wings of the dove which he sees flying over his head, for then he would escape them all; he would fly away from the forest of wild beasts to the open wilderness; there would he be at rest.

This is an emblem of what the Christian oftentimes has to suffer while passing through this world to his eternal home. Sometimes persecution, like the mad *bull* and furious *lion* seen in the picture, rages, and threatens to destroy Christianity itself, and to blot out the remembrance of it from the earth. The prophet Daniel was thus assailed, and cast into a den of lions. The early Christians were subjected to ten fierce and bloody persecutions, which terminated not until the Church had lost its character for holiness.

In the short reign of the bloody queen Mary, (about five years,) of fire and fagot memory, persecution in this form devoured 277 persons, among whom were 5 bishops, 21 clergymen, 8 gentlemen of fortune, 84 tradesmen, 100 husbandmen, 55 women, and 4 children. These were all burned alive, besides numerous confiscations, etc.

Persecution, however, exists very frequently in a different form from the above. The back-biter plies his mean, cowardly trade, in order to injure the character of the righteous. The barking, snarling cur is the most useless of the dog kind: so the backbiter is the most despicable among men. Yet is he able, oftentimes, to vex the soul of the pious.

Sometimes, slander, grown bold, like a hungry *wolf*, attacks the reputation of the man of God, as Shimei assailed David in the day of his adversity.

Envy is known to plot in secret the destruction of that excellence she cannot reach; while *fraud* takes advantage of the unsuspecting child of God, and seeks to draw him into sin and trouble. In the midst of his persecutions, the Christian would fain borrow the wings of the dove, and seek refuge in some vast wilderness, "some boundless contiguity of shade," or rather, the wings of some heavenly cherub; then would he fly to mansions of eternal repose, "where the wicked cease from troubling, and where the weary are forever at rest."

> "When rising floods my soul o'erflow,
> When sinks my heart in waves of wo,
> Jesus, thy timely aid impart,
> And raise my head, and cheer my heart.
>
> "If rough and stormy be the way,
> My strength proportion to my day,
> Till toil, and grief, and pain shall cease,
> Where all is calm, and joy, and peace."

O wretched man that I am! who shall deliver me from the body of this death? Rom. vii. 24.

THE SOUL IN BONDAGE.

Horror of horrors! what a sight is here!
Life linked with death, in terror and despair.
Thus cruel tyrants, when they won the field,
Were wont to punish those compell'd to yield.
The wounded captive, writhing still with pain,
Was made to wear the adamantine chain,
That round the limbs of one new-slain was led,
And bound the living to the putrid dead,
Till, choked with stench, the lingering victim lay,
And breathed in agony his life away.
'Tis thus the soul, enlighten'd by the word,
Descries the path that upward leads to God;
And fain would run, but feels a galling chain,
That quickly drags him to the world again
Corruption's body opens to his eye,
He sees the cause, but oh! he cannot fly.
Who, who! he asks, with trembling, struggling breath,
Will save me from this fearful mass of death?
He calls on Moses now to break his chain,
Moses is deaf—he calls on him in vain;
He calls on Jesus—wondrous name!—he hears,

And breaks his chain, and scatters all his fears.
Now, like the bird that from its prison flies,
On wings of love soars upward to the skies.

This engraving represents the horrid custom of ancient tyrants, who, in order to strike terror into the hearts of their enemies, invented a mode of punishment more terrible than death itself. They chained the living prisoner to the body of a dead person. Virgil, referring to this monstrous practice, says: "The tyrants inflicted a punishment hitherto unheard-of: they bound the living to the dead, limb to limb, and face to face, until suffocated with the abominable stench; in loathsome embraces they gave up the ghost." This mode of torture was considered more appalling than that of burning alive, breaking upon the rack, or even crucifixion itself.

It is, no doubt, to this custom that the Apostle Paul alludes in his Epistle to the Romans. No other image could so well illustrate his meaning. His readers were familiar with it. Peter, *sleeping* in the *prison, bound* with *chains* to the *bodies of two live men*, would not suit the apostle's purpose. It is very important that we try to make out his meaning. I am brought, he says, into "captivity to the law of sin," and wounded, conquered, and chained to this body of death. The soul is under the law or power of sin, and chained to a body of death—a mass of corruption. An evil heart, unholy passions, depraved affections predominate. The light of the Holy Spirit shines into the soul, and the man discovers that the law of God is holy, just, and good, and fain would keep it; that God himself is indeed altogether lovely, and he would acquaint himself with him. He now sees the path that leads to endless life, and he desires to walk in it. But when he would do good, evil is present with him, when he would approach the seat of Divine Perfections, something keeps him back; when he would walk in the path of life, he finds himself enchained. Now he follows the links of his chain, and discovers the body of corruption to which it is secured.

He tries to free himself by some good things he did years ago: this only makes the case worse. He calls on his friends for help; but vain is the help of man. He calls upon Moses, he tries to reform his outward deportment; but by "the deeds of the law" he cannot extricate himself. At length, in the bitterness of his soul, he exclaims, "O wretched man that I am! who shall deliver me from this body of death?" And now the angel of mercy directs him to the Breaker of chains—the Abolisher of death—Conqueror of the grave—the glorious Giver of life and immortality—Jesus Emanuel, God with us. The Saviour is propitious, deliverance is obtained, and the soul, like a bird escaped from the snare of the fowler, sings triumphantly:

"What though I could not break my chain,
  Or e'er cast off my load,
The things impossible to men,
  Are possible to God."

" Love only can the conquest win,
  The strength of sin subdue,
(Mine own unconquerable sin,)
  And form my soul anew.

" Faith, mighty Faith, the promise sees,
  And looks to that alone;
Laughs at impossibilities,
  And cries, ' It shall be done.' "

There is a way that seemeth right unto a man; but the end thereof are the ways of death. Prov. xvi. 25.

DANGER OF SELF-INDULGENCE.

With cheerful step, at blush of early day,
The traveller began his arduous way;
He seeks at noon some pleasant, cool retreat,
Where he may shelter from the noontide heat.
But oh! beneath a tuft of flowery green,
A poisonous serpent slyly lurks unseen;
With deadly aim he from his covert flies,
The traveller, wounded, in the forest dies.

   Thus some begin to run the Christian race,
And for awhile keep up a steady pace;
Till soft indulgence near their path lays wait,
And spreads deceitfully her pleasing bait;
O'ercome by sloth, to sin they fall a prey,
And never more pursue the good old way.

This engraving represents a traveller fatally bitten by a serpent. With a light heart and a firm step he started on his journey at early dawn. Every thing looked lovely around him; he thought of nothing but success. He journeyed on very well until the hour of noon arrived, when he began to grow somewhat tired. He looked round for some cool, sequestered spot, where he might while away a few hours. At a little distance from the path, he discovered a pleasant, shady grove. For a moment he hesitated; but his love of ease prevailed. Now he forgets every thing except his present convenience; he enters the grove; he is delighted with its cool air and agreeable fragrance.

Suddenly he is bitten to the quick. A serpent, concealed hitherto in the grass, fixes in his flesh its poisonous fang; the wound is mortal; his life's blood is poisoned; fires intolerable course through his veins. He now repents of his folly; he wishes he had borne the heat of the day. The venom reaches his heart; he thinks of home and friends; his spirits sink, his head swims, his eyes—they close in death. The leaves of autumn are strown around him, and the place that knew him knows him now no more forever.

This is an emblem of the danger of self-indulgence. With alacrity and delight the convert sets out on his journey to the kingdom of heaven. He anticipates the pleasures he will meet with on his arrival. He thinks not of the dangers of the road, nor of his own besetments. For awhile he makes rapid progress. By and by persecution and trouble come upon him; he grows weary. He looks round for some other way, that has in it less of danger and difficulty. Soon he discovers one apparently more easy and pleasing to flesh and blood. For awhile he stands in doubt; his love of self-indulgence overcomes him. "He will not endure hardness as a good soldier of Jesus Christ." He enters the forbidden path. Now all seems pleasant and delightful. The pleasures of the road lull to sleep his spiritual senses. Sin, now like a serpent, assails him; he has now no strength to resist; he falls a victim to his folly; guilt and remorse now sting him to the quick. "Fool that I was," he exclaims. "Oh! that I had continued in the path of duty." It is too late. Wretched man, self-indulgence has proved his ruin.

The disobedient prophet fell a victim to self-indulgence, when he turned aside to "eat bread and drink water," and a lion met him by the way and slew him. The five foolish virgins also, who "slumbered and slept" when they ought to have been watching, fell by the same insidious foe. They awoke in outer darkness, and found the door of the kingdom of heaven fast closed against them forever.

"If any man will be my disciple," said the Saviour, "let him *deny himself*, take up his cross, and follow me." To them who by *patient continuance* in well-doing seek for glory, and honor, and immortality: eternal life. "He that *endureth to the end*, the same shall be saved."

"*Deny thyself, and take thy cross,*
　Is the Redeemer's great command!
Nature must count her gold but dross,
　If she would gain this heavenly land.

"The fearful soul that tires and faints,
　And walks the ways of God no more,
Is but esteem'd almost a saint,
　And makes his own destruction sure."

Dr. Watts.

Surely thou didst set them in slippery places: thou castedst them down into destruction. Ps. lxxiii. 16.

CARNAL SECURITY.

See here portrayed, a gently rising ground,
With tulips gay, and blooming roses crowned;
Where flowers of various hues, or gay, or fair,
Mingle their sweetness with the balmy air;
While woodland minstrels stoop upon the wing,
Attune their notes, and softest carols sing;
A youth lies sleeping on the roseate bed,
Heedless of dangers, thus to ruin led;
A horrid gulf of thickest night is there,
Where hope ne'er comes, but darkness and despair;
A turn—a move—and in the gulf he'll roll,
Where fiery billows prey upon the soul.

It is by ascending "a gently rising ground," and not by overleaping abrupt precipices, that the youth attains his dangerous position—his bad eminence. "Sin is first pleasing, then easy, then delightful, then confirmed,—then the man is impenitent, then he is obstinate, then he resolves never to repent, and then he is damned."

Sin possesses a peculiar faculty to deceive; this is true of sin in all its modifications. It allures, that it may betray and destroy. It meets the youth with smiles only, that it may plunge a dagger more surely in the heart. It promises to the gambler, the robber, and murderer, wealth, pleasure, kingdoms. But having filled the cup of hope to the brim, with cruel mocking it is exchanged for the chalice of despair.

Sin adapts itself to the various depraved appetites or propensities of man. To all its votaries it promiseth the pleasures of this life. But "the wages of sin is death." To all likewise it offers perfect *security*; crying peace, safety, when sudden destruction is at hand.

As sin is thus deceptive in its promises, and fatal in its results, so also is it in its influence on the human mind. It blinds the eyes, it hardens the heart, it sears the conscience, it fascinates the imagination, it perverts the judgment, it gives a wrong bias to the will, it effaces from the memory recollections of the beautiful and the good. In a word, it throws the pall of the grave over the whole man, and hides from his view, his guilt, his danger, and his immortality.

The man is now wrapped in the mantle of "*carnal security;*" he is insensible to all around him. The path of sinful pleasure is strewed with Plutonian flowers. They breathe the odor of the pit, stupifying to the senses. The bewitching music of the great enchanter, casts the soul into a deep sleep. It is like the sleep of the grave.

Perhaps he is dreaming of happiness that he will never enjoy; perhaps of home, that he shall never behold; or of friends, whom he shall embrace no more forever. In the midst of his dreams of delight, the bow of the Almighty is strung; the arrow is made ready; the dart of death is uplifted, ready to fall upon the unconscious victim; the pit has opened its mouth to receive the prey. Nothing but the voice of God can arouse him from his lethargy.

"What meanest thou, O sleeper! arise and call upon God, if so be that thou perish not. Awake, thou that sleepest; and arise from the dead, and Christ shall give thee light."

"Rejoice, O young man, in thy youth, and let thy heart cheer thee in the days of thy youth; walk thou in the ways of thy heart, and in the sight of thy eyes. But know, that for all these things God will bring thee into judgment."

"Ye sons of Adam, vain and young,
Indulge your eyes, indulge your tongue;
Taste the delights your souls desire,
And give aloose to all your fire.

"Pursue the pleasures you design,
And cheer your hearts with songs and wine;
Enjoy the day of mirth; but know,
There is a day of judgment too.

"God from on high beholds your thoughts,
His book records your secret faults;
The works of darkness you have done,
Must all appear before the sun.

* * * * * * *

"The dust returns to dust again;
The soul, in agonies of pain,
Ascends to God, not there to dwell,
But hears her doom, and sinks to hell."

RELIGIOUS EMBLEMS

Where envying and strife is, there is confusion and every evil work. James iii. 16.——*Wrath is cruel, and anger is outrageous; but who is able to stand before envy?* Prov. xxx. 11.

THE THREEFOLD DEMON, OR ENVY, HATRED, AND MALICE.

Lo! where the threefold demon stalks along,
The work of desolation to prolong;
Envy, and hate, and malice, all combined,
To make afflictions, and torment mankind.
Forward the demon strides in sullen mood,
And chews a viper for her daily food;
Loaded with slanders, and with poison strong,
She deals them largely to the gaping throng:
Her eyes are weak, and in disorder'd plight,
And hence a blinder to keep off the light.
To show that from without proceeds her pain,
She leans with anguish on a thorny cane:
At others' excellence she pines, straightway
Hate brings her malice into active play;
Good name she tears, and scatters to the air
All other epithets of good and fair:
A spotless character, wherever found,
With hate she tramples on the miry ground;

While in her train behold a tempest rise,
That swells and reaches to the topmost skies.

In the engraving is represented a threefold demon striding forward, with sullen pace, in order to torment mankind. On her back she carries a pack of slanders; under her arm a quantity of poison: thus she is thoroughly furnished for her hellish work. She is chewing the flesh of a viper, which, thus introduced in her system, poisons her heart's blood, and disorders her eyesight. In her left hand she grasps a thorny staff; this is to show that she torments herself voluntarily. She banquets on the destruction of human happiness. See! how she tramples upon character, and scatters to the four winds the reputation of others. She leaves behind her, and following in her train, a gathering, blackening tempest, surcharged with the "fire of hell," soon to burst upon mankind.

This emblem represents Envy, Hatred, and Malice united in one person, and forming a being of extraordinary malignity. There are many such in human shape—demons wearing the mask of human form, beings whose eyes are pained at the sight of either excellence or happiness, whose heart is corroded with the poison of envious and malicious thoughts, self-tormented with the thorns of their own creation—beings who never smile but at the tears of others, whose hellish joy consists in the wreck of human happiness, and whose only music is the voice of lamentation and wo—beings of Satanic inspiration. They are always well furnished with slanders, and never want for opportunity to vent them. In this they copy after their great father, the prime enemy of man. When beholding the original happiness of the first human pair in the bowers of Eden, ere he effected their overthrow.

> "———————— Aside the devil turn'd
> For envy; yet with jealous leer malign
> Eyed them askance, and to himself thus 'plain'd,
> 'Sight hateful, sight tormenting!'"

There is great propriety in representing the union of envy, hatred, and malice in one individual. Envy itself is defined to be "pain felt, and malignity conceived, at the sight of excellence or happiness." But when envy conceives, it brings forth hatred; and hatred, when it is finished, brings forth malice. We have a striking example of this union in the conduct of Joseph's brethren towards him. First, "they envied him," probably on account of his superior excellence; then "they hated him," in consequence of the partial conduct of Jacob their father; and finally, in their malice "they sold him" for a slave.

A still greater example occurs in the conduct of the Jews towards the blessed Redeemer, in whom all excellences met, when "for envy they delivered him" into the hands of the Romans; they *envied* him for the splendor of holiness that shone around his path. In their *hatred* they exclaimed, "He hath a devil," and in their blood-thirsty *malice*, "they cried out the more, saying, Let him be crucified."

> If envy, malice, hatred, reigns,
> And binds my soul with slavish chains,
> O Lord, thy heavenly love impart,
> And drive the demon from my heart.

While we look not at the things which are seen, but at the things which are not seen. 2 Cor. iv. 18.——*For we walk by faith, not by sight.* 2 Cor. v. 7.

CHRISTIAN FAITH, OR RELIGION.

High on the world, see where Religion stands
And bears the open volume in her hands;
With eyes upraised, she seeks for heavenly light,
To know its doctrines and its laws aright:
The cross of Christ she bears, and walks abroad,
And holds communion with her Father, God.
Thus with the Christian: filled with love divine,
Above the world he soars in heavenly clime,
The sacred cross his only hope and stay,
The Book of Truth his guide from day to day.

CHRISTIAN Faith or Religion is here represented standing upon a globe. This denotes that the Christian, although he is in the world, yet like a ship at sea, he is above the world. In her hands she holds the opened volume of God's Holy Word. She is looking upward, to show that she expects light from above to shine upon the sacred page. With one arm she embraces the cross, signifying that her only hope of salvation is founded on the death of Jesus Christ.

This is an emblem of that religion which God in his mercy has given to mankind. He who possesses it, rests his all—his soul and body, his time and his eternity—upon the atonement of our Lord and Saviour Jesus Christ. While some are trusting to the mere mercy of God out of Christ, and others to their self-righteousness, others again to the intercession of men, women, and angels, his language is, 'Tis all *my* hope, and all my plea, for me the Saviour died. God forbid that I should glory, save in the cross of our Lord Jesus Christ. The cross of Christ is the mighty lever that is to roll the world back again to God. All true Christians have so understood it.

Constantine the Great took advantage of this fact—the common faith of the early Christians in the power of the cross.—When going to fight against Maxentius, he related to his army that he saw (some say in a vision) a cross in the sky, bearing this inscription, εν τουτω νικα, "*By this, conquer.*" It inspired the soldiers with courage. The cross was seen inscribed on every banner. The emperor led his army to triumphant victory.

The Holy Scriptures are very precious to him who has true faith. He regards them as the words of God—as a divine proclamation of grace to man—as a record of parental love—as a history of his dear Redeemer, and of his own redemption—as the title-deed of his own glorious inheritance—as the only rule of his faith and practice. With its sacred leaves open before him, he looks upward and prays "O Lord, open thou mine eyes, that I may behold wondrous things out of thy law." While some neglect and despise the Holy Book, and others depend upon human creeds, and the musty traditions of "the Fathers," he exclaims, "O how I love thy law. Thy statutes have been my songs in the house of my pilgrimage."

By his faith in the cross, the Bible, the power of prayer, and the influences of the Holy Spirit, the Christian overcomes the world, enjoys communion with God, becomes meet to be a partaker of the inheritance of the saints in light, and finally join in the song of Moses and of the Lamb forever.

Then embrace Religion, " and you shall be presently installed in the possession of all the benefits and immunities of the Redeemer's purchase without deduction, and without qualification; you shall emerge from under the dark shadows of the fall, into the effulgence of the light, and the plenitude of the joy, of a renovated, heaven-born nature; and the silent tide of oblivion shall instantly close forever over all your past sins, and you shall be immediately admitted into the circle of the redeemed of the Lord.

" Your brow shall be encircled with a double diadem of life and righteousness ; a patent to all the titles and illustrious dignities of the nobility of heaven shall be made out for you, which nothing in time or eternity shall alienate or rescind. Paradise shall unlock for you its everlasting gates, and you shall behold the interminable future through a vista of the brightest hopes, and inherit a name immortal in the records of glory."

Which hope we have as an anchor of the soul, both sure and steadfast. Heb. vi. 19.——*For we are saved by hope.* Rom. viii. 24.

HOPE.

On Truth's substantial rock, Hope takes her seat,
While waves tumultuous dash against her feet;
The sky with blackness now becomes o'erspread;
The tempest threatens her devoted head:
Louder, and louder still, the thunders sound;
The lightning flings its fearful glare around;
Creation trembles; but fast anchored there
Hope sits unshaken, never in despair;
With eyes turned upward, whence her help descends,
She waits expecting, till the tempest ends.

Hope is represented in the picture above as being seated upon a rock. Worldly hope has always some supposed foundation on which it relies. But Christian hope has for a foundation the rock of truth, God's most holy word. In the midst of gathering storms she is depicted looking upward; this expresses her confidence in God. She leans upon an anchor; this denotes steadfastness and trust. Hope was compared to an anchor, by ancient writers

Thus Socrates expresses himself: "To ground hope on a false supposition, is like trusting to a weak anchor."

The hope of heaven is represented by the Apostle Paul, as the anchor of the soul. We see the propriety of this figure when we consider that the world is like a tempestuous sea, full of dangers The course of the child of God, the voyage; heaven the port, or harbor, which he expects and desires to gain. Sometimes, when a ship rides at anchor, dreadful storms arise, the wind blows with fury, the tempest howls, and waves roar and beat against the vessel. But if the ship be what is termed seaworthy, that is, firm, strongly put together; if, at the same time, the cable be strong, and the anchor bites, or strikes its fluke deep into good holding ground; all will be well. The storm may rage, rocks and quicksands may lie to leeward, threatening destruction, yet will she be secure. It is true, she will have to send down her topmasts and yards, and keep anchor-watch, yet will she ride out the gale.

By this we may see the proper use of hope to the Christian, which is, to keep the soul calm and secure in the day of adversity. Hope does not remove trouble; it sustains the soul in the time of trouble. The anchor does not dispel the storm; it does not quiet the roaring waves, arrest the rolling thunder, nor bid the winds be still: but it enables the vessel to ride out the fury of the gale; it keeps her from being driven on the rocks of death. The most pious Christian does not find himself exempt from the cares and calamities of this life, or free from the conflicts and difficulties of the Christian life. He often finds himself "toss'd upon life's raging billows," but under these circumstances the hope of heaven, as the anchor of the soul, keeps him steady. "Which hope we have," says the apostle, "as an anchor to the soul, both sure and steadfast." This hope preserves him from being dashed to pieces against the rocks of temptation, destruction, and despair;' it at the same time imparts a delightful sense of security in the day of trial, a blessed sense of peace amid a sea of troubles. It inspires fortitude and boldness in the cause of God. "Hope maketh not ashamed, because the love of God is shed abroad in the heart by the Holy Ghost, which is given unto us."

Among the Arabians, the watermelon is known by the name of "*batech*," which in the Hebrew language signifies *hope*. The melon, by its tendrils, clings to whatever it can lay hold of. Just so, hope: the Christian's hope clings to God, his promises, his faithfulness, his love. "The watermelon is cultivated on the banks of the river Nile," says a traveller. "It serves the Egyptians for meat, drink, and medicine. It is eaten in abundance by even the richer sort of people, but the poor scarcely eat any thing but these." This affords a good illustration. What, indeed, would life be without hope!

"Man never is, but always to be blest."

Take away hope, and you take away the enjoyment of prosperity; deprive man of hope, and you take away the only support and solace of adversity. The most happy, the most prosperous, without hope would soon become the most wretched. The poor and afflicted, without it, would sink at once into the gulf of despair. To deprive man of hope, is to rob him of his dearest treasure. Extinguish hope, and you extinguish life, for who could live without hope? It is the last lingering light of the human breast. "It shines when every other is put out. Quench it, and the gloom of affliction becomes the very blackness of darkness—cheerless and impenetrable."

Bear ye one another's burdens, and so fulfil the law of Christ. Gal. vi. 2

BROTHERLY KINDNESS.

Lo! the poor pilgrim bends beneath his load,
And travels wearily his length'ning road;
Contempt's vast weight, back'd by afflictions sore,
Incline him now to give his journey o'er;
With groaning sick, with labor faint, he stops,
And on the pathway tottering, almost drops:
But ere he prostrate falls, relief is near,
Two brethren of the Christian band appear;
Their cheerful aid they speedily impart,
To ease his burden, and relieve his heart;
His willing shoulder each one runs to lend,
And on he travels to his journey's end

Look at the poor pilgrim. Awhile ago he was bending beneath his burden, unaided, unpitied, and alone. Almost pressed to the earth, he would fain have given his journey over. His heart was sick within him; his bones were wearied; he thought he would lay him down and die. But before he sunk under the pressure, he saw two friends coming towards him. He endeavors now to hold out a little longer. Presently they arrive, and give him a friendly salutation. They do not, like the *Levite*, pass by on the other side; at once they hasten to his relief; each one puts his shoulder to the burden. Now it is lighter; the poor man draws breath; they encourage him with kind words, but still more with their efficient help. Nor do they leave him until he arrives at the end of his journey.

This is a good emblem of Brotherly Kindness. The burdened pilgrim represents the Christian travelling on in the way of duty, bearing affliction and contempt. Afflictions such as are common to men press heavily upon him; contempt and tribulation, peculiar to those who will live godly in Christ Jesus, almost overwhelm him. His soul is among lions; he is ready to sink beneath his burden. His head is sick, his heart is faint. He says, "I shall one day fall by my enemies; I may as well give up first as last." Just now some Christian brethren—signified by the pilgrim's two friends above—hearing of his circumstances, call upon him, find out his trouble, and immediately propose to help him. They furnish him with pecuniary aid, assist him with their prayers and counsel, and being disciples of Jesus, they resolve to bear a part of the reproach of Christ. They unite with their afflicted brother in stemming the torrent of wickedness that runs down the streets, and in advancing the kingdom of God on the earth. All this sympathy and aid makes a new man of him; he again lifts up his head, and goes on his way rejoicing.

The blessed Redeemer established his cross on the earth as the rallying point for all hearts; that being softened *there* by divine love, they might be united to God; and that being divested *there* of all selfishness, they might be united to each other in the bonds of a holy, loving brotherhood. "A new commandment," said the Saviour, "give I unto you, that ye love one another." Hence the words of the apostle, "*Bear ye one another's burdens, and so fulfil the law of Christ.*"

Even under the Jewish dispensation it was ordained that "if thou see the ass of him that hateth thee lying under his burden, thou shalt surely help him." How much better is a man than a beast! and compared with the Jew's, how much more powerful is the weight of the Christian's obligation!

>Blest be the tie that binds
>   Our hearts in Christian love,
>The fellowship of kindred minds
>   Is like to that above.
>
>We share our mutual woes;
>   Our mutual burdens bear;
>And often for each other flows
>   The sympathizing tear.
>
>Before our Father's throne
>   We pour our ardent prayers;
>Our fears, our hopes, our aims are one,
>   Our comforts and our cares.
>
>   *Fawcett.*

Without shedding of blood there is no remission. Rom. ix. 22.—*We have redemption through his blood, even the forgiveness of sin.* Col. i. 14.

DIVINE LOVE AND JUSTICE.

Behold where Justice, with her sword raised high,
In words that echo through the trembling sky,
Demands, in virtue of the Law's just right,
That man should perish in eternal night.
Pale, trembling, fearful, see the culprit stand,
Nor dares to hope deliverance at hand.
On wings of grace, and heavenly motion fleet,
Love hastens, prostrate at the claimant's feet.
"Me! me behold!" she cries, "on me be pour'd
"The wrathful vial that for him is stored.
"Here, in this heart, plunge deep th' avenging blade,
" My life for his! so Justice shall be paid."
'Tis done! the sword is bathed in spotless blood,
And man, released, returns to life—and God.

In this picture Justice is seen standing with her sword raised high, ready to fall upon the guilty one. In her left hand she holds the scales of equity; at her side the two tables of law appear, at the foot of which lies the Holy Bible. In the front of Justice one is seen in the attitude of a culprit; he hangs his head down in acknowledgment of his guilt. Between the offender and Justice, behold one of celestial mien, in a kneeling posture, with wings outspread; her countenance beams with compassion; addressing Justice, she points to her uncovered bosom, and asks that the sword may be plunged therein, and that the guilty one may go free. This is *Divine Love*.

This is an emblem of human redemption. A book of laws is given to man, which is holy, just, and good, the substance of which is contained in the decalogue, or ten commandments. These laws, whether engraved on tables of stone, or written on rolls of parchment, or printed in books, or impressed on the human heart, have been violated by all mankind, for "all have sinned," and consequently have come short of the divine approbation. The penalty is "death." "The soul that sinneth, it shall die." Thus the matter stands when the sinner is brought before the tribunal of Justice.

Justice never forgives, nor makes any allowance for circumstances or human infirmity. The plea put in by Lord Nelson when dying, that "he had not been a very great sinner," will be utterly unavailing. The reply of Justice is, "He that offends in one point, is guilty of all."

But ere the sword of Justice is bathed in the blood of the guilty, Divine Love, in the person of Jesus Christ, interposed, "and poured out his soul unto death, and made intercession for the transgressors." On the hill of Calvary this wonderful scene took place. There Divine Love received the sword of Justice—there the heart of the Son of God bled for guilty man—there he "who knew no sin, became a sin-offering for us." Mercy and Truth now meet together, Justice and Peace kiss each other.

"Greater love than this hath no man, that a man lay down his life for his friends; but God commendeth his love toward us, in that while we were yet sinners, Christ died for us." Shout, heaven and earth, this sum of God to man, that God can now be just, and the justifier of him who believes in Jesus.

"Infinite grace! Almighty charms!
　Stand in amaze, ye rolling skies!
Jesus the God extends his arms,
　Hangs on a cross of love, and dies!

"Did pity ever stoop so low,
　Dress'd in divinity and blood?
Was ever rebel courted so,
　In groans of an expiring God?

"Again he lives, and spreads his hands—
　Hands that were nail'd with torturing smart,
By these dear wounds! he looks and stands,
　And prays to clasp me to his heart."

Five bleeding wounds he bears,
　Received on Calvary;
They pour effectual prayers,
　They strongly speak for me;
Forgive him, O forgive, they cry,
Nor let that ransom'd sinner die.

He ever lives above,
　For me to intercede;
His all-redeeming love,
　His precious blood to plead.
His blood atoned for all our race,
And sprinkles now the throne of grace.

RELIGIOUS EMBLEMS.

And all things are of God, who hath reconciled us to himself by Jesus Christ..... God was in Christ, reconciling the world unto himself..... Be ye reconciled to God. 2 Cor. v. 18, 19, 20.

RECONCILIATION.

Between the bleeding victim, cut in twain,
Two, once at variance, meet, at one again;
Gladly the hand of fellowship impart,
And pledge the honor of a faithful heart,
And by the God of life and death agree
The past to bury in oblivion's sea;
They vow each other's interest to befriend,
And when in need, to succor and defend.
And as the parted victim lies in death,
So they adjudge who breaks his solemn oath.

THIS engraving represents two men standing between the two parts of a divided calf. They hav been for a long time enemies to each other. Now they earnestly desire to become friends again; they wish to bury all past differences in the ocean of forgetfulness, and to enter into an agreement mutually to assist and defend each other in time to come.

To accomplish this object, they have met together
As a proof of their sincerity, they offer a sacrifice
to the object of their religious adoration. The blood
of the victim is poured out, the animal is divided into two equal parts. The parts are placed opposite
to each other, space enough being left for the parties
to enter between. When this is done, they meet in
the middle of the divided beast, where the contract
is read or repeated, and by a solemn oath sanctioned
and confirmed. This was an ancient and almost
universal mode of making contracts. It is referred
to by Jeremiah the prophet: "And I will deliver up
the men that have transgressed my covenant, which
have not performed the words of the covenant which
they had made before me, when they cut the calf in
twain, and passed through the parts thereof."

The above is a significant emblem of that reconciliation which is proclaimed by the everlasting
gospel. The holy God and sinful man constitute the
parties. Man had, by his sins, separated himself
from God, and had, in fact, become an "enemy."
God, the offended party, proclaims a truce, and proposes a reconciliation. The place of meeting was
Mount Calvary. There Mercy and Truth met together, Justice and Peace embraced each other; the
victim, the Lord Jesus Christ. Without shedding of
blood there is no forgiveness, and without forgiveness there is no reconciliation; but "God was *in
Christ*, reconciling the world to himself," and "Christ
is our peace, who hath made *both one*." The terms
of the covenant are, "He that believeth shall be
saved, and he that believeth not shall be damned."

On this ground, i. e., "*in Christ*," God has sworn
to receive to friendship all who come to him. Here
he opens his heart of love—here he bestows more
than kingly dignities—here the kingdom of grace is

exhibited, and the splendors of the kingdom of glory shadowed forth. But for those "who count the blood of the covenant an unholy thing, there remaineth no more sacrifice for sin, but a certain fearful looking for of fiery indignation, which shall devour the adversaries."

The reconciliation of a soul to God is perhaps the greatest event that can come to pass on the earth. It affects three worlds: heaven, earth, and hell. When this takes place, angels, in their flights of mercy, passing over fields of renown, where empires are won and lost, stoop upon the wing, and stringing their harps to a loftier melody, they sing the anthem of all-redeeming love, " Glory to God in the highest on earth peace, and good-will toward man."

> God, the offended God Most High,
>   Ambassadors to rebels sends;
> His messengers his place supply,
>   And Jesus begs us to be friends
>
> Us in the stead of Christ they pray,
>   Us in the stead of God entreat,
> To cast our arms, our sins, away,
>   And find forgiveness at his feet.
>
> Our God in Christ! thine embassy,
>   And proffer'd mercy we embrace,
> And gladly reconciled to thee,
>   Thy condescending mercy praise.

Wesley

That we might receive the adoption of sons . . . . and if a son, then a heir of God. Gal. iv. 5, 7.

ADOPTION.

See here the king, in regal splendor clad,
Comes forth to meet the ragged, friendless lad;
Attended by his sons, a princely race,
He comes to manifest his royal grace:
In one hand, see! he bears a crown of light,
And with the other takes the hapless wight,
And up the steps he leads him, pale with dread,
And sets the diadem upon his head.
His rags removed, with regal robes he's dress'd,
And o'er his shoulders thrown the purple vest.
The royal youths look on with mute surprise,
While pleasure dances in their generous eyes.
The imperial gates on golden hinges swing,
And crowds advance, and hail the new-made king.

A MONARCH is here seen standing arrayed in his robes of state, and crown of glittering gems. He has left his guests within the palace; he has come forth he holds in his hand a crown of purest gold. On the steps he meets a poor, ragged boy; he intends to make him an object of his especial favor. He takes him kindly by the hand, and leads him up the steps. The poor boy trembles; he is greatly afraid. The king places the crown upon his brow; he commands that royal robes be brought forthwith, to clothe him withal. Moreover, he orders that proclamation be made, announcing that he is received among the princes of the realm.

Some of the king's sons are seen standing behind. They look on with wonder, but not with jealousy They appear delighted at what they see; they embrace him as a brother. The news reaches the inside of the palace; the inmates hasten out to congratulate the new-made king. He returns with them and takes his seat at the banquet, amid strains of music and the voice of song.

This is an emblem of Adoption. The king represents the Almighty Father, King of heaven and earth. The king's sons signify the angels, who have never sinned. The boy in rags represents the sinner, man. The sinner, "wretched, and miserable, and poor, and blind, and naked," is driven by the storms of guilt and anguish that beat upon him, to seek a place of refuge. "Whither shall I flee?" he asks, in the agony of his soul. He resolves, " I will arise and go to my Father." Thus, in all his misery, he presents himself before the King, Jehovah.

Whereas the king is seen coming forth from his palace, and taking the poor boy by the hand; this is to show how willingly God receives the poor penitent who comes to him in the name of the Mediator. When he was yet a great way off, he saw him, and had compassion on him. He takes him by the hand, saying, " Him that cometh unto me, I will in no wise cast out." He places a crown on his head, that is, he adopts him as his own son; he makes him an heir of his eternal glory.

Now he has a childlike confidence in God as his Father; God having sent forth the spirit of his Son into his heart, crying, Abba, Father. He takes his place among the children of God, lost in wonder, love, and praise. "Behold what manner of love the Father hath bestowed on us, that we should be called the sons of God."

The angels, those elder sons of the Almighty, gladly welcome the adopted to their number; they receive him as one that was lost, and is found, that was dead, and is alive again; and henceforth minister to him as an heir of salvation.

> Not all the nobles of the earth,
> Who boast the honors of their birth,
> Such real dignity can claim,
> As those that bear the Christian name.
>
> To them the privilege is given
> To be the sons and heirs of heaven;
> Sons of the God who reigns on high,
> And heirs of joy beyond the sky.
>
> On them, a happy, chosen race,
> Their Father pours his richest grace;
> To them his counsels he imparts,
> And stamps his image on their hearts.
>
> *Dr. S. Stennett.*

RELIGIOUS EMBLEMS.

For they loved the praise of men, more than the praise of God. John xii.

SPIRITUAL PRIDE.

See where the Pharisee inflated stands,
And sounds his praise abroad to distant lands
Himself his trumpeter, he blows, not faint,
That all may hear, and own him for a saint;
His lengthen'd notes in sonorous accents say,
"I do—I think—I give—I fast—I pray!"
No bankrupt he, for lo! to feed his pride,
See bale on bale, close pack'd, stand by his side.
The beggar comes, worn down with grief, and old;
He's soon discharged, for Pride has little gold.
He doles his pittance into misery's hat,
And loud applause he asks, in full for that.
The gaudy peacock, strutting in the rear,
Is but a figure of this trumpeter;
It struts, and swells, and spreads its plumes abroad:
So he, absorb'd in self, forgets his God.

This engraving represents a man who appears to be on very respectable terms with himself. He is sounding a trumpet before him; he is very anxious that everybody should know when he performs what he conceives to be a good action. A poor man is asking charity; he never refuses a trifle, provided he has his trumpet with him. Up it goes, and with a long blast, he calls the distant passengers to behold him. At the side of the trumpeter are seen several bales of goods; these are his stock in trade. Behind, is seen the peacock, strutting, swelling, and displaying her brilliant train. A proper emblem of this proud trumpeter.

The above cut is an emblem of Spiritual Pride. The trumpeter, giving a little small-change to the beggar, and apprizing everybody of the fact, denotes one who loves to make a parade of his religious performances. Does he give to benevolent objects? It is that he may receive the praise of men. Does he fast, or pray, or worship? It is that he "may be seen of men." On the house-top, through the newspapers, and other sources of circulation, he proclaims his good deeds. He conjugates all his verbs in the first person only: "I visited," "I preached," "I prayed," "I gave," etc. Thus the praise of worms becomes necessary to his existence; on this food he grows fat. Deprive him of it, and he will pine away, and die of atrophy. He sacrifices to his own net; he burns incense to his own drag. Self is the god he adores. The "bales of goods" denote that he is well stocked with self-righteousness. In his own opinion, he is "rich and increased in goods, and has need of nothing." The peacock, after all, has just as much religion as he has.

The hypocritical Pharisees of the Saviour's time were men of this stamp. They sounded a trumpet before them under pretence of calling the poor together; but in reality it was to say, "Look at me." They had "their reward." In the East, the practice varies. It is said that the dervishes, a kind of religious beggars, carry with them a horn, which, when receiving alms, they blow in honor of the giver.

All pride is pretty much alike in its nature and effects. It is produced in some persons by noble birth, and great natural abilities. In others, by wealth and learning. In others again, by certain ecclesiastical endowments, such as an office in the church, the gift of praying, or of preaching, etc. These things are all alike good in themselves, but the hearts of the possessors being unsanctified, the gifts are abused, and the Giver neglected.

He who possesses true religion will be truly humble. Humility is the only proper antidote for pride. When humility enters, pride departs, as flies the darkness from the sun. To slay pride, and teach man humility by example, the blessed Saviour took upon him the form of a servant. He made himself of no reputation; he humbled himself unto death, yea, even unto the death of the cross. O wonderful humility! O boundless grace!

Pride renders its possessor truly miserable in this life. The Father of spirits alone can fill an immortal spirit. The man of pride rejects the blessed God, and depends for happiness on the applause of man. This is uncertain, unsatisfying, and transitory. Witness the case of Haman, who, notwithstanding "the glory of his riches," "the multitude of his children," and his princely preferments, was truly wretched. "All this availed him nothing," so long as his voracious pride went without its accustomed fee—so long as one man refused to bring his tribute of homage. But pride will render its possessor miserable to all eternity. "How can ye be saved who seek honor one of another, and not the honor that cometh from God only?"

Beware of false prophets, which come to you in sheep's clothing; but inwardly they are ravening wolves. Matt. vii. 15.

HYPOCRISY.

See in the distance, there, those harmless sheep;
Nor watch or ward at any time they keep;
Well pleased, along the pastures green they tread,
And unsuspecting crop the flowery mead:
The shepherd slumbers in the noontide's shade,
His flock forsaken, and his trust betray'd.
The wolf draws near, in sheepskin shrewdly dress'd,
He bleats aloud, and mixes with the rest;
They prick their ears, and look with some surprise,
But can't detect him in his deep disguise.
He marks his time; when they are all asleep,
He slays the lambs, and tears the silly sheep.
Thus all false teachers are on ruin bent,
And by Apollyon on their mission sent;
Without, the clothing of Christ's flock they wear,
Within, the heart of ravening wolves they bear.

THE engraving shows a wolf in disguise, and a flock of sheep in the background. The shepherd is absent from his charge; the sheep wander on, without any to control their movements. The green pastures and verdant meadows afford them plenty of employment. Innocent themselves, they suspect no danger. But the wolf comes; he comes, too, in deep disguise, not in his true character; not as a wolf, but as a sheep. The flocks are deceived; he mingles with them; he marks his time. First one straggler, and now another, fall victims to his tooth of blood. At length, in an unguarded moment, he kills all the lambs, and tears and worries the entire flock. But think not that the ravening wolf escapes without punishment. No; the owner of the flock sees what has been done; he discovers the enemy, and kills him. He leaves his carcass on the ground, a warning to all wolves in sheep's clothing.

In comparing small things with great, the Saviour compared the false prophets, or teachers, to a wolf in sheep's clothing. "Beware," said he, "of false prophets, who come to you in sheep's clothing; but inwardly they are ravening wolves." Hypocrisy consists in acting a part or character not our own. There are hypocrites in all professions, and a great deal of hypocrisy in the world. Men of low degree are vanity, and men of high degree are a *lie*. Both of them together, laid in the balance of sincerity, would be found wanting.

Of all hypocrites, the false teacher of religion is the most dangerous. He it is that scatters firebrands, arrows, and death. True Christians are honest themselves in their professions of piety, and unsuspecting of others; they do not mistrust. This exposes them to the schemes of hypocrites. Sometimes, also the true teacher is absent from his charge. Of this circumstance the false teacher will avail himself. Satan is never asleep or absent. It is his business to sow tares; he selects his time, "when men sleep;" he selects his agents, his own children; he assists them in disguising themselves, and sends them forth to their hellish work.

Armed with the whole armor of Satan, the false teacher approaches the children of God. He begins by cant; he talks gospel truth sometimes; he insinuates, wheedles, and flatters, until he has gained confidence; then he addresses himself to his task in good earnest. Young converts are beguiled from the simplicity of the gospel; the weak in the faith are perplexed and turned out of the way; the rest have their confidence weakened, their peace destroyed, and their souls put in danger. His object is to scatter, tear, and kill, and secure the fleece for a prey. Some are satisfied with the fleece, and suffer the sheep to live; but this son of Satan comes also to tear and destroy. Wolves are now abroad in sheep's clothing. Let the flock of Christ beware. Let the false teachers also beware, because the Chief Shepherd will appear, and cut them in sunder, and appoint them their portion with the hypocrites.

"By their fruits ye shall know them." Fruits are the conduct of a man; his actions are the language of his heart. If the flock would wait awhile before they suffer themselves to act, they would know that "an evil tree cannot bring forth good fruit."

Let the following marks be attended to in passing judgment:

1. The false teacher goes to the fold of true Christians, and labors not to convert sinners from their evil ways.

2. The false teacher persuades Christians to leave the fold, instead of helping them to grow in grace and in knowledge, and rejoicing in their prosperity, as did Barnabas.

3. The false teacher speaks evil against the true teachers of the Gospel, instead of regarding them as co-workers with the Lord.

For the wicked bend their bow, they make ready their arrow upon the string, that they may privily shoot at the upright in heart. Ps. xi. 2.—
.... *their tongue a sharp sword.* Ps. lvii. 4.

SLANDER AND BACKBITING.

    Mark! where the good man unsuspecting treads,
    No evil meditates, nor evil dreads;
    The base assassins from their covert start,
    And sheath the dagger in his bleeding heart;
    Or shoot their arrows, strung by hate, unslack,
    With deadly aim at the defenceless back.
    So smites the slanderer, with poison'd tongue,
    The man—his neighbor—who has done no wrong;
    Thief-like, he steals what gold cannot replace,
    And, like a coward, dares not show his face:
    A brutish cur, that sneaks along the track,
    Awaits his time, then springs upon the back.

BEHOLD the good man! He walks leisurely along towards his home; very likely he has been visiting the house of mourning—drying the poor widow's tears, or feeding and clothing the forsaken orphan He is probably anticipating much pleasure from the recital of what he has seen and heard, to his beloved family He may be revolving in his mind schemes of future benevolence, or meditating on the goodness of his heavenly Father; perhaps contemplating the vast concerns of the eternal state. He sees no foe, he hears no hostile step; he feels himself suddenly wounded, his head swims, he reels, and falls to the ground.

The base poltroons had carefully watched their time, and, with the sharp dagger and empoisoned arrow, had cruelly murdered the innocent. The deed is done in secret; yet all the heavenly world beheld it; and under cover of darkness they escape, but not forever. The earth refuses to cover the blood of the murdered.

This emblem sets forth the sin of slander or backbiting, which is, of all things whatsoever, the most abominable, and to be detested. The slanderer contains within himself almost all the vices of other transgressors. He is for the most part a *liar* of the very worst class. Whether he forges the calumny himself, or retails that of others, it matters not; he is still a liar in the sight of God and man. Not only so, the slanderer is also a *thief*—a robber of the first magnitude, for

"—— He who steals my purse, steals trash.
* * * * * * *
But he who filches from me my good name,
Robs me of that which not enriches him,
And makes me poor indeed."

Look again at the brow of the slanderer, and you will see another title of infamy—that of *coward*. He dares not say to the face what he so freely utters behind the back. Thus he *bites* the *back*. He resembles a snappish dog often seen in the streets, running after passengers, and biting their heels. Furthermore, the slanderer is in the sight of God a *murderer*. He must necessarily hate the person slandered; but "he who hateth his brother is a murderer." Injury is added to hatred, which renders the case worse. Reputation is more precious than life. Thus the man or woman who makes or vends a slander, must be known and read of all men as a *liar, coward, thief*, and *murderer*.

The slanderer's tongue is a four-edged sword. It wounds the hand of him who uses it; it wounds the ears of those who listen to it; it wounds the heart of him who is the object of the thrust; it strikes at the throne of God, and breaks his law. Slander excludes the miserable perpetrator from the kingdom of heaven. "Who shall dwell in thy holy hill, O Lord?" "*He that backbiteth not with his tongue.*" Death and life are in the power of the tongue. A wholesome tongue is a tree of life; a polluted tongue is a *upas* of death. It may be warmed with a seraph's flame, or set on fire of hell; a world of iniquity, or a universe of good; an unruly evil full of deadly poison, or a well-ordered system, transmitting the blessings of an endless life. Therewith bless we God even the Father, and therewith curse we men made after the image of God.

The Jewish Rabbis tell the following story: "A certain man sent his servant to market to buy some good food. The servant returned, bringing with him some tongues. Again he sent the same servant to buy some bad food. The servant again brought tongues. The master said, 'What is the reason, that when I sent you to buy good and bad food, you brought tongues?' The servant answered, 'From the tongue both good and evil come to man. If it be good, there is nothing better; if it be bad, there is nothing worse.'"

The tree corrupt, and his fruit corrupt; for the tree is known by his fruit Matt. xii. 33.—— *Every tree which bringeth not forth good fruit is hewn down, and cast into the fire.* Matt. iii. 10.

THE TREE OF EVIL.

Here, in dread silence, on the blighted heath
Behold! the Tree of Evil, and of Death;
No heavenly breeze throughout the region blows;
No life of Love exists where'er it grows;
No flowers of Hope around it ever bloom;
No fruit of Faith e'er yields its rich perfume;
Fell Unbelief strikes deep its deadly root;
The branches bend with most pernicious fruit;
The Pride of Life, and Fleshly Lusts hang there,
Emblems of misery, anguish, and despair.
Two men employed in different ways you see,
To rid the groaning earth of this bad tree:
One, only lops a branch just here and there,
That makes its neighbor more productive bear;
The other, by experience taught to know,
Aims at the root his well-directed blow;
Blow after blow through the wide heath resound,
And with a crash, it falls and shreds the ground

The Tree of Desolation stands alone upon the blasted heath. It sheds its baleful influence far and wide. No dewy meads, nor grassy plains, or verdant lawns, are seen around; no blushing fields, waving luxuriantly the golden ear; no laughing flowers bestudding the earth with their starry gems; nor spicy groves breathing the odor of delight, can live or flourish here. The lowing kine, the bleating, fleecy tribe, the choral songsters of the woods, are never heard; here, in these regions, eternal silence reigns. This corrupt tree is altogether of a poisonous quality. Its roots, bark, branches, leaves, and fruit, are all poison.

Two men are seen at work upon the tree; their object is to deliver the country from so great an evil The one on the right hand has been employed many years, without effecting any thing; he merely lops off a branch here and there: this only adds strength to the remaining branches, and makes them more fruitful; meanwhile, the excised limb sprouts again. The one on the left, more wise, wants to cut the tree down; to this end, he comes prepared with a good sharp axe; he directs his blows at the root of the tree; blow follows blow in quick succession, every stroke tells, and soon the monster tree lies prostrate on the ground.

The Tree of Evil is an emblem of an evil heart; the bad fruit, of a bad life. The unconverted man sheds a deleterious influence all around him. In his soul there is a lack of spiritual graces: faith, love, hope, peace, joy, long-suffering, are all wanting. A spiritual death exists. Unbelief is the poison that corrupts the heart. Thoughts, words, actions, are all poisoned. Faith is put for the whole of religion, and unbelief for an ungodly life. Hence it is said, "He that *believeth* shall be saved," etc.

The fruit of the evil heart is the pride of life, i. e., a love of the honors and glories of the world, the lust of the flesh, i. e., intoxicating drink, gluttony, and adultery, and the various pleasures of sin; the lust of the eye, i. e., love of fine dress, fine furniture, and the vanities of this life. He spends his wretched strength for naught, who labors to reform his outward conduct only. He may make a good Pharisee, but he will never make a Christian. His heart still continues "deceitful and wicked." "First make the tree good, and the fruit will be good also."

He alone is the wise man who "lays the axe at the root of the tree;" who strikes at unbelief; who believes the truth as it is in Jesus. He prays with David, "*Create* in me a clean heart;" relying on the promise of God, "A new heart will I give unto you." Thus he is "created anew in Christ Jesus unto good works." "He has his fruit unto holiness, and the end everlasting life."

Travellers inform us of a poison tree found in the island of Java, which is said by its effluvia to have "depopulated the country for twelve or fourteen miles around the place of its growth. It is called '*Bohan Upas*.' Poisoned arrows are prepared with the juice of it. Condemned criminals are sent to the tree to get this juice, carrying with them proper directions how to obtain it, and how to secure themselves from the malignant exhalations; and are pardoned if they bring back a certain quantity of the poison; but by the register there kept, not one in four is said to return

Anger resteth in the bosom of fools. Eccl. vii. 9.——*Cease from anger and forsake wrath.* Ps. xxxvii. 6.

ANGER, OR MADNESS.

Upon the margin of the silvery flood,
Come, see the Lion in his wrathful mood.
His roar terrific echoing rocks rebound,
And nature trembles at the dreadful sound;
His furious tail he works from side to side,
His bristly mane he shakes with awful pride;
His eyes, wild rolling, glare with startling light,
With paw upraised, he stands prepared for fight.
And wherefore stands he thus with warlike look?
He sees his image in the quiet brook.
 Man, born to reason, like the foolish beast,
Lets rage hot boiling fester in his breast;
The cause as futile: he himself possess'd
Of evil tempers, colors all the rest.

Look! here is the Lion, the king of beasts. See where he stands, maddened with rage. The savage monarch is alone; the beasts of the field hide themselves when he is angry; his dreadful roar makes them tremble in their dens; the echoing hills reply to the sound thereof. Now he becomes hot with passion. He lashes with his furious tail his heaving sides; he shakes thunder from his shaggy mane; his eyes dart lightning. See! he has raised his murderous paw; he is ready to grapple with his foe. Terrible he looks in the season of his wrath.

But what has enkindled his rage? What is the cause of this fierce commotion? Nothing but his own shadow. He sees his reflected image in the placid stream. Face answers to face; every indication of passion is faithfully reflected. He beholds no common foe. He prepares himself for mortal combat.

The above engraving is an emblem of Anger, and of the worthless causes that oftentimes give rise to it. Anger is one of the most fierce and deadly passions that agitate the human breast, and afflict mankind. Let anger ascend the throne of the human mind, and all other passions, affections, and interests are trampled under foot. A brother lies swimming in his blood; a village is depopulated with the edge of the sword; cities burn amid the conflagration of fire: and kingdoms, given over to the horrors of wrath, become desolate, pass into oblivion, and are known no more. But who can declare the miseries that flow from anger?

Anger, as a sinful passion, is never justifiable; but it oftentimes exists without any real cause whatever. Like the lion in the picture, the man is angry at the reflection of himself; it is his own image that he sees. He imagines, and this is all; his own evil temper colors all besides. The object of his wrath is innocent, perhaps as quiet as an unruffled lake.

Be sure, before you give way to anger, that your neighbor has injured you, and then—forgive him. But even if an apparent cause does exist, suppose some one has injured me. Is not this enough? He that sinneth, wrongeth his own soul; shall I therefore sin and wrong mine? To have an enemy, is bad; to be one, is worse. And why should I inflict self-punishment for the crime of another?

There is a degree of madness connected with anger. The angry man is brutishly insane. This is so wherever it is seen; whether we regard it in the conduct of Xerxes, who flogged the waves, and cast fetters into the sea to bind it, because it broke his bridge of boats—or in its daily outbreaks around us.

But is there no cure for this contagious evil? There is. What is it? When Athenodorus was about to retire from the court of Augustus Cæsar, he gave the emperor this advice: "Remember, whenever you feel angry, that you neither say nor do any thing until you have repeated all the letters of the alphabet." This is good; but the following is better: When a man feels himself sinking into the gulf of angry passion, looking by faith on the Lord Jesus Christ, let him exclaim, "Lord, save or I perish!" The rising storm will pass away, and all will be calm and peaceful.

"The wise will let their anger cool,
    At least before 'tis night;
But in the bosom of a fool,
    It burns till morning light."

"Anger and wrath, and hateful pride,
    This moment be subdued:
Be cast into the crimson tide
    Of my Redeemer's blood."

The sacrifices of God are a broken spirit. Ps. li. 17.——*He that covereth his sins shall not prosper: but whoso confesseth and forsaketh them shall find mercy.* Prov. xxviii. 13.

REPENTANCE.

On bended knees, replete with godly grief,
See, where the mourner kneels to seek relief;
No "God, I thank thee," freezes on his tongue,
For works of merit that to him belong;
Deep in his soul conviction's ploughshare rings,
And to the surface his corruption brings;
He loathes himself, in lowest dust he lies,
And all abased, "Unclean, unclean," he cries.
From his full heart pours forth the gushing plea,
"God of the lost, be merciful to me!"
The light of life descends in heavenly rays,
And angels shout, and sing, "Behold, he prays."

BEHOLD here an individual on his knees, weeping. He is in great distress of mind; he has retired from the busy walks of life, and come to this place of solitude, to give vent to his feelings. His groans break the surrounding silence; they return in soft, but melancholy echoes, to his ears. Above his head are seen descending particles of heavenly light; a little in the rear stands the plough, imbedded in the opening earth.

This is an emblem of Repentance. The man bowed on his knees represents the true penitent, whose soul is humbled under the mighty hand of God. He withdraws from the vanities of the world; he is sick of sin; he breaks the silence of solitude with his inquiries of, "O that I knew where I might find him!" He does not, in the pride of self-righteousness, exclaim, "God, I thank thee that I am not as other men," etc. O no! too deeply he feels the plague of his own heart.

As the plough enters the hard soil, and lays bare furrow after furrow: even so has conviction penetrated the heart of the true penitent, and laid bare its deceitful folds, and discovered its once hidden depths of pollution and guilt. He abhors himself in dust and in ashes; he can only say, God, be merciful to me a sinner. The ploughshare of God's convicting spirit has entered and broken up the fallow ground of his heart; hence he brings the sacrifice with which God is well pleased—that is, "a broken and contrite heart;" and the light of Jehovah's countenance falls full upon his soul, as a token of divine acceptance.

Repentance consists in a change of mind or purpose, wherein the penitent "ceases to do evil," and "learns to do well." The prodigal repented when he said, "I will arise and go to my father," and departed. The farmer's son, who, when he had refused to go and work in the vineyard, and afterwards altered his purpose and went, repented. Saul of Tarsus, when he refused any longer to obey the mandates of the chief priests and scribes, and inquired, "Lord what wilt thou have me to do?" repented. Thus we see it consists in actually doing the will of God. It is not mere anxiety: Simon Magus had this; nevertheless he was still in the "bonds of iniquity." Nor mere trembling: Felix trembled, yet retained his sins. Nor remorse: Judas had this, and died in despair; and Dives also, though in the regions of the lost.

Repentance is the gate of heaven. It is the condition, upon the fulfilment of which depends eternal life. "You repent, and I will forgive." Hence the ambassadors of heaven have invariably directed the attention of sinners to this as a first step towards obtaining the favor of God, and every promised blessing. The prophets, in their denunciations, John of the Desert, in his fiery exhortations, the Saviour, in his divine instructions, and the apostles, in their warm appeals, enjoined upon every soul "repentance toward God."

Through this gate all have passed who have at any time been recognised by the Almighty as his servants. The children of Israel passed through it, typically, when they ate the bitter herbs—before they beheld the pillars of cloud and of fire in the wilderness; Isaiah, ere he touched the sacred harp of prophecy; Elijah, ere he ascended in the chariot of ethereal fire; Ezekiel, before he gazed upon the visions of the Eternal; Daniel, before the Angel of God pronounced him "Blessed;" Paul, ere he was "caught up to the third heaven;" and John of Patmos, before the glorious Revelations of "Alpha and Omega" filled him with wonder and astonishment; and "the hundred and forty-four thousand," ere they sung the song of Moses and of the Lamb. Repentance is a sacred duty. God "now commands all men everywhere to repent." Why! "Because all have sinned, and come short of the glory of God;" and, "Except ye repent, ye shall all likewise perish."

The wicked flee when no man pursueth, but the righteous are as bold as a lion. Prov. xxviii. 1.

FEARFUL AND FEARLESS.

Here is depicted plainly to the eye,
The wicked fleeing when no foe is nigh.
The thunder echoing in its deep-toned peals,
Alarms his conscience, and awakes his heels.
The wind low whistling through the hollow tree,
A call from justice is, from which they flee,
The rolling torrent, in its murmurs loud,
Appears the shout of the pursuing crowd;
Each object looming through the gloom of night,
His fear increases, and augments his flight.
Not so the Righteous; see him walk along,
Bold as a lion, as a mountain strong.
Courageous heart, he fears no rude surprise,
He trusts in *Jesus*, and all else defies.

This engraving shows a man running as it were for his life. On the other hand is seen one who walks steadily and boldly forward. The former is

Fearful; he is alarmed at every thing he sees and hears; he is afraid of his own shadow. The distant echo of reverberating thunder strikes terror into his heart; the autumnal breeze, rustling through the falling leaves, makes him afraid; the neighboring torrent, as it tumbles down the mountain ravine, causes him to fear. He cannot endure darkness, neither can he bear the light. He is afraid of company, yet he fears to be left alone. Now he is fleeing when there is none pursuing.

How different the fearless man! See how boldly he walks along. The gloom of night is nothing to him; he appears to fear no evil. While others are running, he stands his ground; while they are afraid, his heart is strong.

This emblem is descriptive of two characters: of the Righteous and of the Wicked. It is the *wicked* who flee when none pursue. Their guilty conscience transforms every object into an enemy; therefore they are in fear where no fear is, and flee away in terror.

A Christian king of Hungary, talking one day with his brother, who was a gay, thoughtless courtier, upon the subject of a future judgment, was laughed at by his brother for indulging in "melancholy thoughts." The king made no reply. There was a custom in that country that if the executioner sounded a trumpet before any man's door, that man was led instantly to death. The king ordered the trumpet to be sounded that night before the door of his brother, who, on hearing the dismal sound, and seeing the messenger of death, was greatly alarmed. He sprang into the presence of the king, beseeching to know how he had offended. "Alas, my brother!" replied the king, "you have never offended me; but if the sight of my executioner is so dreadful, shall not we, who have so greatly offended God, fear to be brought before the judgment-seat of Christ?"

M. Volney, a French infidel, it is well known, was frightened during a storm, while some Christian ladies, his fellow-passengers, bore all with unruffled composure. M. Voltaire, a Frenchman also, and of the same stamp, affected to despise the Christian religion during life; yet on his death-bed he sent to Dr. Tronchin, a priest, to administer to him the sacrament. It was affirmed of him that he was afraid to be left alone in the dark.

The righteous man is afraid of nothing but sin. He goes forward in the path of duty, though dangers grow thick around him. He enters the burning, fiery furnace, and grapples with its curling flames. He descends into the den of lions, the king of beasts crouches at his feet. In the storm at midnight, tossed upon the raging billows, he is calm in the presence of the God he serves, and to whom he belongs. In earthquake's shock, when temples are falling, earth opening, and ruin reigns around, he stands fearless amid the desolation, exclaiming, " Therefore will we not fear, though the earth be removed out of its place." Descending the dark vale of death itself, he says exultingly, " Though I walk through the valley and shadow of death, I will fear no evil." And when the last enemy stands full in his presence, he sings triumphantly:

"Lend, lend your wings; I mount—I fly
O grave, where is thy victory?
O death, where is thy sting?"

They profess that they know God; but in works they deny him. Titus i. 16.——— *If any man love the world, the love of the Father is not in him.* 1 John ii. 15.

THE TWO WORLDLINGS.

View here spread out the plains of heavenly light,
And narrow way, that ends where all is bright.
Behold, with globes, upon the lightsome green,
To different work address'd, two men are seen.
With careless ease one rolls his globe along,
And follows after, full of mirth and song;
The other strives to move his world's vast weight,
Uphill, toward the brightly shining gate:
He strives in vain; the globe, though in the track,
Still downward tending, drives him farther back,
And though they seem contrary roads to go,
They meet together in the vale below.
  Thus some pursue an open course of sin;
Some Christ profess, yet hold the world within.
Though these appear to play a different game,
Their fate is equal, and their end the same.

IN the engraving, two men are seen employed in rolling globes. The one on the right hand has very

easy work of it; he is going down hill; his globe
rolls on rapidly. He follows after with great glee
and merriment; soon he is out of sight below. The
one on the left is seen with his globe in the path
that leads to the gate of brightness. He is striving
to make his way toward the gate of light, with the
ponderous world before him. In vain he struggles,
and heaves, and lifts; it still presses down upon
him, and bears him backward, till at length he finds
himself at the bottom of the valley, where he meets
his neighbor, who laughs heartily at him for taking
so much trouble to effect what he accomplished so
easily.

This picture represents two kinds of worldly
characters, who both equally miss of heaven in the
end. The gate of light shows the entrance to the
New Jerusalem; the pathway signifies the way of
holiness, leading thereunto; the man on the right,
rolling his ball along so gayly, represents the professed
man of the world. He has chosen *honors,
riches*, and *pleasures* for his portion. These, combined,
form the deity that he worships. Where they
lead, he follows; where they tarry, there he also
abides; hence he turns his back upon the way of
life, and upon the glories of the upper world. He is
no hypocrite—not he; he glories in his conduct; he
will have nothing to do with church or minister,
prayer-book or Bible. He says in his heart, "There
is no God," and casting off all fears, he hastens
down the road that leads to death, and receives the
doom which awaits "all those who forget God."

He on the left represents one who, while professedly
a follower of Christ, yet loves the *honors, riches*
and *pleasures* of the world. He thinks the Bible may
be a true book, and heaven worth having when he
can have no more of earth, therefore he is found in

the way. *He* professes to love God, but in works he denies him; he makes, consequently, no progress heavenward. The world is too much for him; it obtains more and more power over him, until it, after having made him miserable on earth, sinks him into the gulf of wo, where he receives his portion with the " *hypocrites and unbelievers.*"

> When in the light of faith divine,
>   We look on things below,
> Honor, and gold, and sensual joy,
>   How vain and dangerous too!
>
> Honor's a puff of noisy breath;
>   Yet men expose their blood,
> And venture everlasting death,
>   To gain that airy good.
>
> While others starve the nobler mind,
>   And feed on shining dust,
> They rob the serpent of his food,
>   T' indulge a sordid lust.
>
> The pleasures that allure our sense
>   Are dangerous snares to souls;
> There's but a drop of flattering sweet,
>   And dash'd with bitter bowls.
>
> *Dr. Watts*

Seest thou how faith wrought with his works, and by works was faith made perfect? James ii. 22.

FAITH AND WORKS.

    Lo! where the Boatman stems the flowing tide,
    And aims direct his little bark to guide;
    With both oars working, he can headway make,
    And leave the waters foaming in his wake;
    But if one oar within the boat he lays,
    In useless circles, round and round, he plays.
    So Faith and Works, when both together brought,
    With mighty power, and heavenly life are fraught,
    To help the Christian on his arduous road,
    And urge him forward on his way to God:
    If Faith or Works, no matter which, he drops,
    Short of his journey's end he surely stops.

Look at the honest waterman plying at his daily occupation. He has just left a passenger on the other side. See with what precision he guides his little boat. By pulling both oars with equal strength, he makes rapid progress, and steers straight. He leaves the waters foaming in his track; this is called his wake. If he should lay in either of his oars, his progress would at once be stopped. As long as he plies both, he goes ahead; but let him pull but one ever so hard, and he could not advance a foot. Round and round he would float, in eddying circles, forever. In vain would his passengers await his arrival—in vain would his wife and little ones expect his return; he would never more return; probably he would drift out to sea, and be lost in the immensity of old ocean.

The above engraving is an emblem of Faith and Works united. The Christian has a "calling," or occupation, in which he makes progress so long as faith and works are united. They are to him as a propelling power, urging him forward in his pathway to immortality. He exerts a holy influence wherever he goes, and leaves a brilliant track behind him. It is seen that a man of God has been there. But let him lay in one of his oars; let it be said of him, "He hath left off to do good," and his progress in the divine life will at once be checked. Let him lay aside "Faith," and the effect will be the same. He may, indeed, go round and round, like a mill-horse, in a circle of dry performances, but he will never reach the Christian's home. In vain will his friends, who have gone before him, expect his arrival; he will never see the King in his beauty The current of sin will bear him outward, and downward, and land him eventually in the gulf of the lost.

Some there are who have "faith," yet who are destitute of "good works." "The devils believe," but they neither love nor obey—devils they continue. Deists again, men who believe in the being and unity of God, but reject the Bible as an inspired book, have faith. But are their works perfect [good] before God?—will their faith save them? All antinomians are of this class.

Some, on the other hand, strive to abound in "works," who yet are destitute of "faith." Cain, who brought his offering, and slew his brother Abel, was of this class. The Pharisees, who paid tithes of all they possessed, and who cried out, "Crucify him! Crucify him!" were also of this number. The professors of "good works," in our own day, who have no true faith in Christ, are of this number; for all offerings whatsoever, that are not perfumed with the odor of Christ's sacrifice, they are an abomination to the Lord.

In Abraham we see faith and works admirably combined. "He believed God, and it was counted to him for righteousness," "and he was justified by works, when he had offered Isaac his son upon the altar." "Thus faith wrought with his works, and by works was faith made perfect."

In fine, where there is a scriptural "faith," that faith which is the evidence or conviction of unseen realities, there will be "works" corresponding thereto, as surely as there is life while the soul is in the body.

On the other hand, where there is no true faith, there can be no "works" acceptable to God, no more than there can be life when the soul has left the body. "For as the body without the spirit is dead, so faith without works is dead also."

With a furious man thou shalt not go. Prov. xxii 24.——— *The simple pass on, and are punished.* Prov. xxii. 3.

PRECIPITATION, OR RASHNESS.

Behold the rash, impetuous charioteer,
Who reckless urges on his wild career;
Dangers and darkness thick around him grow,
High cliffs above, and yawning gulfs below;
Yet much at ease. In neither fear nor pain,
He smacks his whip, and freely gives the rein;
Rocks, vast, precipitous, he dashes by,
But frightful chasms now before him lie;
Down, down the dreadful precipice he flies,
And dashed to pieces, for his rashness dies.
   Thus wilful youth to passion gives the reins,
And lengthen'd grief, for pleasures short, obtains;
By passion drawn, before he's well aware,
He sinks o'erwhelm'd in misery and despair.

The youth above is seen driving furiously along paths replete with danger. The road, if road it may be called, becomes more and more hazardous. He labors not to curb the fiery steeds, whose speed increases every moment. Instead of restraining them, he cracks his whip, and loosely gives the rein. He appears to be wholly unconscious of his imminent peril. Abrupt cliffs hang over his head, and deep, awful ravines open on each side of his path. His situation becomes still more dangerous; right ahead a frightful gulf presents itself to his eyes, now beginning to open. With the rapidity of lightning he approaches the dreadful brink; on the coursers fly Now he sees his danger, and strives to check them It is in vain; they have had the rein too long; their blood is up. With a fearful bound, over the precipice they go; horses and driver are dashed to atoms against the rocks, and are seen no more.

Ancient philosophers used to compare human passions to wild horses, and the reason of man to the driver, or coachman, whose business it was to control and guide them at his pleasure. But many men have more command over their horses than they have over themselves. This is a melancholy truth. Their proud chargers are taught to stand still, to gallop, to trot, and to perform, in short, all kinds of evolutions with perfect ease; while the passions run away with their rightful owners; they will not submit to be guided by reason. It is of far more importance that a man should learn to govern his passions than his horses. Our passions, like fire and water, are excellent servants, but bad masters. Horses, to be useful, must be governable; but to be governable, they must be broke in betimes, and thoroughly. So with the passions, otherwise their power will increase over that of reason, and in the end lead to ruin.

Philosophy may do much in enabling us to govern the passions; religion, however, can do more. It is said of Socrates, who had a wretched scold for a wife, that one day, when she was scolding him at a great rate, ne bore it very patiently, controlling himself by reason. His unruffled composure enraged her still more, and she threw a bowl of dirty water in his face. Then he spoke. "It is quite natural," said he, smiling, "when the thunder has spent its fury, and the lightning its fires, that the teeming shower should descend."

But religion is more easily obtained than philosophy, and it is far more powerful. It imparts a gracious, influential principle that enables whosoever submits to it to govern his passions, and even to love his enemies, and thus to conquer them.

Many have conquered kingdoms, who could not conquer themselves. Thus Alexander, who, being a slave to his passions, slew Clytus, his most intimate friend. And, notwithstanding the laurels that have been woven for the conquerors of ancient and modern times, the Almighty himself has prepared a diadem of glory for the self-conquered, bearing in letters of heavenly light this inscription: "*He that ruleth his own spirit, is better than he that taketh a city*"

<blockquote>
Madness, by nature reigns within,
  The passions burn and rage;
Till God's own Son, with skill divine,
  The inward fire assuage.

We give our ⸺ is the wounds they feel,
  We drink the poisonous gall,
And rush with fury down to hell,
  But heaven prevents the fall.
Dr Watts.
</blockquote>

Wherefore do ye spend money for that which is not bread? and your la-bor for that which satisfieth not? Isa. lv. 2.

VAIN PURSUITS.

The truant urchin has forsook the school,
To learn betimes how best to play the fool;
O'er hedge and brake, beneath a burning sun,
With breathless haste, he perseveres to run;
His folly's cause is pictured to the eye:
The object what?—A painted butterfly.
At length outspent, he grasps the trembling thing,
And with the grasp, destroys the painted wing;
Chagrined he views, for that once beauteous form,
Nothing remains, except a homely worm.
  So larger children leave important deeds,
And after trifles oft, the truant speeds;
And if by toil he gains the gaudy prize,
Alas! 'tis changed—it fades away, and dies.

THE foolish boy, leaving the useful and delightful pleasures of study, runs after a pretty butterfly that has attracted his attention. On he runs, through brake and brier, over hedges and ditches, up hill and down dale; the sun, at the same time, pours down its burning rays upon his uncovered head. See how he sweats, and puffs, and toils! 'Tis all in vain —just as he comes up with the prize, away it flies far above his reach. Still he follows on; now it has settled upon a favorite flower. He is sure of it now; he puts forth his hand. Lo! it is gone. Still he pursues—on and on he runs after the glittering insect. Presently it alights, and hides itself within the leaves of the lily of the valley. For awhile he loses sight of it; again he discovers it on the wing, and again he renews the chase. Nor is it until the sun descends the western sky, that he comes up with the object of his laborious race. Weary of the wing, the butterfly seeks shelter for the night within the cup of the mountain blue-bell. The boy, marking its hiding-place, makes a desperate spring, and seizes the trembling beauty. In his eagerness to possess it, he has crushed its tender wings, and marred entirely those golden colors. With deep mortification, and bitter regret at his folly, he beholds nothing left but a mere grub, an almost lifeless worm, without form and without loveliness.

This emblem aptly shows the folly of those who, whether young or old, leaving the solid paths of knowledge, of industry, and of lawful pleasure, follow the vanities of this life. Corrupt and unbridled passions and vitiated tastes lead, in the end, to ruin.

The way of transgressors is hard, as well as foolish and vain. To follow after forbidden objects is far more laborious than to pursue those only that are lawful. It is said of *wisdom*, that all her ways are ways of pleasantness, that all her paths are paths of peace.

The mind of the youth who is in pursuit of vanities, or of unlawful pleasures, is ever raging, like a tempest. Now up, now down—he knows nothing of true pleasure, nothing of solid peace. The object he desires and pursues so ardently mocks him again and again. "To-morrow," he says to himself, "will give me the object of my wishes." To-morrow comes—once more it eludes his grasp. Now he becomes uneasy, then impatient, then fretful, then anxious, and then desperate; now he resolves at all hazards to seize upon the prize—it is his own; but ah! the flowers have faded, the beautiful colors have disappeared; the angel of beauty is transformed into a loathsome object. His eyes are opened; and alas! too late, disappointed and remorseful, he learns the truth of the maxim, that "it is not all gold that glitters."

"Man has a soul of vast desires;
He burns within with restless fires:
Toss'd to and fro, his passions fly
From vanity to vanity.

"In vain on earth we hope to find
Some solid good to fill the mind;
We try new pleasures, but we feel
The inward thirst and torment still.

"So when a raging fever burns,
We shift from side to side by turns;
And 'tis a poor relief we gain,
To change the place, but keep the pain.

"Great God! subdue the vicious thirst,
This love to vanity and dust;
Cure the vile fever of the mind,
And feed our souls with joys refined."
Dr Watts.

The high ones of stature shall be hewn down, and the haughty shall be humbled. Isa x. 33.

DANGER OF GREATNESS.

The clouds assemble in the blackening west,
Anon with gloom the sky becomes o'ercast,
United winds with wide-mouth'd fury roar,
Old ocean, rolling, heaves from shore to shore;
With boiling rage the waves begin to rise,
And ruffian billows now assail the skies;
The hardy forests, too, affrighted quake,
The hills they tremble, and the mountains shake;
The oak majestic, towering to the skies,
Laughs at the whirlwind, and the storm defies:
Spreads wide its arms, rejoicing in its pride,
And meets unbending the tornado's tide;
The winds prevail, one loud tremendous blow
The monarch prostrates, and his pride lays low;
While the low reed, in far more humble form,
Unknown to greatness, safe, outlives the storm.

The storm rages. The sturdy oak, the growth of centuries, lifts its proud head towering to the heavens it spreads abroad its ample branches, giving shelter to birds and beasts. For a long time it resists the fury of the hurricane, but 'tis all in vain: with a mighty crash it is overturned; its very roots are laid bare, its branching honors are brought low; birds, beasts, and creeping reptiles now trample upon its fallen greatness.

But see: the humble reed, bending to the storm, escapes unhurt. Its lowly position has preserved it. from destruction; while its mighty neighbor is no more. It still lives, and grows, and flourishes.

This is an apt emblem of the danger attending upon high stations, and of the security afforded in the less elevated walks of life. It is calculated to damp the ardor of ambition, of at least that ambition that seeks to be great only that self may be enriched, or vanity gratified.

This kind of greatness is indeed the most dangerous, and the most uncertain. It is sure to be a mark for others, equally aspiring and unprincipled, to shoot at; while the possessor of this greatness, not being protected by the shield of conscious integrity, falls to rise no more, and the flatterers and dependents being no longer able to enrich themselves, unite in trampling under foot the man they formerly delighted to honor.

Love is not an evil of itself, neither is ambition; they may both be expended on worthless or sinful objects. Let the youth seek out a proper object for the lofty aspirings of the soul; let him learn to direct them by the providence and word of God. True greatness consists in goodness—in being useful to mankind. Those individuals usually called great have been the destroyers, not the benefactors of our race. A private station is as much a post of honor as the most elevated. Indeed, properly speaking, there are no private stations; every man is a public man, and equally interested with others in the welfare and progress of his fellows. The lowly reed is as perfect in its kind as the lofty oak, and answers equally the end of its creation.

It is true, however, that the more elevated the station a man holds in society, the more responsibility he is under both to God and man. He is also exposed to more dangers and temptations. Envy, that hates the excellence she cannot reach, will carp at him, and slander shoot her poisoned arrows at him. Happiness seldom dwells with greatness, nor is safety the child of wealth and honors. "But he that humbleth himself—in due time—shall be exalted."

A striking instance of the danger of greatness may be found in the fall of Cardinal Wolsey. This ambitious man lived in the reign of Henry VIII., king of England. He was that monarch's favorite minister. He is said to have been "insatiable in his acquisitions, but still more magnificent in his expenses; of great capacity, but still more unbounded in enterprise; ambitious of power, but still more ambitious of glory." He succeeded—he was raised to the highest pinnacle; but he fell under the displeasure of the king. The inventory of his goods being taken, they were found to exceed the most extravagant surmises. Of fine holland, there were found eleven hundred pieces; the walls of his palace were covered with cloth of gold and silver; he had a cupboard of plate, all of massy gold; and all the rest of his riches and furniture were in the same proportion, all of which were converted to the use of the king. A bill of indictment was preferred against him; he was ordered to resign the great seal, and to depart from his palace. Soon after, he was arrested for high treason, and commanded to be conducted to London to take his trial.

When he arrived at Leicester Abbey he was taken sick—men said he poisoned himself. His disorder increased. A short time before he expired, he said to the officer who guarded him: "O had I but served my God as faithfully as I have served my king, he would not have forsaken me in my gray hairs." He died shortly after, in all the pangs of remorse, and left a life rendered miserable by his unbounded ambition for greatness.

For every one that doeth evil hateth the light. John iii. 20.

GUILT.

In splendor rising, view "the king of day,"
And darkness chasing from the earth away;
The beast of prey escapes before the sun,
To thickest covert, ere his work is done;
The birds of night now flee away apace,
And hide securely in some gloomy place;
While the blithe lark, elate, pours forth its lays,
And warbles to the sun its notes of praise.
 So guilty men pursue, in devilish mood,
The trade of plunder, and the deed of blood;
They work in darkness without shame or fear,
And skulk in darkness when the day draws near;
While conscious innocence walks forth upright,
And, like the lark, rejoices in the light.

SEE where the glorious sun is rising in majesty and strength. Darkness has fled from his presence, and now there is nothing hid from his rosy light. See the beast of prey, slinking off to his den. Stung with hunger, and athirst for blood, he roamed round in the darkness of night. Lighting upon a sheep cote, he breaks into the enclosure; the bleating, helpless lambs become his prey; some he devours, others he leaves mangled and torn upon the ground. Detected by the light, he sneaks away; he plunges into the forest, and hides him in its thickest shade.

The birds of night—the bat, and others—fly away before the rising light. The music of the awakening choir, blooming fields, and spicy gardens, possess no charms for them. Mouldering ruins, among thickest shades, where the toad finds a shelter, and the serpent hisses—this is their favorite dwelling-place; while the gay lark, high mounting, pours forth his praises to the solar king. He is gladdened by his beams, and welcomes his approach with all the melody of song.

"Thou, O Lord, makest darkness, and it is night, wherein all the beasts of the forest do creep forth. The sun ariseth, they gather themselves together, and lay them down in their dens."

The engraving is emblematical of guilt; for happy would it be for mankind, were the beasts of prey and birds of night the only disturbers of the world's repose—the only destroyers that walk abroad in darkness. Alas!

"———————————— When night
Darkens the streets, then wander forth the sons
Of Belial, flown with insolence and wine."

Then, too, the robber goes forth to perpetrate his deeds of violence and rapine; then, too, the adulterer, and kindles a fire that will burn to the lowest hell; and shrouded in the mantle of night, the man of blood stalks forth, and works his deeds of death.

In this way, man, made in the image of God, becomes allied to the most malignant part of the brute neation, companions and co-workers with them What degradation! Alas, alas! how are the mighty fallen!

Look again at the folly and ignorance of wicked men in supposing themselves concealed because *they* cannot see. It is related of the ostrich, that she covers her head only, with reeds, and because she cannot see herself, thinks she is hid from the eye of her pursuers. Thus it is with the workers of iniquity in the night-time; they may indeed be hid from the sleeping eyes of mortals, but the ever-wakeful eye of Jehovah looks full upon them. When they say, "Surely the darkness shall cover me," even then "the night is light" all around them. "Clouds and darkness are round about Him;" they are Jehovah's habitation, therefore what is mistaken for a covering is the presence-chamber of the Holy God, who "compasseth thy path, and thy lying down, and who is acquainted with all thy ways."

"Every one that doeth evil hateth the light, neither cometh to the light, lest his deeds should be reproved. But he that doeth truth, cometh to the light, that his deeds may be made manifest, that they are wrought in God."

"When men of mischief rise
In secret 'gainst the skies,
Thy hand shall sweep them to the grave;
And oh! beyond the tomb,
How dreadful is their doom,
Where not a hand is reach'd to save!"

"His enemies, with sore dismay,
Fly from the light, and shun the day:
Then lift your heads, ye saints, on high,
And sing, for your redemption's nigh."

Be patient in tribulation. Rom. xii. 12.——*An example of suffering, affliction, and patience. Behold, we count them happy who endure.* James v. 10, 11.

PATIENCE AND LONG-SUFFERING.

With sore afflictions, and with injuries too,
One deeply loaded, in the picture view;
Above, beneath, and reigning all around,
Trouble, and chains, and slanderous foes are found;
Her own sweet home no more a shelter stands,
Consumed by fire, it falls by cruel hands:
Amid this widely-devastating stroke,
No cry is heard, no voice of murmur spoke;
Like the mild lamb that crouches by her side,
She bears with meekness all that may betide;
She leans on Hope, and upward casts her eyes,
Expecting succor from the distant skies.

THE above engraving represents a female, loaded with a heavy burden of afflictions and injuries; fast bound by chains and fetters of iron, she is unable to help herself. Before her lie whips, chains, and slanders; behind, her house, her only asylum, is on fire : ignited by wicked hands, it falls a prey to the devouring flames; while the barking cur assails her with all his spite. In the midst of her wide-spread calamity, she murmurs not, she makes no complaint. Like the innocent lamb at her side, she bears all without repining. She leans on the anchor of hope, and looks upward.

This is an emblem of Patience and Long-suffering. The figure represents one who is oppressed with manifold wrongs, upon whose shoulders is laid a heavy burden of grievous outrages, and who is incapacitated, by the force of circumstances, from extricating herself; at the same time, she discovers that she has not yet drunk the full cup of her woes. Other evils lie in prospect before her.

One, who, instead of receiving the commiseration and assistance of her neighbors in the season of adversity, is assailed with the venom of the slanderer, the malice of the backbiter, and the wickedness of the incendiary; but who, in the midst of her sufferings, refuses to complain. Though cast down, persecuted, and perplexed, she yields not in despair. With lamblike meekness, she arms her breast, and possesses her soul in patience. All-sustaining hope imparts new strength to her spirits; she commits herself to God, who judgeth righteously; and looking to God for grace to enable her to endure till he shall send deliverance, calmly awaits the issue.

Wicked and unreasonable men abound in the world, and the path of duty is often beset with present difficulties and dangers; yet it ends where all is easy and delightful. Let no one recede from the path of duty, nor tamely yield to despair. We may be tempted to flee, like the prophet Jonah, from our proper work; like Joshua, we may throw ourselves on the ground, and exclaim, despondingly, " Alas, O

Lord God!" Like David, we may say, "I shall perish by the hand of Saul;" or like Elijah, the fearless advocate of truth, say inquiringly, "What good shall my life do me?" Yet let us remember, that "light is sown for the righteous." The seed of deliverance is already in the ground; the crop is not far distant; we shall reap, if we faint not.

The conduct of Job affords the most perfect example of patience. Despoiled of his worldly property, his children taken from him at a stroke, his body tormented with one of the most painful and loathsome diseases, distressed by the foolish infidelity of his wife, and slandered by his professed friends; yet his patient soul triumphed over all. Still clinging to God, his Rock, he exclaimed, exultingly, "Though he slay me, yet will I trust in him. The Lord gave, and the Lord hath taken away: blessed be the name of the Lord."

In your patience, possess ye your souls. *Luke* xxi. 19.—— Be patient, brethren, unto the coming of the Lord. *James* v. 7

Take, my brethren, the prophets, who have spoken in the name of the Lord, for an example of suffering affliction, and of patience. *James* v. 10.

Let us run with patience the race set before us; looking unto Jesus, the author and finisher of our faith; who, for the joy that was set before him, endured the cross, despising the shame, and is set down at the right hand of the throne of God. *Heb* xii. 1, 2.

My brethren, count it all joy when ye fall into divers temptations; knowing this, that the trying of your faith worketh patience. But let patience have her perfect work, that ye may be perfect and entire, wanting nothing. *James* i. 2, 3 4

And lead us not into temptation, but deliver us from evil. Matt. vi. 13

TEMPTATION.

See where the tree its richest foliage wears,
And golden fruit its laden branches bears;
Behold conceal'd beneath its shade sidelong,
The glossy serpent, with his poisonous tongue;
The simple boy, far from his father's care,
Is well-nigh taken with the gilded snare.
The tempting fruit, outspread before his eyes,
Fills him with rapture and complete surprise;
Nor hidden dangers will he wait to see,
But onward hastens to the fatal tree.
His father sees him, and, with faltering breath,
Recalls his loved one from the brink of death,
Nor waits reply, but on the spot he springs,
And saves his darling from the serpent's stings.

THE tree rich in foliage, and rich in fruit, spreads out its delicious produce to the passer by. See also the subtle serpent, as if aware of the powerful attractions that the tree affords, conceals itself under-neath its branches, ready to spring upon the unwary traveller. That little boy has been in great danger: he left the house, and wandered on till he came in sight of the tree; the fruit attracted his attention; he stopped, he was delighted with its appearance. Thoughtless of danger, he was just going to pluck and eat, when the voice of his father alarmed him; he had seen his danger. In another moment he was on the spot, and seizing him by the hand, pointed out to him the serpent, and led him from the place of danger.

This is an emblem of Temptation—of the danger to which youth especially are exposed. The tree, with its rich foliage and golden fruit, represents those things that are objects of temptation. The serpent, shows the danger that invariably attends those objects that entice to sin. The artless boy represents the simplicity of youth, who, attracted by the outside appearance of things, consider not the evil of sinful gratification. The anxious father exhibits the ever-watchful care of our Father who is in heaven, over his children, whom, as long as they confide in him, he will deliver from evil.

This emblem sets forth also somewhat of the nature of temptation. Thus: the *object* is presented to the eye; the *mind* takes pleasure in beholding it; then the *will* consents to embrace it. " Then when lust hath conceived, it bringeth forth sin; and sin, when it is finished, bringeth forth death."

The youthful Joseph, when in the house of Potiphar the Egyptian, was assailed by temptation. The object was presented to him in its most attractive form; while master of himself, he fled from it, and escaped. His memory is blessed.

David, king of Israel, when walking upon the battlements beheld a similar object of temptation.

He looked till the fire of lust was enkindled in his soul, and his will determined upon possession. Lust, when it hath conceived, bringeth forth sin; sin, when it is finished, bringeth forth death. This was to David the beginning of sorrows.

Temptation, at the commencement, is "like the thread of the spider's web; afterwards, it is like a cart-rope." The poor slave, Joseph, broke the thread, and became a king, nay, more than a king; while the king, David, was fast bound by the cart-rope, and became a slave.

The theatre, the card-table, the intoxicating cup, the painted harlot, are all so many objects of powerful temptation, under which lurks the serpent with its sting of death. Fleeing to God, in Christ, by earnest prayer, is the only way of escape therefrom.

> "How vain are all things here below!
> How false, and yet how fair!
> Each pleasure hath its poison too,
> And every sweet a snare.
>
> "The brightest things below the sky,
> Give but a flattering light;
> We should suspect some danger nigh,
> Where we possess delight.
>
> * * * * * * *
>
> "Sin has a thousand treacherous arts
> To practise on the mind;
> With flattering looks she tempts our hearts,
> But leaves a sting behind.
>
> "She pleads for all the joys she brings,
> And gives a fair pretence;
> But cheats the soul of heavenly things,
> And chains it down to sense."
>
> *Dr. Watts*

See that ye walk circumspectly. Eph. v. 15.——*A prudent man foreseeth the evil.* Prov. xxii. 3.

PRUDENCE AND FORESIGHT.

Where some would thoughtless rush, with skip and dance,
See Prudence there with cautious steps advance:
Behind, the faithful mirror brings to view
The roaring lion, that would her pursue;
Before, she knows, by telescopic glass,
How many things will shortly come to pass;
Betimes, conceal'd where fragrant roses hang,
She sees the serpent with his poison'd fang:
And thus she learns, what youth should always know,
That pleasures oft with fatal snares may grow.

PRUDENCE is here seen proceeding with slow and cautious steps. She has in her right hand a telescope, by means of which she is enabled to bring things that are far off nigh to view; thus she sees things that would otherwise be hidden entirely from her sight; while other things are magnified in their proportions, so that she can discern their nature more truly, and thus adapt her conduct to the cir cumstances of the case. In this manner she applies her wisdom to practice. She carries also, in her left, a mirror, by which she is enabled to detect objects that are behind her. A lion is discovered descending from the mountains, hungry, and ravening for its prey. Nor in her attention to remoter objects is she regardless of those nigh at hand; she espies concealed behind a rose-bush a serpent; it is of the dangerous kind. By her timely discovery, she saves herself from its poisonous fang.

This is an emblem of Prudence; for what is prudence but wisdom applied to practice? Wisdom enables us to determine what are the best ends, likewise what are the best means to be used in order to attain those ends. But prudence applies all this to practice, suiting words and actions to time, place, circumstance, and manner. O! how necessary is prudence for the purposes of the present life. Without prudence, the mighty become enfeebled, the wise become foolish, and the wealthy, inhabitants of the poorhouse.

There are duties to be done, pleasures to be enjoyed, dangers to be guarded against—all of which cannot be effected unless prudence guides the helm. Pleasures and dangers are so artfully mingled together, as the serpent among the roses, that the prudent only can possibly detect the snare. The youth cannot be rich in experience; still, he can cultivate prudence, which will beget an habitual presence of mind, ever watchful and awake. Misfortunes are common to all; the prudent, considering that he is not exempt from the common lot of mortals will guard against them; and, as if they were sure to come, he will prepare himself to endure them. Like the mariner, who, when sailing in windy latitudes, sweeps the horizon with his telescope to see if there are signs of squalls: towards evening, he shortens sail, sets his watch, and keeps a good look-out.

Now, if prudence is so necessary and profitable when applied to the things of this life, it is much more so when applied to the life which is to come, because the *soul* is of more value than the *body*, and *eternity* of more importance than *time*. Events not *contingent*, but *certain*, will come upon us, against which, if we are *prudent*, we shall provide—events *solemn*, *momentous*, and deeply *interesting*. What more solemn than death? What more momentous than the judgment to come? What more interesting to an immortal spirit than the final issues of that judgment? Shall I my everlasting days with fiends or angels spend? "The prudent man foreseeth the evil, and hideth himself. The simple pass on, and are punished."

> "O may thy Spirit guide my feet
> In ways of righteousness!
> Make every path of duty straight
> And plain before my face.
>
> "My watchful enemies combine
> To tempt my feet astray;
> They flatter with a base design
> To make my soul their prey.
>
> "Lord, crush the serpent in the dust,
> And all his plots destroy;
> While those that in thy mercy trust,
> Forever shout for joy."

The righteous shall never be removed. Prov. x. 30.——*Behold, we count them happy who endure.* James v. 11.

FORTITUDE AND CONSTANCY.

As stands the pillar on the solid ground,
Nor heeds the tempest that prevails around,
Unmoved, though tempests bluster from on high,
And thunders rolling shake the trembling sky:
So *Fortitude* is strong in Virtue's cause,
Nor fears contempt, nor covets vain applause;
But when the storms of evil tongues prevail,
And envy rises like a furious gale,
She bears on high her ample spotless shield,
Her own fair fame, and still disdains to yield;
Enduring greatly, till the storm is gone,
Then sees triumphant, that her cause is won.

BEHOLD here the emblems of Fortitude and Constancy. The pillar stands upright amidst the storm, and upright in the midst of sunshine, bearing the summer's heat and winter's cold, by night and by day; still it stands, regardless of passing events, and answering at the same time the end of its erection. Thus Constancy continues at the post of duty. For-

titude is seen standing by the pillar of Constancy
See how she braves the fury of the tempest! Winds
whistle, thunders roll, and night seems gathering together a magazine of storms to let loose upon her
head; yet she continues at the post of patient endurance; with her shield she is enabled to protect herself against all the storms which beat around.

Courage resists danger; fortitude endures pain
either of the body or of the mind, or both. True fortitude is always connected with a holy, a righteous
cause. Adversity, or opposition, is the test of fortitude and constancy; it is the fiery trial which tries
the virtuous; they come out of it as gold seven times
purified, losing nothing save the alloy. Holiness of
character, faith in God's word, constitute the shield
of Fortitude, and render her altogether invulnerable.

It is easy for a man to profess attachment to a
good cause, when that cause meets with the general
approbation. It is an easy thing to boast of virtue
that has never been tried by temptation, and to exult
in fortitude that has never had to bear the storm of
opposition; but true fortitude is found to consist in
supporting evils with resignation, and in enduring opposition with resolution and dignity. "He that
loseth wealth," say the Spaniards, "loseth much:
he that loseth his friends, loseth more; but he that
loseth his spirit, loseth all." The man of fortitude,
strong in conscious integrity, and in the knowledge
of the right, though wealth may desert him, though
his friends may forsake him in his greatest need, yet
he *possesses his soul* in patience; he rejoices that
his soul is free. The cause of truth he knows can
never fall. This makes him magnanimous, both to
do and to dare.

One of the most conspicuous instances of true for

titude is found in the conduct of the Apostle Paul. After having for some time served the Church at Ephesus, his duty called him to Jerusalem, where he knew he was to encounter the deadly opposition of his enemies. Before he set out, he preached his farewell sermon. The people were greatly affected. The thoughts of losing their beloved pastor, and of the dangers that awaited him, melted them into tears. " They all wept sore, and fell on Paul's neck, and kissed him, sorrowing most of all for the words which he spoke, that they should see his face no more." These circumstances were sufficient to have overwhelmed the stoutest heart. Paul's reply is the language of true fortitude : " Bonds and afflictions await me ; *but none of these things move me;* neither count I my life dear unto me, so that I may finish my course with joy."

> " Beset with threatening dangers round,
> Firm Fortitude maintains her ground :
> Her conscience holds her courage up.
> The soul that's fill'd with virtue's light,
> Shines brightest in affliction's night ;
> And sees in darkness beams of hope.
>
> " Ill tidings never can surprise
> That heart, that fix'd on God relies ;
> Though waves and tempests roar around,
> Safe on the rock he stands, and sees
> The shipwreck of his enemies,
> And all their hope and glory drown'd."

Both sure and steadfast. Heb. vi. 19.

THE FAST-ANCHORED SHIP.

Lo! where the war-ship, with her tattered sail,
Tho' late escaped the fury of the gale;
At anchor safe within the bay she rides;
Nor heeds the danger of the swelling tides:
Though high aloft the furious storm still roars,
Below, she's sheltered by the winding shores.
  The church of Christ a war-ship is below,
She spreads her sails to meet her haughty foe;
Satan assails her with his furious blasts,
Her sails are riven, broken are her masts:
A night of darkness finds her in some bay,
She drops her anchors, and awaits the day;
Faith, Hope, and *Prayer,* her steadfast anchors prove,
With *Resignation* to the powers above.

THIS engraving represents a ship riding by four anchors. To escape the rage of the storm at sea, she has sought shelter in the bay. Her sails are torn, and cordage damaged; she needs to undergo repairs. The gale still howls fearfully overhead;

but protected by the land, she rides comparatively in smooth water.

The Church of God may be compared to a ship, and to a ship of war, built by the great Architect who made heaven and earth—first launched when Adam fell overboard—chartered by divine love to take him in, with all his believing posterity, and convey them to the port of glory.

Jehovah is her rightful owner; Immanuel is her captain; the Holy Spirit is her pilot; the Holy Bible is both chart and compass; self-examination is her log-book; her pole-star is the star of Bethlehem. Under her great Captain, the ministers of religion take rank as officers; besides whom, there are a number of petty officers. Her crew consists of all those who "follow the Captain." Passengers, she carries none—all on board are "working hands."

This world is the tempestuous sea over which she makes her voyages. It is a dangerous sea; rocks, shoals, and quicksands hide their deceitful heads beneath its dark blue waves; mountainous billows roll, furious storms descend, and treacherous whirlpools entice only to destroy.

The voyage is from time to eternity. The good ship never puts back; well stocked, she carries bread of life, and waters of salvation, in abundance; no "southerly wind" ever afflicts her. The Church is a ship of war; she carries a commission authorizing her to "sink, burn, and destroy" whatever belongs to Beelzebub, the great enemy of mankind, and to ship hands in every quarter; therefore, Beelzebub, being a "prince of the power of the air," comes out against her, armed with the four winds of heaven, and attacks her as he did the house of Job's eldest son.

Bravely does she behave amid the storm. She

would weather the gale, were it not that there is treachery on board; some "Achan" compels her to "about ship." She runs into the bay of Promise, and casts first of all the anchor of *Hope*. Though "perplexed," she is "not in despair." Hope is as an anchor to the soul in the day of adversity. Hope, however, is not sufficient; another anchor divides the parting wave, even that of *Faith*. Faith takes hold of the promises made to the Church in her times of trial, especially this one: "Call upon me in the day of trouble, and I will deliver thee." *Prayer*, consequently, "is let go" next. Ah! now she "takes hold on God;" now the vessel rightens; now she is steady. Nevertheless, she is not yet delivered. What more can she do? There is yet one more anchor on board: *Resignation*, last of all, is received by the yielding wave. The good ship has done her duty; now she may lie still, and wait for the salvation of God. Soon it comes; heavenly breezes fill her flowing sails; she is again under weigh for the *port of glory*—

> "Where all the ship's company meet
> Who sail'd with their Saviour beneath;
> With shouting, each other they greet,
> And triumph o'er trouble and death.
> The voyage of life's at an end,
> The mortal affliction is past,
> The age that in heaven they spend,
> Forever and ever shall last."

Endeavoring to keep the unity of the Spirit. Eph. iv. 3.——*So we being many, are one body in Christ.* Rom. xii. 4.

UNANIMITY.

Look! where the soldiers form a hollow square,
And thus the fortunes of the day repair;
On every side a bristling front present,
On which the fury of the foe is spent;
"Union is strength"—'gainst odds they win the day,
And proud their banners o'er the field display:
The camp, the Christian Church may sometimes teach,
To gain a triumph, or to mount a breach:
So when the armies of the cross *unite*,
They quickly put the alien foe to flight;
When, up and doing, *united* and awake,
They drive back Satan, and his kingdom shake;
The standard-bearer with his brethren stands,
By love united. Love binds hearts und hands,
The flag of Jesus high aloft he bears,
That tolls of vict' ies won, by groans and tears;
Of future victories, too, this is the sign,
When all the kingdoms, Saviour, shall be thine;
Then let the heroes of the cross *unite*,
And quickly put the alien foes to flight;
And win the *world* in great Messiah's right.

The soldiers are here seen formed into what is termed a hollow square. They have been well-nigh beaten on the field of battle; this position is resorted to as a last effort; on every side they present an array of glittering arms. The foe advances: still they stand their ground; they repel the onset; they change the fortunes of the day. By union, they route the enemy, and gain a complete victory.

Behold, says the Psalmist, how good, and how pleasant it is for brethren to dwell together in *unity*. It is not only good and pleasant, but essential to success. Christians have a work to do—a great work. Union is strength in religious warfare, as well as in military tactics. "United, we stand—divided, we fall." It is a part of the plans of military commanders, to divide the forces of the enemy, both in the council and in the field; so likewise it is the plan of the grand adversary of souls to divide Christians. The great Head of the Church has provided a principle which binds, nourishes, and consolidates the various members of the body together,—for we are all members one of another. If this principle is neglected, the army of the cross becomes easily dispersed. The principle is LOVE.

An aged father, when dying, called his sons around his dying bed, and in order to show them the necessity of union among themselves, he commanded a bundle of sticks, which he had provided, to be brought before him. Beginning with the eldest, he requested him to break the bundle of sticks; he could not. The next was called, and so on down to the youngest: all failed; upon which, the old man cut the cord which bound the sticks together, and they were easily broken, one by one. *Love* is the cord that binds together. *Union* alone supplies the lack of numbers of talents, and of wealth. The minister of the gospel is the standard-bearer in the Christian army; the membership are the soldiers of Jesus. If every soldier rallies round the standard, and all are determined to conquer or die, nothing can stand before them; they would drive back the powers of darkness, and make Apollyon fly. For want of *union*, antichrist and infidelity prevail, and sinners go unreclaimed. When professing Christians cease to vex each other, and turn the whole tide of their strength against the common foe, the kingdoms of this world will become the kingdoms of our God, and of his Messiah, and he will reign forever and ever.

THE END

CHRISTIANITY,

Represented by a woman coming out of the wilderness, clad in beautiful garments. Confiding in the eternal God for protection and support, she advances: the gods of the heathen, and the temples of superstition fall on her approach; her enemies retire abashed and confounded, while the Angel of the everlasting Gospel is dispersing the clouds of darkness that surround the globe.

RELIGIOUS ALLEGORIES:

BEING A SERIES OF

EMBLEMATIC ENGRAVINGS,

WITH WRITTEN EXPLANATIONS, MISCELLANEOUS OBSERVATIONS, AND RELIGIOUS REFLECTIONS,

DESIGNED TO ILLUSTRATE

DIVINE TRUTH,

IN ACCORDANCE WITH THE CARDINAL PRINCIPLES OF

CHRISTIANITY.

I have used similitudes. Hosea, 12 chap. 10 v.

BY REV. WILLIAM HOLMES,
MINISTER OF THE GOSPEL; AND
JOHN W. BARBER,
AUTHOR OF "THE ELEMENTS OF GENERAL HISTORY," ETC.

NEW YORK:
GEO. F. TUTTLE, PUBLISHER,
No. 147 FULTON STREET.
1860.

ENTERED
ACCORDING TO THE ACT OF CONGRESS, IN THE YEAR 1846,
BY JOHN W. BARBER,
IN THE OFFICE OF THE CLERK OF THE DISTRICT COURT OF
CONNECTICUT.

TO THE READER.

It is now about two years since the Religious Emblems, a work by the Authors of the present publication, was first issued. The manner in which that work was received by the Christian public, has encouraged another effort of the same kind, which, it is believed, will be found equally worthy of attention.

Looking unto Jesus. Heb. xii. 2.

LOOKING UNTO JESUS.

Amid the world's vain pleasures, din and strife,
The Christian treads the upward path of life;
Though sorely tempted to forsake the way,
He presses onward still from day to day;
On worldly *honors* he with scorn looks down,
Content if he at last shall wear a crown;

And worldly *wealth* without regret he leaves,
He treasure has beyond the reach of thieves.
The Syren *Pleasure* with voluptuous strain,
Strives to ensnare him, but she strives in vain;
His ear he closes to their idle noise,
And hastens upward to celestial joys;
At God's right hand he owns an ample store,
Of joys substantial, lasting evermore;
He *looks to Jesus*, his Almighty Friend,
Nor fails at last to reach his journey's end.

The Christian is here depicted making his way up the path of life. The wealth of this world is offered to him on condition that he will turn aside. He rejects the offer with disdain: he points upward, intimating that his treasure is in heaven. Honors are presented; these he despises also, content with the honor that comes from God. The votaries of sinful pleasures next address him; they promise all sorts of delights if he would stay and dwell with them. He closes his ear to their deceitful song: he looks upward to Jesus his Lord and his God, and taking up the song of an old pilgrim, he goes on his way singing:—

"Thou wilt show to me the path of life,
"In thy presence is fulness of joy,
"Pleasures at thy right hand for-evermore.

But what will not men in general do in order to obtain those very things which the Christian rejects with so much disdain? What have they not done? Answer, ye battle fields that have heard the dying groans of so many myriads! Answer, ye death beds that have listened to the lamentations of the votaries of pleasure! Answer, ye habitations of cruelty, where the life's blood of the victims of avarice oozes away from day to day, under the rod of the oppressor! And who or what is the Christian that these things have no influence over him? Is he not a man? Yes; an altered man from what he was once; a new man. Old things have passed away. All things have become new. *He looks to Jesus.* Here is where his great strength lies. Here is the power by which he overcometh the world, ven by looking to Jesus. Do you ask what is this looking to Jesus? What magic is there in this so powerful? Listen! Our sins have separated us from God, for " all have sinned and come short of the glory of God." Death temporal has passed upon all men, as the forerunner of eternal death, except we repent and be converted. But how shall we repent and be converted? How shall we guilty ones dare to approach the Holy God? He is of purer eyes than to behold iniquity. What shall we bring to gain his favor? Alas for our poverty if it were to be bought with money! Alas for our sinfulness if our own righteousness could have sufficed to recommend us to God! Alas for our impotence if we had been left unaided to descend Bethesda's Pool! Alas for our blindness if we had been left to ourselves to discover a door of Hope.

While in this plight Jesus comes to our relief. He brings a price—a righteousness—a strength—a light. He is the light of the world—the Sun of righteousness. He shines and dispels the gloom. O how cheering are His rays! As the beams of the morning give hope and consolation to the benighted traveler in some dreary wilderness, so does Jesus, the "day spring from on high," give light and hope to those who sit in "darkness, and in the shadow of death." The light of love and the hope of heaven. The path of duty is revealed, the promise of immortality is given. Do you ask yet again, what is meant by looking to Jesus? Again listen. The exercise of faith in the Lord Jesus Christ. This is what is meant. Man is made capable of confidence, of confidence in man. In this consists the charms of domestic felicity. A man without confidence in his race is an isolated being; he is cut off from all the sympathies of his kind. Just so, man without confidence in God, is separated from him. He is in the world without God, and without Hope. Faith unites man to God. The Christian is a man of faith. He is united to God; he walks by faith, he lives by faith. The life which he lives is a life of faith in the Son of God who loved him, and gave himself —O wondrous gift—for him.

He looks to Jesus, as unto an "offering for sin." He receives it as a faithful saying, worthy of all acceptation, that "He hath made Him who knew no sin, to be a sin-offering for us, that we might be made the righteousness of God in Him." That is, that we might be completely saved by Him. This is the ground of his rejoicing, that Jesus hath made "a full, perfect, and sufficient sacrifice, oblation, and satisfaction for the sins of the whole world," since "he by the grace of God tasted death for every man." He regards his sins as being of such a nature that nothing but the "precious blood of Christ" could avail to purge them away. Thus the man of God considers Jesus. He goes from strength to strength, making mention of his righteousness, who died for his sins, and rose again for his justification.

Such, however, is man's nature, such are his wants, trials, and destiny, that the Lord Jesus Christ has for his sake assumed various offices and titles. Does man feel his helplessness, that he cannot of himself do anything that is good, he is invited to look from self to Jesus as the "Mighty God." Look unto me, and be ye saved all ye ends of the earth, for beside me there is no God. While others look at their own weakness, at the difficulties of the way, at the strength and number of their foes, the man of faith looks from these to Jesus. Is he tempted to think that after all he shall never see the King in his beauty? He may look to Jesus as his "Advocate" with the Father, who takes care of his interest in the court of heaven, and who is no less watchful over his affairs below. Does he need a subject calculated to fill his mind with mean ideas of self? he looks to Jesus as "*the wonderful*," wonderful indeed. God made man for man to die. In his birth, in his life, in his death, in his resurrection, and ascension, He is wonderful. In his character, in his operations, both of nature and of grace, in drawing, softening, sanctifying, and glorifying the believer, He is wonderful! O the depth both of the wisdom and the goodness of God!

Does he find the affairs of earth too intricate for him, and that the children of this world are wiser in their generation than the children of light? He looks to Jesus as "the Counsellor" who is able to guide the feet of his saints.

In the time of trouble the Christian looks to his counsellor and finds him a "very present help," and no expensive charges, or ruinous issues follow. He looks to Jesus as the Author or Beginner of Faith, who has called him to be a Christian, who has pointed out to him the proper path of duty, and who will at last award to him a crown of righteousness.

Painters, sculptors, and others have, in order to be perfect in their art, studied models of excellence. The Christian studies Jesus; he is his "model" or "example." Are his trials many? is his cross heavy? He considers Jesus who "endured the cross and despised the shame." Is he poor? "The Son of man had no-where to lay his head." Is he rich? for the rich are also called; he considers him "who was rich, and for our sakes become poor." Is he tempted with the glories of the present world? To the Savior "all the kingdoms of this world and the glory of them" were offered. Is he persecuted? He looks to Jesus on the cross and prays "Father forgive them." Thus he looks from earthly glory to that far more exceeding and eternal weight of glory. From earthly possessions to that "inheritance that fadeth not away, and from earthly pleasures to those that are spiritual and eternal. Adopting the language of the poet, he looks unto Jesus as

"His all!
His theme, his inspiration, and his crown;
His strength in age, his rise in low estate,
His soul's ambition, pleasure, wealth, his world,
His light in darkness, and his life in death,
His boast through time, bliss through eternity,
Eternity too short to sing his praise."

"I send the joys of earth away;
  Away, ye tempters of the mind,
False as the smooth, deceitful sea,
  And empty as the whistling wind.

Now to the shining realms above,
  I stretch my hands and glance mine eyes;
O for the pinions of a dove,
  To bear me to the upper skies!

In vain the world accosts my ear,
  And tempts my heart anew;
I cannot buy your bliss so dear,
  Nor part with heaven for you."
                              Dr. Watts.

For we walk by faith, not by sight. 2 Cor. v. 7.

WALKING BY FAITH.

The convert here turns on the world his back,
And walks by faith along the narrow track;
Before him mists arise, and o'er his head
Thick clouds of darkness roll, and round him spread,
A bottomless abyss beneath extends,
And still new danger to his pathway lends,

While ever and anon a lurid wreath
Comes rising upward from the pit of death.
Though all around him spreads the gloom of night,
His footsteps sparkle with a brilliant light;
His Lamp—the Book of God—doth brightly shine,
And pours upon his path a light divine.
Between the murky columns as they rise,
Sometimes he sees a palace in the skies;
His heart is cheered, nor death nor danger dreads,
While circumspectly on his way he treads.
Thus step by step, he walks the narrow road,
Till at the end he finds himself with God.

HERE is depicted a man just starting from what appears to be solid ground, to walk upon a narrow plank, stretched across a deep gulph, and which ends nobody knows whither. Before him thick clouds of mist and vapor slowly but continually ascend from the gulph or pit, rolling clouds of pitchy blackness also ascend. They spread themselves around him; in wreathy columns they stand before, and hide the future from his vision. Still he proceeds; he is a wonder to many, who cannot tell what to make of it. The man himself, however, appears to know very well what he is doing. He holds in his hand a book which he reads as he goes along; though it may seem to some unsafe, yet he finds it advantageous rather than otherwise. The book, he thinks, throws light upon his path; now and then the wind blows the clouds of smoke a little on one side, and he beholds, apparently far off in the distance, a splendid mansion—this is the palace he has heard of; it is thither the way leads, thither he would go.

The sight of the mansion above, whenever he is so fortunate as to behold it, inspires him with courage and fortitude; he bears cheerfully his present labors and sufferings, and meets without fear any new foe. He walks onward step by step, looking well at his footsteps; at last he arrives at the end of his journey—this opens upon him quite abruptly. Suddenly he beholds right before him the mansion shining gloriously. He enters—he is made heartily welcome—he is amply repaid for all his labors and sufferings.

This may be considered as an allegorical representation of the Christian walking by faith through this world to the next; the young Christian, when he embraces Christ, turns his back upon the world, its vanities, and sinful pleasures. He renounces it as an object of trust and hope; he leads a new life; he walks a new path. It is the path of Faith. He knows not what is before him in the present life, whether sickness or health, prosperity or adversity; clouds of darkness, of temptation, and trouble, are sometimes made to arise in his path, by the enemy of his soul, to discourage him in the way he has chosen. Yet he pursues. The word of God is his constant, best companion—it is a light unto all his goings; by it he cleanses his way; though it occupies much of his time, so that many think it will prove his ruin, yet he finds it exceedingly helpful, nay he would not be without it for all the world.

In the midst of his labors and sufferings, he frequently enjoys rich foretastes of the happiness of heaven; these are refreshing to his soul, strengthening and inspiring him with zeal for the Lord of hosts. His light afflictions he reckons are not worthy to be compared with the glory of which he has had an earnest. Not knowing what shall befall him from hour to hour, and from day to day, he goes forward trusting in God, to whom he has committed the keeping of all his concerns, soul and body, for time and eternity. By and by he finishes his course; he has kept the faith, and an abundant entrance is administered to him into the everlasting kingdom of Jesus Christ. The man who walks by sight, looks only at the things which are seen, and which, of course, are temporal. He looks at and regards the things of earth, as worthy of his esteem, of his love, of his labor, of his sufferings; houses and lands, power and renown, and whatsoever tends to supply, the lust of the flesh, the lust of the eye, and the pride of life—these are the objects to which he directs all his prayers, all his purposes, and all his toils—he lives for this, and if necessary he will die for it.

He puts faith in nobody. He will have bonds and seals and witnesses for all and in all his transactions He will not trust the Almighty with any of his concerns, but manages them all himself. He asks no favors at his hands; if indeed he does at any time put up a petition to God, it is that he will ask nothing of him.

How different with the man of Faith. He sees the things of earth and knows their value. It is enough for him that they are temporal. He values them simply as they bear upon Eternity. He looks at the things that are not seen, which are eternal: his soul—and whatever tends to inform and purify it—his Savior, and whatever will advance his cause on the earth; his God,—and what will glorify him: Heaven—and whatever will help him on his way thither: Hell—and what will enable him to escape it. He looks at man as a fellow traveler to Eternity—to the Judgment—puts a generous confidence in him and labors to benefit him temporarily and spiritually. His thoughts, his words, his actions, are all regulated according to his eternal interest. A man must live before he can walk. So it is spiritually. He lives a life of faith in the Son of God. Hence it is not difficult to walk by faith. He is but a sojourner here. His citizenship is in heaven. He is a denizen of immortality. Hence to him—

"Faith lends its realizing light,
"The clouds disperse, the shadows fly,
"The Invisible appears in sight,
"And God is seen by mortal eye;
"The things unknown to feeble sense,
"Unseen by reason's glimmering ray,
"With strong commanding evidence,
"Their heavenly origin display."

Faith is the foundation of things hoped for, the conviction of things not seen. Faith becomes a foundation on which Hope builds her glorious temple of future happiness. The spies who brought an evil report of the land of Promise, walked by sight. They saw nothing beside the high walls; the number of inhabitants; the gigantic Anikim. Not so Joshua and Caleb. They saw only the promise, and the power of Jehovah, which they believed was sufficient to bring it to pass. While the former perished with those who believed not, they, walking by Faith, entered the goodly land and possessed it for an inheritance forever.

In the days of the Redeemer, there were some who saw only the Babe of Bethlehem—the Carpenter's Son—the Nazarine—the Man of sorrows—the crucified Malefactor, and who dreamed of a temporal kingdom. These all walked by sight. Others beheld in him, the mighty God—the everlasting Father—the Prince of Peace—the Messiah—the desire of all nations—the Lamb of God—the Son of God—The King of Israel—who looked for a spiritual kingdom that would fill the whole earth, whose dominion should be forever and ever. These all walked by faith, and according to their faith even so was it done unto them.

By faith, the good old Simeon took up the child Jesus in his arms, and said, "Lord, now lettest thou thy servant depart in peace, for mine eyes have seen thy salvation." By faith, the friends of the man sick of the palsy broke open the roof of the house, and lowered the sick man down into the midst where Jesus was, and experienced his salvation. By faith, Joseph of Arimathea, went to Pilate and begged the body of Jesus, and layed it in his own sepulchre, not doubting but that it would be raised again according to the scriptures. By faith, Paul, when brought before kings and princes of the earth, declared boldly the gospel of Christ and his hope in the resurrection of the dead. By faith, the disciples, who were in Jerusalem when it was encompassed by the Roman armies, left the city and fled to the mountains, and thus escaped punishment in the overthrow thereof. By faith, John Huss, and Jerome, of Prague, delivered their bodies to be burned, not accepting deliverance. By faith, Luther burnt the Bull of excommunication, and repaired to the city of Worms, not fearing the wrath of Pope, Emperor, or Devil. By faith, the Pilgrim Fathers braved the fury of the ocean and the violence of the savage, and planted a habitation for God in the wilderness, yea, a refuge for the children of men.

The time would fail to speak of Elliot and of Brainerd, of Martyn and of Carey, of Wilson and of Schwartz, of Wesley and of Whitefield, and of others whose names are recorded in heaven, who, through faith, unlocked the fountains of truth, broke down the barriers of opposition, subdued nations to faith of Christ, wrought righteousness, and preached to the poor the acceptable year of the Lord.

Thy word is a lamp unto my feet, and a light unto my path. Ps. cxix. 105. *Ye do well that ye take heed, as unto a light that shineth in a dark place.* 2 Peter i, 19.

THE SURE GUIDE.

Alone, bewildered, and in pensive mood,
A traveler wanders through a pathless wood;
Forward he goes, then back, then round and round,
And lists in vain to catch a friendly sound.
Soon night o'ertakes him on her ebon car,
Robed in thick darkness, without moon or star;
No lonely light gleams through the misty air,
And tremblingly he wanders in despair;

At length he sinks, and now for once he prays,
And lo! a compass close beside him lays;
A light he gets and holds it at its side,
That he may well consult the faithful guide;
Within his breast hope now exulting springs,
And painful doubt, and fear away he flings;
But now false guides advance across his track;
One strives with speeches fair to turn him back;
Another bawls with bold and blust'ring shout:
Here! through this pleasant opening lies your route."
I tell you, says a third, it is not so;
This, and this only, is the way to go;
He shuns them all, and trims his light anew,
And heeds his compass, and it guides him through.

An honest traveler having, on his way home, to pass through a lonely forest, loses his way. Bewildered, he knows not which way to turn. Now he goes forward; now backward. Then after wandering about for some time, finds himself where he first starts from. He is discouraged; he listens, hoping to catch from the whispering winds, some tidings of companionship or safety. 'Tis all in vain. Thick mists now gather beneath the leafy canopy. The shadows of evening prevail, and night wraps the earth in her mantle of pitchy darkness. He gropes his way with fear and trembling; he becomes exhausted; hopeless and overcome, at last he sinks on the wet ground. For a while he muses. A thought strikes him—he will pray. He lifts up his hands in prayer, and as they fall again at his side, he feels a something. Behold! it is a compass. Now he strikes a light, and looks with intense interest on his new found guide. Hope now swells his bosom; he will again see his beloved home. Doubt and fear are thrown to the winds, and he springs up to pursue his journey.

As he moves forward with a light in one hand and compass in the other: several persons, attracted by by the light, rush towards him and proffer their assistance; one pointing out an opening to the left, roomy and level withal, with many fair speeches and much earnestness, presses him to take it. Another pointing to the right, in a very confident manner, urges him to take that. It is smoother and less obstructed than the way ahead. The traveler, honest in his purpose of finding home, and relying upon his compass, rejects all their offers of advice. He trims his lamp afresh; looks again at his guide, and following implicitly the way it directs, he gets out of the wood and arrives home in peace.

The lonely forest denotes this present world. The traveler, man; home, happiness; the compass, the Holy Bible; the light, the Holy Spirit; the false guides, those deceitful directors and false doctrines that abound in the world. The world, apart from the sacred light and holy influences of heaven, is dark, cheerless, and impenetrable. Through sin, the darkness of ignorance and the shadows of death prevail. "Darkness has covered the earth, and gross darkness the minds of the people."

Every where, snares and pitfalls abound; dangers, pain, and death. With the desire of happiness strongly implanted in his bosom, man wanders in the midst of misery and uncertainty. What he is; what he must do; whither he is going; he cannot tell. What is life? what is death? He knows not. He tastes of life with bitterness; he approaches death with horror. If there is a God,—what is His character? how shall he worship him? If there be a state after death, what is its nature? where is the place of its abode?

In this state of distressing anxiety, he wanders on, pathless, guideless, lightless, hopeless—he is lost! In the anguish of his soul, he exclaims, "Who will show me any good?" "God, for ever blessed," hears his prayer. He has been tenderly watching him while in trackless mazes lost, and in His providence presents him with a BIBLE. He opens it—he reads. Wonderful Book! It tells him all about the darkness; of what it is made, and how it came to overspread the earth. It tells too, of a sun, a glorious sun, that can disperse the gloom: who he is, and how he becomes the light of the world. It points out to him more distinctly than he ever saw, the snares and pitfalls, and the way to escape them. Wherefore pain, and how to endure it. Why the desire of happiness is implanted in the human breast, and how it may be gratified. It makes known to him, what he is; what he ought to do; where he is going, and what he may become. It tells him of life, and how to enjoy it: of death, and how to strip it of its terrors.

It reveals to him a God, tremendous in power, glorious in holiness, accurate in justice, infinite in love. The Almighty Maker and Ruler of the Universe. It prescribes the way in which He would be worshiped, through "Jesus Christ the Righteous." The sacrifices He would accept, "a broken and a contrite heart;" this is more acceptable to Him than

"Arabia sacrificed
And all her spicy mountains in a flame."

The Bible reveals to him Futurity. It raises the curtain of the hidden world. Here he beholds the tormenting flame, the parched tongue, the useless prayer; there, the glory of Paradise, the bliss of Heaven, the song of praise. It becomes to him just what he needs. He has found a way, a guide, a light, to happiness. Still, he understands its mighty truths but imperfectly, yet he reads on: scales fall from his eyes; he beholds men as trees walking. But the consolations of hope are his; he has found God; he seeks for wisdom at its fount—for light at its source. "Open my eyes," he prays, "that I may behold the wonders of thy Law." Light celestial shines upon the sacred page; he reads and understands enough for knowledge, enough for duty, and enough for happiness.

As soon as the honest inquirer after truth has discovered the right path, begins to walk in it, and lets his light shine, numerous false guides appear and proffer their services. While he was stumbling along in darkness and in ignorance, the devil gave himself no concern about him. Now he is very much interested in his welfare. He sends his servants to put the poor man right. One of these endeavors to dissuade him from using the Bible, for, says he, "it is full of mystery; it is impossible to understand it. I, for one, will never believe what I can not understand. Follow reason, that is the surest guide." "Indeed, friend," replies the enlightened man, " it was by following reason that I was led into the possession of the Bible, and my Bible has led me to God. I acknowledge it is mysterious, wonderfully so; yet it has led me right hitherto, and I am determined to follow it. The nature of its secret influence over my soul, I can not tell. The nature of the power by which it guides aright, under all circumstances of life, I know not. Neither does the mariner understand the power by which the compass operates, so beneficially under all circumstances; of storm and calm, light and darkness, heat and cold. It is ever a sure guide. He believes in it; he follows it. Were the sailor no more to weigh anchor and spread the flowing sail, until he understands the mysteries of the compass, verily, he would have to learn another trade, for ships would rot in harbor, commerce would cease, and intercourse between nations come to an end. And what is worthy of remark, the common sailor boy understands just as much of the practical use of the compass, as the captain; cease then to persuade me further. The Bible is my compass, my sure guide, I will follow it."

Other false directors of different names, but all of them having the same end in view, viz : to make him distrust his guide, and turn him out of the way, offer to him their services; some press the matter one way, and some another. His reply to all is, "Wherewithal shall a young man cleanse his way, but by taking heed thereto according to thy word."

Thus he believes in it practically, follows its directions implicitly, and it guides him safely by every slough of despond, over every mountain of difficulty, through every strait of distress, and every storm of tribulation, and conducts him at last in triumph to the home of the blessed.

"Take from the world the Bible, and you have taken the moral chart by which alone its population can be guided. Ignorant of the nature of God, and only guessing at their own immortality, the tens of thousands would be as mariners, tossed on a wide ocean, without a pole star and without a compass. The blue lights of the storm-fiend would burn ever in the shrouds; and when the tornado of death rushed across the waters, there would be heard nothing but the shriek of the terrified, and the groan of the despairing. It were to mantle the earth with a more than Egyptian darkness; it were to dry up the fountain of human happiness; it were to take the tides from our waters, and leave them stagnant, and the stars from our heavens, and leave them in sackcloth; and the verdure from our valleys, and leave them in barrenness; it were to make the present all recklessness, and the future all hopelessness; the maniac's revelry, and then the fiend's imprisonment; if you could annihilate the precious volume which tells us of God and of Christ, and unveils immortality, and instructs in duty, and woos to glory. Such is the Bible. Prize ye it, and study it more and more. Prize it, as ye are immortal beings, for it guides to the New Jerusalem. Prize it, as ye are intellectual beings for it " giveth light to the simple."

Above all these things put on charity. Col. iii. 14. *Love is the fulfilling of the law.* Rom xiii. 10. *God is love.* I. John, iv. 8.

CHARITY OR LOVE.

The seraph Charity from heaven descends,
And o'er the world on shining pinions bends;
Round mourning mortals tender as a dove,
She spreads her wing and soothes in tones of love;
Pours living balm into the wounded breast,
And aids the beggar though in tatters drest;
The orphan's plaint she heeds, and widow's sigh,

And smiles away the tear from sorrow's eye.
Like some fair fount that through the desert flows,
Fringed with the myrtle and the Persian rose,
She scatters blessings all along her track,
And hope and joy to want and woe brings back,
And when the last faint sob is heard no more,
Up to her native bowers again she'll soar.

Behold here a being of heavenly appearance. The light of love irradiates her brow; her eyes melt with tenderness; her countenance wears the aspect of benevolence; her heart bleeds with sympathy; her hands are strong to save; the commisserating Angel has come from a far distant part; on the wings of love and compassion she has come; she has left all to succor and to save the helpless, the wretched, and the lost.

See her at her Godlike work. In the foreground she is raising a miserable being in rags and tatters from a pit of mire and filth. With her right hand she is pouring the balm of life into the wounds of the dying. Look behind her; see the widow and the fatherless. They have come to bless her; with hearts gushing with grateful emotion they follow her with their praise; she has rescued them from the gripe of the oppressor; they were hungry and she fed them, naked and she clothed them, and their prayers like a cloud of incense go up to heaven in behalf of their compassionate friend. Before she leaves the district of pain, want and wretchedness, CHARITY, for that is her name, builds a house for the reception of the distressed; here she provides what is necessary, appoints her officers and attendants, leaves wholesome instructions, then amid the praises, thanksgivings and benedictions of those whom her love has blessed, she spreads again her wings and soars to her own abode, there to banquet on the remembrance of her deeds.

This engraving represents, first of all, the divine Charity of the ever blessed Redeemer. He left the glories and happiness of heaven to visit our diseased, our lost world. Beaming with love, melting with tenderness, filled with benevolence, on the wings of compassion he flew to our relief. How compassionate! how sympathizing! He becomes a slave himself that he may preach deliverance to the captives, and the opening of the prison doors to them which are bound, and that he might proclaim the acceptable year of the Lord. See Him at his work of mercy. The world is an aceldama, a vast Lazar house, a conquered province, subject to sin and death. He scatters health around him; he gives eyesight to the helpless blind; he bids the lame to walk: the hungry he fills with good things; the very dead he restores to life and joy. He beholds the weeping widow, and hastens to wipe away her tears. He visits the house of mourning and fills it with the song of praise.

Behold Him ascend the Mount of Blessing. He takes his seat; heavenly light shines around him; the majesty of holiness encircles his brow. Love, divine love, looks out from his wondrous eyes; the manna of wisdom drops from his lips; he assembles around him the poor—the mourners—the persecuted, and showers upon them the blessings of an endless life. He rescued the conquered province from the grasp of the foe; destroyed the power of death, and opened unto man the portals of immortal Life. "He wept that man might smile; he bled that man might never die; he seized our dreadful right, the load sustained, and hove the mountain from our guilty world." He established his Church as an Hospital for the spiritually diseased; appointed his own ministers and officers; gave his own laws for the guidance thereof, and having perfected his work of Charity, he ascended again to the mansions of bliss, there to see the effects "of the travail of his soul and be satisfied." As was the divine Founder, such is the religion he established. Christianity is a noble system of Charity. It teaches man to feel another's woe; to seek another's good; to breathe, instead of revenge, forgiveness and affection; for the aged, the halt, the maimed and the blind, it erects asylums of comfort and repose; for the suffering and the sick, Hospitals; and above all, taking into account man's spiritual wants, man's deathless interests as a candidate for eternity, it provides temples for religious worship, where the ignorant may be instructed, the guilty pardoned, the polluted sanctified, and made meet for heaven. Other religions are a fable—a delusion—a shadow. Christianity is alone benevolent; in its Founder, in its essence, and in its operations, intensely benevolent.

Infidelity, in all its appeals, professes Charity and benevolence. What have its apostles done to benefit mankind? In what book are their "Acts" recorded? To what lands have they carried the blessings of civilization? what prisons have they opened? what chains have they snapt asunder? where are the tombs of their martyrs? where the trophies of their success? Infidelity is cruel, earthly, sensual and devilish. Witness its day of triumph in France. True, it opened the doors of the Bastile, but it was only to lead the inmates to the guillotine. It demolished the walls, but it was only to build out of the ruins thereof a hundred dungeons, if possible still more gloomy and terrible. The reign of Infidelity is the "reign of terror." "The infant comes into the world without a blessing, the aged leaves it without hope." The house of mercy is closed; the book of mercy is burnt; the ministers of mercy are slaughtered; the God of mercy is banished; yea, a watch is set upon the tomb that the dead may rise no more. Infidelity

> "like Samson in his wrath,
> Plucking the pillars that support the world,
> Fair Charity in ruins lies entombed,
> "*And midnight, universal midnight reigns.*"

As is the founder of Christianity, and as is Christianity itself, such also is the disciple; he goes about doing good; he is the Jordan in its fullness; he, like the Nile, leaves behind him the seeds of a new creation; he seeks out the helpless and the destitute; he visits the widows and the fatherless in their affliction, and soothes and wipes away their tears; he understands and appreciates the heaven-born sentiment, "*It is more blessed to give than to receive.*" Hence, "when the ear hears of him it blesses him, when the eye sees him it gives witness for him, and the blessing of him that was ready to perish comes upon him."

The disciple however views man in his relation to both worlds, as possessing a deathless spirit; as a candidate for eternity; as an ignorant, helpless and guilty sinner, unholy and unclean, and yet redeemed by the blood of Christ. He will, as far as possible, instruct his ignorance and point him to the Savior. True Charity acts from motives of love to God as well as man. Hence ingratitude does not restrain him, nor opposition make him afraid. He lays up a foundation against the time to come; and when he shall have sown the seeds of Benevolence here, he will reap a harvest of everlasting love; for "whatsoever a man soweth, that shall he also reap."

> "True Charity, a plant divinely nursed,
> Yet by the love from which it rose at first,
> Thrives against hope, and, in the rudest scene,
> Storms but enliven its unfading green..
> Exuberant is the shadow it supplies,

Its fruits on earth, its growth above the skies,
To look at him, who formed us and redeemed,
So glorious now, though once so disesteemed,
To see a God stretch forth his human hand,
To uphold the boundless scenes of his command;
To recollect that in a form like ours,
He bruised beneath his feet the infernal powers;
Captivity led captive, rose to claim
The wreath he won so dearly in our name.
Like him the soul, thus kindled from above,
Spreads wide her arms of universal love;
And, still enlarged as she receives the grace,
Includes creation in her close embrace."

" Charity is placed at the head of all the Christian virtues by St. Paul, the ablest divine that ever graced a pulpit or wielded a pen. It is the sub-stratum of philanthropy, the brighest star in the Christian's diadem. It spurns the scrofula of green-eyed jealousy, the canker of tormenting envy, the tortures of burning malice, the typhoid of foaming revenge. It is an impartial mirror, set in the frame of love, resting on equity and justice. It is the foundation and cap stone of the climax of all the Christian graces—without it, our religion is like a body without a soul—our friendships, shadows of a shadow—our alms, the offsprings of pride, or, what is more detestable, the offerings of hypocrisy—our humanity, a mere iceberg on the ocean of time—we are unfit to discharge the duties of life, and derange the design of our creation. Wars and rumors of wars would cease—envy, jealousy, and revenge, would hide their diminished heads—falsehood, slander, and persecution would be unknown—sectarian walls, in matters of religion, would crumble in dust. Pure and undefiled religion would then be honored and glorified—primitive Christianity would stand forth, divested of the inventions of men, in all the majesty of its native loveliness—the victories of the cross would be rapidly achieved—and the bright day be ushered in, when Jesus shall rule, King of nations, as he now does King of saints.'—*Probs.*

Pride goeth before destruction, and an haughty spirit before a fall. Prov. xvi. 18. *He giveth grace unto the lowly.* Prov. iii. 34.

PRIDE AND HUMILITY.

Rising in fair proportion side by side,
Behold the stages of Progressive *Pride;*
Respectability begins the course;
'T is his who has—all told—a well filled purse;
High as his neighbor sure he 'd like to feel,
So takes the next step, and is quite *Genteel;*
By many acts for which he 'd fain write—blank,

He swells and struts at length a man of *Rank;*
The chair of state he next ascends, that *Fame*
May faithfully transmit his *Honored* name;
He meets a rival here, and—woe to tell,
He sends his rival in a trice to—hell;
A thousand shots like that, and strange to say,
Right up to *Glory* he has won his way.
Pride walks a thorny path; it nothing bears
But swords and pistols, blood, and groans, and tears.
   Far different in the happy vale, behold
Humility at ease, uncursed with gold;
With competence content, with wisdom blessed;
In peace he dwells, caressing and caressed;
No thorns beset his path, there only grows
The bending corn, the violet, and the rose;
Truth, beauty, innocence, at once combine,
And o'er his pathway sheds a light divine;
And when he leaves the vale, to him 't is given,
To walk amid the bowers of bliss in heaven.

This engraving shows a rude mass of rocks rising from the valley below. They appear to be thrown up by some volcanic explosion, or forced up by the agency of subterranean fires, they are so steep, rugged and unequal. On the tops of the ledges are seen bushes of thorns, high, and spreading in all directions. On the first ledge is a man who has scrambled up with some difficulty to the place he now occupies. His object is to get as high as he can, and he is seen about to place himself on the elevation of Gentility. On the next ridge is seen a man and woman, who appear to think a good deal of themselves. They strut and swell like peacocks, although behind and before danger threatens. A little higher see! there is murder committed. One man has shot at, and killed his brother, just because he would not move faster out of his way, although there was room enough for both. At the end of the rocks and above all, is a man in uniform. He has attained the highest pinnacle. Thunder and lightning attend his path; storms gather round him. A man of thick skin, no doubt; thorns could not scratch him, nor daggers pierce him, nor bullets kill him. His glory, however, is almost gone. The next step he takes he falls, and disappears.

A more pleasing picture presents itself to us below A lovely vale opens enriched and adorned with the choicest of fruits and flowers of paradise; there the fountains pour forth their living streams. The corn bends gracefully to the passing zephyr. The lowly violet rears her beauteous head in the friendly shade the rose of Sharon decks the border; the father mother, and little one are seen walking together along this beautiful valley, with Wisdom for their guide. The air is filled with fragrance and sweet sounds; no thorns grow there to obstruct their path; no lightning's flash, nor thunder's roar, makes them afraid. Safe, peaceful and happy, they pass along, while Truth, Beauty, and Innocence, irradiate their pathway that leads directly to their own sequestered cottage.

This is an allegorical representation of Pride and Humility. The shelving rocks denote the rugged and thorny path of Pride. The way is raised by the agency of the devil. Having ruined himself by pride, he seeks to bring man into the same condemnation; he tempts the children of men to walk on it. The Most High has planted it with thorns, made it difficult in order to deter men from walking on it. Notwithstanding this merciful precaution, it is crowded with adventurers. Nothing shows the fallen character of man, more than his silly and presumptuous pride, at once stupid and wicked.

> " Of all the causes which conspire to blind
> " Man's erring judgment, and misguide his mind,
> " What the weak head with strongest bias rules,
> " Is *Pride*, the never-failing vice of fools;

" Whatever nature has in worth denied,
" She gives in large recruits of needful pride;
" For as in bodies, thus in souls, we find
" What wants in blood and spirits, swelled with wind;
" Pride, where wit fails, steps in to our defense,
" And fills up all the mighty void of sense."

A man becomes possessed of a little gold, and he all at once becomes blind, or at least he sees things in a very different light from what he did once. He himself is altogether another man. He wonders that he never before discovered his own merit. He no longer associates with his former friends; Oh no! they are not respectable. He wishes to be considered a gentleman; he will no longer work; he is above that. He sees his neighbor living in a higher style than he does, he is discontented. The thorns already begin to scratch him. Pride, however, can bear a little pain. Pride is very prolific. The man under its influence soon gets peevish, envious, and revengeful. The remonstrances of conscience are silenced, and he gives himself up to the guidance of Ambition.

He next aspires after *rank* and fashion; but Pride is very expensive. In order to keep up appearances, he does many things that at one time, he would never have thought of doing. He can lie, and be very respectable. He can overreach and defraud his neighbor, and yet be respectable. He can seduce the innocent and unsuspecting, and destroy the happiness of entire families, and still be considered respectable. By his slanders he has ruined the reputation of more than one. By his unrighteous schemes he attains the present object of his proud heart, and moves among the circles of rank and fashion.

Yet his soul is restless. It is like the troubled sea; he pants for Power. He pursues after honors, that the trump of fame may sound his name abroad, and hand it down faithfully to posterity. He becomes now a candidate for high office. In his own opinion he possesses every qualification; he is astonished that the world should be so blind to his many excellencies. He here meets with a competitor—he wishes him out of his way. "From pride comes contention;" he picks a quarrel with his rival. The challenge succeeds; the duel is fought, and his antagonist falls weltering in his blood. He triumphs. Ah! unhappy man! Remorse is his companion forever—the ghost of the murdered haunts him continually.

He is installed in office. He scruples at nothing that will but increase his power; the man's pride knows no bounds—he aspires now after conquest and dominion. He will be a Hero; he will attain the high pinnacle of military renown and glory. War, fearful, devastating war, goes before him; Famine and Pestilence attend him; Ruin and Misery follow close behind, but "Pride goeth before destruction!" There are others who wish him out of the way. A shot from his own ranks cuts him down. From his high elevation he is brought low. His glory is departed.

"Heroes are much the same, the point's agreed,
"From Macedonia's madman to the Swede;
"Mark by what wretched steps their glory grows,
"From dirt and seaweed as proud Venice rose;
"In each how guilt and greatness equal ran,
"And all that raised the hero sunk the man."

The man with his family in the happy vale, represents *Humility*. The passions seldom operate alone; humility begets contentment and peace. He is satisfied with the position God has given him. He has learned from the book of wisdom that happiness consists not in the abundance of things which a man may possess; hence contentment is his safe-guard. He has no desire to ascend the rugged path of pride; he drinks wisdom and knowledge from the fountain of Truth—he quaffs pleasure at the springs of domestic bliss. His greatest treasure is a good conscience—his highest ambition to walk humbly with his God. Free from the consuming cares, the torturing desires, the fierce passions, the dreadful fears and gnawing conscience of the man of Pride, he enjoys peace. He labors to discharge all the duties of his station, with an eye single, doing all to the glory of God. His present path is safe, peaceful and happy, and his hope of the future, blessed and glorious.

" Far from the madding crowd's ignoble strife,
" Their sober wishes never learned to stray;
" Along the cool, sequestered vale of life,
" They keep the noiseless tenor of their way."

Behold how great is the difference between Humility and Pride. Pride assumes an elevated position, and looks down with contempt on all beneath. Humility is content with a lowly seat, and mingles kindly with the brotherhood of man. Pride climbs a steep, dry, and rugged path, beset with thorns and briars. Humility walks the verdant vale amid rippling brooks, blushing corn, and flowers of vernal beauty. Pride occupies a dangerous place; even nature contends against him. The thunder, the lightning, and the storm, encompass him about. Humility walks with nature, and her path is safe. Pride is tormented with cares, fears, and vain desires. Humility enjoys the peace of God that passeth understanding. Pride works all, and endures all, to be seen of dying men. Humility courts the eye only of the living God. The path of Pride leads to shame and everlasting contempt; that of Humility to Honor, Glory, and Eternal Life.

Whosoever will lose his life for my sake shall save it. Luke ix. 24.—*He died for all.*—2 Cor. v. 15. *We ought to lay down our lives for the brethren.* —1 John, iii. 16,

THE SACRIFICE.

See here the Warriors on the battle-field,
In dread array with gleaming spear and shield ;
They rush together with the mighty roar
Of stormy ocean on a rock-bound shore ;
Shields strike on shields, helmets on helmets clash,
In pools of purple gore the Legions splash.

From Latium's host the sound of triumph rings,
And Victory guides them on her crimson wings:
Then the brave Roman, fired with patriot zeal,
His life devoted for his country's weal;
The victors then in dire amazement stood,
As on he swept like a destroying flood;
His blood-stained sword through crest and corselet sank,
Like Death's own angel, swift he strewed each rank:
At length he fell,—and Rome's proud banner waved
Its folds triumphant o'er a nation saved.

BEHOLD, here, the battle-field; the warriors are seen arrayed in all the pompous circumstance of war. Armed with shield and javelin, they stand prepared for dreadful combat. See! the ranks are broken; one is seen rushing into the midst of the enemy—on he sweeps like a tornado—right and left he hurls the blood-stained spear; he cuts his way through—the foe, astounded at his daring intrepidity, give back. Again they rally, and the hero falls covered with a hundred wounds; he has, however, effected his object—the ranks are broken; his comrades follow up the advantage thus gained—rushing into the breach they rout the foe; and soon victory sits perched upon their banner.

The Romans, being at one time engaged in battle against the Latins, the latter had the advantage, and victory was about to decide in their favor, when Publius Decius, observing how things went, fired with a generous zeal, determined to sacrifice his life for his country's welfare. He threw himself upon the ranks of the enemy, and after having committed great slaughter among them, fell, overwhelmed with wounds. His countrymen, inspired by his heroic example, rallied their forces, renewed the combat, fought with great bravery, and gained a complete victory. Decius left behind him a son, who in like manner sacrificed his life in a war with the Etruscans; also, a grandson who sacrificed himself in the war waged against Pyrrhus. His example influenced his countrymen down to the last of the Romans.

The hero sacrificing his life for his country's good, represents the Christian Missionary falling in the midst of heathen lands. The young man already belongs to the sacramental host; devoutly attached to his Saviour, burning with zeal for his glory, he longs to do something to advance his kingdom on the earth. The two armies he knows are in the field; long, fierce and bloody, has been the contest. O! if he were permitted to turn the battle to the gate. That he may see distinctly the state of things, he ascends the mount of Vision; in one direction he beholds Africa bleeding and prostrate beneath the powers of evil—he sees tribe waging against tribe bloody and cruel wars; rivers run red with the blood of its slaughtered millions; its mountains are crimsoned with human sacrifices; its vallies resound with the wild yells of demon-worshippers. In Central Africa he sees forty millions ignorant, cruel and superstitious, covered with the blackness of night; every where cruelty reigns rampant, enslaving and destroying millions of immortal souls; and as he bends over this mass of woe, he thinks he hears Africa "weeping for her children" as she "stretches out her hands unto God."

He turns his eyes in another direction, and he beholds China—vast, populous China: an infidel refinement, mixed with abominable vices prevails; one vast chain binds them fast to the pictured idols of their own creating; there they are ignorant of Jehovah, and Jesus Christ whom he has sent; without hope in the world.

He ventures to look still further. Now he beholds the myriads of India crushed beneath a gigantic system of error—the growth of ages. The rivers as they roll, the mountains as they rise, the vallies as they open, all proclaim the deep degradation of the people. "They have priests, but they are imposters and murderers; and altars—but they are stained with human blood; and objects of worship—but they acrifice to devils and not to God. The countless nass is at worship—before the throne of Satan, glowing as with the heat of an infernal furnace— with rage, lust, and cruelty, for their religious emotions. He looks again; their demon-worship is over, but are they satisfied? How eager their looks! how objectless and restless their movements! how the living mass of misery heaves and surges, and groans and travails in pain together. He beholds them "as travellers into Eternity; how vast the procession they form, how close their ranks, how continuous the line, how constant and steady the advance! an angry cloud hangs over them—which moves as they move —and ever and anon emits a lurid flash; it is stored with the materials of judicial wrath. Thousands of them have reached the edge of a tremendous gulph— it is the gulph of perdition, and they are standing on the very brink. God of mercy, they are falling over. They are gone!"

Finally he looks at home; here, in his own beoved land, he sees millions of immortal souls, for whom Christ died, shut up in unbelief and ignorance. Slaves, doomed to labor in despair, and to die without hope.

"From Greenland's icy mountains,
 From India's coral strand,
Where Afric's sunny fountains
 Roll down their golden sand;
From many an ancient river,
 From many a palmy plain,
They call him to deliver
 Their land from error's chain."

He hears the call; it sinks deep into his heart. He burns to carry to Africa the tidings of the God of Love—to China the system of Eternal Truth—to India the sacrifice of the Son of God—to his oppressed countrymen the Liberty that maketh "free indeed." Viewing the vast and deadly plague that desolates the earth, he longs to carry into the midst thereof the censer of incense, that the plague may be stayed, and spiritual health every where established. In the spirit of devotion he exclaims, "here am I, send me."

> "My life and blood I here present,
> If for thy truth they may be spent."

Now he selects his field of labor; the tear of love and friendship bedews his cheek—the parting hand is given—the last farewell breaks from his trembling lips—he flies on the wings of the wind to meet the foe. Soon he is at the post of duty; he flings the torch of heavenly love into the midst of midnight darkness; powerfully he wields the sword of truth against gigantic forms of error. He wrestles with the man of sin and prevails; the might of God is with him; the enemy falls before him; he takes possession of his strong places. The banner of Emmanuel opens its folds triumphant to the breeze; soon the infant Church lifts up its voice, "hosanna, hosanna in the highest."

But in the struggle the Hero falls. Through the influence of the deadly climate, or through the deadlier passion of the ferocious natives, he falls. Far from home and friends he falls, and "unknelled and uncoffined" he is borne to the house appointed to all the living; the earth closes over him; not a stone tells where he lies; but his object is effected, the seed is sown. The tree of Life is planted, whose leaves shall be for the healing of a nation's curse. The nation that smote him by and by shall remember him whom they pierced, and mourn deeply because of the madness of their guilt. He is crowned with glory, honor, and immortality; the brightest diadem in heaven's own gift is his; he wears it as his due.

He has fallen, but like Samson, he slew more dying than when he was alive. The Temple of Error is overthrown, the tree of gospel liberty is watered by the blood of its martyrs; thus has it ever been, from the time of the proto-martyr to him of Erromanga. Every stroke received is a victory gained, every death a triumph. The sacrificing spirit of the brave Roman lived in his immediate descendants and fired a whole nation with the love of heroic deeds; it is so with the Christian Hero, and to much better purpose. Living he was located; his sphere of usefulness was limited; now he possesses a ubiquity of presence; he is every where animating the Church of God by his example; and she is animated—the spot where he fell becomes a recognized part of her possessions. Others rush forward and secure the prize. Every one of his wounds become more effective and eloquent than the mouth of the living orator, speaking through all time. Dying, he becomes an immortal, his very name becomes a watch-word—his deeds, a memorial unto all generations; his heroic example, a glorious inheritance. If the offering of the widow's mites have constituted so rich a treasury to the Church, how much more shall the sacrifice of the Christian Hero open to her a mine of wealth, at once precious and inexhaustible.

> "'T is now the time of strife and war,
> The contest sounds on every side;
> Nations are bound to Satan's car,
> And who shall meet him in his pride?
> Is there no arm his power to break?
> Are there no hearts that deeply feel?
> Sons of the kingdom! rise, awake!
> Obey, at length, your Saviour's will.
> Go, bear the gospel banner forth,
> Its glittering web of light unroll,
> To gleam sublime from south to north,
> And scatter light from pole to pole"

Whosoever therefore, shall be ashamed of me—of him shall the Son of Man be ashamed. Mark, viii. 38.

NO CROSS, NO CROWN.

    See where the Cross of duty stands upright,
    Above it, shines the Crown with radiant light;
    Right in the narrow way the Cross it stands,
    And all the space completely it commands;
    On either side behold! vast rocks arise,
      Expand their width, and reach the topmost skies:

See numbers there, who fain the Crown would have,
But will not touch the Cross, their souls to save;
They seek some other way, but 't will not do,
They wander on, and find eternal woe.
　But one is seen advancing right ahead.
And like his Lord—the Cross he will not dread;
He takes it up—'t is feathers—nothing more—
He travels onward faster than before;
He loves the Cross, nor ever lays it down,
'Till he receives instead the starry Crown.

　On a gently rising ground, a Cross of somewhat large dimensions is seen to stand erect; above it, and suspended in the air, a bright Crown sparkles with a brilliant light. On both sides of the Cross rocks, vast and precipitous, lift up their tops to the heavens; on either side they extend as far as the eye can reach. Many persons are seen going round the base of the mountain chain; their object appears to be to get the Crown; it is theirs, if they will but get it according to the condition proposed. They have been trying to go through the narrow passage, but the wooden cross blocks up the entrance; they never think of moving that, although they try to climb the mountain barrier, which is much more difficult. See! one is now attempting to ascend, but it is all in vain—there is no other way than through the chasm. Away they go, wandering round and round; some are seen falling off a precipice, they are dashed to pieces; others lose themselves among dark labyrinths, and some are torn to pieces by wild beasts. All come to a bad end—not one of them obtains the Crown.

　One, however, is seen alone, marching up to the terrible Cross; he walks with a firm step. Decision is his name; he goes right up to the Cross, he quickly throws it down—it is only a few inches in the ground; he takes it up, its weight is nothing, for it is hollow. He carries it to the place appointed, lays it down, and receives the glittering Crown, and bears it away in triumph.

By the Cross here is signified religious duties; by the Crown—immortality in heaven; those who pass by the Cross and wander round the wall, represent those who think of heaven, but neglect duty; the man who boldly takes up the Cross—the faithful Christian. Many persons think about heaven, who, alas! will never arrive there; nay, they do more, they actually set out for it—perhaps make a profession of religion; they do not like the idea of being lost; submit to a partial reformation, and make an approach toward the performance of religious duties. They just obtain a sight of them, and they are frightened; this is the Cross. What is there in the Cross so dreadful? Let us see. Of all who present themselves as candidates for heaven, it is required that they *become* poor in spirit—humble as a little child—penitent for sin—"perfect and pure, as He is pure"—that they do deny self—crucify the flesh—mortify the body—subdue inordinate desires—set the affections on things above—hunger and thirst after righteousness—forgive enemies—submit to persecution for Christ's sake—to exercise a constant watchfulness over themselves, and against the world and the devil. The hand, if it offends, must be cut off—the eye plucked out.

They are told of the straight gate—the narrow way—the yoke—the burden—the race—the warfare, etc. Yea, the whole man is to be brought under new influences, governed by new principles, and to live for new ends. Self-denial, self-discipline, and self-conquest, are made indispensable prerequisites for the kingdom of Heaven. This is the Cross, it stands in the path of life; to proceed, it must be em braced. Christ is "the way" to God. His atonement, example, doctrines, commandments—there is no other way, there can be no other—a wall of adamant, wide as earth, high as heaven, meets us in our attempts to find one; on which stands inscribed in letters of light, "He that entereth not by the door, but climbeth up some other way, the same is a thief and a robber."

Religious duties are irksome and disagreeable to the carnal mind—to the unconverted; it is their nature to be so. By them a man may know what he is, whether he is converted or not; the Cross is a mirror. Religious duties are imposed, not that by performing them we may earn a title to heaven, but because they are necessary for the purification of our moral nature, through the grace of Christ, that we may become meet to be partakers of the inheritance of the Saints in light. To neglect the Cross is to neglect all; it is to go to the feast without the wedding garment; it is to go forth to meet the bridegroom without light, and without oil in our vessels.

We may substitute something else for the Cross; such as morality, philosophy, or even works of painful pennance. It will be all in vain; as long as we continue unwashed, unjustified, unsanctified, we are unsafe—in momentary danger of hell fire. There is no neutrality in this war. In revolutions of States and Empires, those who do not take up arms against the foe, are deemed as enemies; it is so here. "He that is not with me is against me, and he that gathereth not with me scattereth abroad." This is the conclusion of the whole matter. When Christ comes to judge the world, all who will not now take up the Cross will be regarded as enemies; instead of the Crown they will have the curse; instead of Heaven, everlasting fire with the Devil and his angels

Hence it is that so many "draw back to perdition." Ignorant of the great principles of religion, of its power to save, they wear it as a cloak to hide the deformity within; so inadequate are their conceptions of its excellency, that they will not sacrifice a single lust, a momentary gratification, one darling idol, to insure the "eternal weight of glory" which it promises.

"*No Cross, no Crown!*" Some of the early disciples of the great Messiah, when the spiritual nature of Christianity was presented to them, were "offended." Their carnal stomachs loathed "the bread which came down from heaven." Companions of the world, they rejected the "fellowship with the Father, and with the Son, Jesus Christ;" the Cross displeased them, and with their own hands they inscribed their names with those "who, having put their hand to the plough, looked back, and so became unfit for the kingdom of God."

"No Cross, no Crown!" See! that young man running toward the great teacher; what can he want with him? He is a noble man, a ruler of the Jews. Strange sight, indeed, to see! A ruler of the Jews running after the despised Gallilean. What is his business? He inquires about the way to heaven; he seems a good deal in earnest; he runs, and kneels at the Saviour's feet; listen to him. O, says he, "what shall I do that I may inherit eternal life?" "Take up the Cross, and thou shalt have treasure in heaven," said the Saviour, as he looked kindly upon him. The young man looks 'sad,' he is 'sad,' and 't is a 'sad' sight to see. He wants the "treasure in heaven." But he wont take up the Cross, and they go together; God has joined them, and what God has joined no man can put asunder. He looks at the Saviour again inquiringly, as much as to say, "Is there no other way?" The Savior understands him; he points him to the Cross again, saying "Except a man deny himself, and take up his Cross, he cannot be my disciple." Fearful crisis, what will he do? The Saviour is looking at him—the disciples—the multitude standing around—God—the holy angels—glorified spirits—all are looking—yea, hell is looking on this spectacle. What is the issue? O, dreadful infatuation; 'heaven that hour let fall a tear.' He who knew the commandments by heart, and who had kept them from his youth up; he turns his back on Christ and heaven, and goes away "sorrowful," to be yet more "sorrowful" long as eternal ages roll.

Have the Cross and have the Crown. Look again at that young man walking boldly up to the Cross; he lays hold of it exclaiming, "when I am weak then am I strong; I can do all things through Christ strengthening me." He finds it 'easy' and 'light,' pleasant and delightful; he bears it faithfully in palaces and in prisons—in the wilderness and in the city—on the sea and on the land—among Jew and Greek—Barbarian and Scythian—Bond and Free—every where exclaiming as he goes, "God forbid that I should glory, save in the Cross of my Lord and Saviour Jesus Christ," and having carried it the appointed time he lays it at the Saviour's feet, singing triumphantly:

> "I have fought a good fight;
> "I have finished my course;
> "I have kept the faith:
> "Henceforth there is laid up
> "For me—A CROWN OF RIGHTEOUSNESS."

They cry unto the Lord in their trouble, and he bringeth them out of their distresses.—Ps. cvii. 28. *Then the waters had overwhelmed us.*—Ps cxxiv. 4.

THE LIFE-BOAT.

 Loud yell the winds escaped from caves beneath,
And summon Ocean to the Feast of Death;
Ocean obeys, high lifts his hoary head,
With fearful roar, impatient to be fed;
With maddened rage his mountain billows rise,
And shake the earth and threaten e'en the skies.
See the poor bark engulphed—with precious freight—
Who, who can save her from impending fate?

Old Ocean strikes her with tremendous shock,
And, oh! she's stranded on a sunken rock;
Horror and grief now seize the hapless crew,
To hope and life they bid a last adieu:
Thousands on shore behold their awful plight,
But cannot save them; 't is a piteous sight.

At this dread crisis, on the mountain wave
Is seen the "*Life-boat*," with intent to save;
Onward she dashes o'er that sea of strife,
Buoyant, and hopeful, 't is a thing of life,
She makes the wreck, and from its drifting spars,
She takes on board the drifting mariners;
Trip after trip she makes—with mercy fraught—
Till they are safely carried into port.

HERE is portrayed the life-boat hastening to the rescue; the winds, escaped from their prison-house, issue forth roaring indignantly at having been confined so long. Ocean is summoned to the feast of Death; Neptune obeys the summons—instantly he is all commotion, stirred up from his lowest depths, impatient to satiate his devouring appetite; he dashes his billows against the earth—he assails the very heavens. Behold the frail ship exposed to all the fury of his rage; she is laden with precious treasure. Her ruin appears inevitable. Loud roars Neptune; loud roar the winds; loud too, snap and crack the cordage and the sails; high rises the mountain surf. The bark "mounts up to the heaven," deep yawns the gulph beneath; she goes down again into the depths; the crew are "at their wits end," their soul is melted because of trouble. But instead of calling "upon the Lord in their trouble," that He might "bring them out of their distresses," they drink and are drunken. Still the waves and the billows go over them; at length a mountain wave dashes the vessel on a sunken rock, she falls to pieces; the men cling to masts, spars, and broken pieces; despair sits on every countenance; multitudes from the shore behold the catastrophe, but cannot succor. Lamentable sight!

At this appalling moment, when all hope is taken away of their being saved, the Life-boat is launched into the terrific ocean. Will not she also fall a prey to the watery monster? See! she lives above the waves; her gallant crew impel her forward; on she dashes—she leaps from billow to billow; soon she reaches the wreck, and begins her work of mercy. Quickly she takes the drowning wretches from the drifting spars, giving back to them life and hope. Some, indeed, not yet sobered, will not be saved; others in the same condition take the "life-preservers" for pirates, that have come to take and sell them for slaves, therefore refuse to leave the raft. No time is to be lost. All they can, they receive on board, and carry safely into port, amid the acclamations of the multitude.

O what is this but a picture of the goodness of our God in Christ, in establishing his Church on the earth. The tempestuous sea is this world, the wreck is man; the life-boat is the Church, and the multitudes on shore may represent the heavenly host who look with interest into the affairs of man's redemption.

The world is indeed a "troubled sea," a tempestuous ocean; it is raised into fury by the breath or spirit of the "evil one," "the prince of the Power of the air," who, having escaped from his prison-house, the "bottomless pit," descends in great wrath and summons all the powers of evil to aid him in the destruction of mankind. Here roll the waves of profanity—there those of impurity; here dash with fury the breakers of Revenge—there rise impetuous the mountain billows of Pride; on the right are seen the rocks of Infidelity—on the left the quicksands of

Destruction, while the whirlpools of Mammon abound in every part.

Man, shipwrecked by the first transgression, is cast upon this troubled sea, exposed to all its dangers; ignorant and helpless, he is "tossed upon life's stormy billows." Wave after wave rolls him onward to destruction; the whirlpool opens wide its mouth to "swallow him whole, as those that go down into the pit." Is all lost? must he become a prey to the devouring elements? Ah! is there no eye to pity? no arm to save? Oh, divine compassion! "God so loved the world," that the Life-boat is launched; Jesus is in the midst of her; he guides her movements! his disciples form the crew; they encounter the storm that Satan has raised; they spring from wave to wave, from billow to billow,

> "With cries, entreaties, tears, to save,
> And snatch them from the gaping grave."

They take sinners from off the waves that are beating them on to death, and place their feet upon the Rock of Salvation. Some are too proud to accept deliverance; such are left in their sad condition.

To speak without a figure, the Lord Jesus Christ has established his church upon the earth, for the salvation of men. This is the proper business of the Church, even as of the life-boat, to save men; its sacraments, ordinances, and various means of grace, all leading to Christ, the Saviour, are well adapted to do this; and when used aright, they never fail to ensure salvation. Believe, love, obey, "this do and you shall live."

And whereas the usefulness of the "*Life-boat*" consisted in having her bottom and sides hollow and filled with air, so the usefulness of the Church depends upon her being filled with the Holy Spirit, with the atmosphere of heaven; and as boats not made air-tight fail to be useful in the storm, and prove the destruction of those who venture in them, in like manner, Churches lacking the atmosphere of heaven, being destitute of the power of the Holy Ghost, fail in being serviceable to the souls of men, and sink into the "dead sea" of forms and ceremonies.

The Church of Christ—that is, a company of true believers—being filled with the Holy Spirit, become inflamed with zeal, and animated with love for perishing sinners. The love of Christ constraineth them, for they thus judge: if Christ died for all, then were all dead—and that he died for all, that they which live should not henceforth live unto themselves, but unto him that died for them and rose again. In seeking to save souls, they seek Christ's honor and glory, by establishing his dominion on the earth; daily the Church influenced thus, makes efforts for the salvation of men; her grand effort is on the Sabbath-day. On this day, worldly business is laid aside; the Angel of Mercy rings her bell around the earth; the Ambassadors of Heaven appear, and issue their proclamation unto the children of men life and immortality are offered without money and without price; Mercy is active on the earth. Fountains of living waters are opened in dry places; heaven's gates are thrown wide open, and streams of light and love issue from the King of Glory. Every where sinners, perishing sinners, are affectionately invited to escape from their sins, and take refuge beneath the sanctuary of the Most Holy;— " Wisdom" herself "uttereth her voice in the streets, she crieth in the chief place of concourse, in the opening of the gates; in the city she uttereth her words, saying, how long, ye simple ones, will ye love simplicity, and the scorners delight in their scorning, and fools hate knowledge." Nevertheless

> "Millions are shipwrecked on life's stormy coast,
> "With all their charts on board, and powerful aid
> "Because their lofty pride disdained to learn
> "The instructions of a pilot, and a God."

As we saw in the case of the wreck, that some actually refused to enter the life-boat, so it is with sinners; alas! alas! that it is so; they, too, are intoxicated, "drunken, but not with wine," sin has intoxicated them; they are beside themselves. Some will not yield their heart to God, and be saved, simply because *they will* not; others do not believe the record God has given of his Son, and continue exposed to the damnation of those "that believe not." Others again, mistrust the motives of the pious, who seek to lead them from the way of death, and think they want only to bring them into bondage; and as the mariners had power to remain on the wreck and be drowned, so the sinner has power to continue in his sins and be damned. Awful power! fearful responsibility! and yet if man be not free, "how shall God judge the world."

The Church, however, as a Spiritual Life-boat, continues her benevolent excursions, and daily lands some saved ones, at the port of glory; and when she shall have made her last trip, through that tempest that shall make a wreck of earth, then shall arise from countless myriads the song of triumph and of praise;—

> "Blessing, and honor, and glory, and power,
> "Be unto Him that sitteth upon the throne,
> "And unto the Lamb for ever and ever."

For the wisdom of this world is foolishness with God.—Cor. 1, iii. 19. *If they have called the Master of the house Beelzebub, how much more shall they call them of his household?* Matt. x. 25.

OBEDIENCE AND WISDOM.

Here is Self-Will, so called by men below,
Struggling alone his upward path to go;
Though steep and rugged he will persevere;
The way he knows is right, then wherefore fear?
His friends and foes alike pronounce him mad;
His *friends* are sorry, but his *foes* are glad;

One pulls him by the skirt to keep him back,
Another runs before to cross his track;
One with a club resolves to stop his course,
And right or wrong, to bring him back by force;
But they are wrong, and wrong the title given,
Self-will on earth—Obedience is in heaven.

Next Folly—nicknamed—here is seen to rise
And climb the path that leads to yonder skies;
Honors and shining gold his pathway cross,
Yet he esteems them but as dung and dross;
Old fashioned things prefers, o'ergrown with rust,
And stars and garters tramples in the dust.
Judging the man by earth's acknowledged rule,
The lookers on denounce him for a fool;
The world is wrong again, the man is right;
His name is Wisdom in the realms of light.

In this picture, on the one hand, is seen a man urging his way up a steep and rugged path; his name is recorded. He is opposed, still he doggedly perseveres; friends and foes alike are astonished at his proceedings. The former are grieved, the latter rejoice at the prospect of his certain ruin. Some of his friends are determined to arrest his progress; one seizes hold of him by the skirt, another, more intent, tries to get ahead of him in order to stop him; a third, yet more violent, pursues him with a bludgeon, and is determined, if fair means fail, to employ force. Nevertheless, he obstinately persists in the path he has chosen; he believes it to be right; he will not give in. They employ threats and promises, but all to no purpose; out of all patience with him, they use up a whole vocabulary of opprobrious epithets. He is self-willed, obstinate, stubborn, etc.; one by one, however, at length they leave him, and go about their business, and the man, no longer molested, goes along the way which to him appears to be right, and which he is determined to follow.

On the other hand, one is seen pressing forward

up a rough and difficult pass; his name, also, is apparent. On his path lie scattered profusely, Riches and Honors, of various kinds; there is the trumpet of Fame, with Stars and Garters, and many other things of equal value; these appear to be at his command—he may ride in a coach drawn by six beautiful horses, and yet he prefers to toil and tug along that rough road on foot. This strange conduct excites the scorn, ridicule, and laughter of those who behold him; they denounce him as a fool—they know that they would act very differently, and they are wise men. The man, however, regardless alike of their scorn and jests, goes his own way; and after a while, they go theirs.

The traveler here called Self-will, represents the Christian, or man of Piety, in every age; the steep and rugged way, Christian conduct; the traveler's opponents, the Christian's adversaries, or men of the world. The Christian is one who is anointed with the Spirit of Christ; he receives a heavenly call; he is not disobedient thereto; he knows in whom and in what he believes. The path he is commanded to follow may be a difficult one, very difficult to flesh and blood; it is a new and a strange way; it is so to himself in many respects, but God has called him to walk in it—he will obey. He walks by faith, not by sight, merely. His friends become alarmed at his conduct, and at first approach him with tenderness, beseeching him to give up his new fangled notions; though he loves them sincerely, he cannot, he dare not yield to their solicitations. They remonstrate, they threaten, but all in vain; he is determined, nothing will move him; he even invites them to go with him; nothing would give him greater satisfaction than to have them for companions; they will not be persuaded, and mourning over what they consider his self-will and stubbornness, permit him, at length, to have his own way.

Others of a more hostile character, but equally blind, who know nothing of the Christian's motives and aims, who put darkness for light, and light for darkness, call sweet bitter and bitter sweet, beset the man with foul and abusive language. They revile and slander him, they maltreat and persecute him; they believe him to be an obstinate, stupid fellow—one who will have his own way at all hazards.

The man of God endures all things, and hopes all things; he prays for those who oppose him; he gives them good advice, and tells them "As for me and my house, we will serve the Lord." But God sees not as man sees; Heaven approves of his conduct; hallelujahs resounded above when first he started on the way; new shouts of angelic applause might have been heard, when he persisted to walk in it. God has enrolled his name among his obedient ones, and when earth's records, doings, and opinions, shall be no more, he will receive amid ten thousand thousand witnesses, the welcome plaudit of "Well done, good and faithful servant, enter thou into the joy of thy Lord."

A wonderful example of what the world calls self-will, lived many years since. An old man who knew nothing about the business, took it into his head to turn shipwright and build a ship. Such a thing had never been heard of; of such enormous dimensions, too, that it was very clear there could not be water enough to float it; and a thousand idle things were said about the old man and his wild and willful undertaking. Yet he was self-willed; day after day found him at his work—he knew what he was about—he knew who had commanded him; he doubted not but that there would be water enough to float his ship by and by, nor was he mistaken. His obedience had its full reward, and the lone Ark, floating majestically on the world of waters, testified that it is better to obey God than man.

The man Folly, his path, and the treatment he meets with, serve also to illustrate Christian character. The Christian is called to forsake home and friends, houses and lands, riches and honors, whenever they in any measure stand in the way of duty. The heavenly commission he has received makes incumbent on him to deny self, take up his cross, to bear the yoke, and to become a pilgrim in the world. He is faithful to his calling. Pleasure courts him, but he embraces her not. Wealth entices, but he consents not. Honors and glories solicit him, but all in vain. He rejects them all. He will not have a clog to his soul. He is free, and he knows the value of his freedom. The poor slaves of sin and earth know no more of the man and his pursuits, than of the angel Gabriel and his employments in paradise. To them, this spurner of gold, this rejector of honors, this trampler on earth, is a fool and a madman; he is beside himself, and so he is denounced accordingly. They judge of him and his conduct by the rules of earth, but he follows another standard. As well might the oyster buried in the sand attempt to pass judgment on the towering eagle when he flies on the wings of the storm, mounts and mingles with the new born light, and rejoices in the boundlessness of space.

The Christian rejects what he knows upon the authority of Truth, and the God of Truth to be worthless in themselves, unsatisfactory in their nature, and transitory in their continuance. He receives and holds fast what is invaluable, satisfying, and eternal. And when the light of the last conflagration shall reveal the secrets of all hearts, and declare the value of all things, then will it be seen that the Christian has governed himself according to the rules of the highest *Wisdom*.

Thus it was with the man of meekness; he gave up kingship and royalty, and formed an alliance with a troop of slaves; he relinquished the splendors of a court for the terrors of a desert; a life of luxurious ease for one of peril and fatigue. By the men of his generation his conduct was regarded as foolish and absurd, but his appearance on the glorious mount of transfiguration, as an Ambassador of the skies, encircled with the splendors of Heaven, proclaims to the world that " the fear of the Lord is the beginning of *Wisdom*," and the love of him its highest consummation.

Look again at the young man of Tarsus; see him resign the professor's chair to become a teacher of barbarians. The ruler of the Jews becomes the servant of the Gentiles; the friend of the great and powerful becomes the companion of the weak and contemptible; the inmate of a mansion becomes a vagabond on the earth, " having no certain dwelling place." He embraces hunger, thirst, and nakedness; the dungeon, the scourge, and the axe. The world has pronounced its verdict upon him—he was a " madman," " a pest," " a disturber of the public peace," " a ringleader of the despised." The case, however, is pending in a higher court, and when those who " sleep in the dust of the earth shall awake," and Paul, " shining as the brightness of the firmament," takes rank among the " wise," the verdict of Heaven will have been recorded.

> " Wisdom is humble, said the voice of God,
> 'T is proud, the world replied. Wisdom, said God,
> Forgives, forbears, and suffers, not for fear
> Of man, but God. Wisdom revenges, said
> The world; is quick and deadly of resentment;
> Thrusts at the very shadow of affront,
> And hastes by Death to wipe its honor clean.
> Wisdom, said God, is highest when it stoops
> Lowest before the Holy Throne; throws down
> Its crown, abased; forgets itself, admires,
> And breathes adoring praise."

If sinners entice thee, consent thou not.—Prov. i. 10. *Lean not unto thine own understanding.* Prov. iii. 5.

DANGER OF PRESUMPTION.

Behold where Winter on his stormy throne,
With icy scepter sways the world alone;
From arctic regions fierce the whirlwinds blow,
And earth, all shivering, wears her robe of snow;
The leafless forest murmurs to the blast,
The rushing river now is fettered fast;

And clouds and shadows settling over all,
Wrap lifeless nature in her funeral pall.
Some youths now hasten to the frozen lake,
And on to school their way with pleasure take;
Nor go alone, but others they entice
With them to frolic on the slippery ice;
The way is pleasant, smoother far to go,
Than o'er the mountain through the drifted snow:
One, and one only, makes a wiser choice;
He will not hearken unto Pleasure's voice:
Awhile the others glide along the lake,
When all at once the ice begins to break;
In—in they plunge! In vain their piteous tones—
The waters quickly hush their gurgling groans.

HERE we see the danger of presumption—the fruits of disobedience. It was a winter's day, the snow had fallen, and earth was clad in her robes of white; the north wind had moaned through the forest, and the ponds and rivers were partially frozen over. Some village school boys, about to start for the school-house, which was situated at some distance on the other side of a mountain, were admonished by their parents not to go by the way of the lake that lay round the foot of the mount; the parents judging it to be unsafe, the command was given with all possible earnestness and tenderness. Well would it have been for the boys had they obeyed; as soon as they were out of sight, Harry whispered to Charles that "it would be much more pleasant to go by the way of the lake, than to trudge it over the mountain, and nobody could know any thing about it." After a few moments pause Charles agreed; others now are invited to accompany them—"the more the merrier" say they; one by one they give their assent, and all, except Samuel, who forgot not his parents' injunction, and who preferred trudging through the drifts of snow over the mountain, to disobeying his parents' command—all resolve to take the smoother and pleasanter way across the lake. They doubt not but it will bear; they anticipate a fine time; they hesitate not to trust the ice, though they will not trust the word of their parents. On they venture—away they glide o'er the slippery surface, with the wind behind them—full of delight they slide along; they see Samuel working his way through the snow; full of fun and laughter, they with difficulty stop to ridicule him, when behold! their entire weight is more than the ice will bear; suddenly it breaks—in, in they go, down! down! they sink;—the cold waters close over them—they are lost. The school-bell rings, but they are not there; one only of the party has arrived to tell to the teacher and the rest of the scholars, the dismal tale.

From the commonest events in life we may gather instruction; the bee disdains not to gather honey from the meanest flower. The Almighty is the great Parent of all, the Father of the Spirits of all that live; He has not forgotten the work of his own hands, he takes pleasure in the security and happiness of his children; he governs the world by laws, —fixed, unalterable laws—except when he alters them for some especial purpose, as in the case of miracles. His natural laws prevail in the heavens above, in the earth beneath, and in the waters under the earth; the law of gravitation, by which a body unsupported falls, exists every where, extends to the remotest star or planet, and binds all material objects to a common center; the law of motion, by which a body once put in motion continues in that state, if it be not resisted by the action of an external cause—these laws and others govern the universe of matter, and they are uniform. Fire always burns, water always drowns, and ice supports bodies in exact proportion to its quality and thickness.

But for Spirits, God has given laws that are spiritual; in wisdom he has given them to his creatures; these, too, are all fixed and unalterable, "Except ye repent ye shall perish." The way of sin always leads to disgrace, sorrow, and eternal death; the path of duty or piety always to honor, happiness, and everlasting life; they have always done so, they ever will do so; God has admonished the children of men of this truth; he has plainly pointed out the two paths, their character, tendency, and end; and having done this, he in the most affectionate manner urges us to follow the path of life. "Behold!" says He, and wonder at the announcement, "I set before you Life and Death, Blessing and Cursing, choose Life that you may live."

> "Placed for his trial on this bustling stage,
> From thoughtless youth to ruminating age,
> Free in his will to choose or to refuse,
> Man may improve the crisis, or abuse;
> Else, on the fatalist's unrighteous plan,
> Say to what bar amenable were man?
> With nought in charge he could betray no trust;
> And if he fell, would fall because he must.
> If Love reward him, or if Vengeance strike,
> His recompense in both unjust alike.
> Divine authority within his breast
> Brings every thought, word, action, to the test;
> Warns him or prompts, approves him, or restrains,
> As reason, or as passion, takes the reins;
> Heaven from above, and conscience from within,
> Cries in his startled ear—abstain from sin
> The world around solicits his desire,
> And kindles in his soul a treacherous fire;
> While all his purposes and steps to guard,
> Peace follows virtue as its sure reward;
> And Pleasure brings as surely in her train
> Remorse, and sorrow, and vindictive pain."

The boys who broke through the ice and perished, had been faithfully warned; the two ways had been distinctly marked out to them, they followed their own course; they *presumed* their parents might not know every thing, they might not know how hard it had frozen during the night—that the ice was strong enough to bear them—there was no danger. The fact was, the way of duty looked difficult, and the way forbidden easy and delightful; they had their reward. So it is with the sinner, man; he *presumes* that he may violate the laws of God with impunity, that he will not punish, that the way is a safe one—although God has said "the end thereof is death." The truth is, the way of piety seems hard, steep and difficult, and the way of sin smooth and agreeable to his carnal nature; hence he ventures on, at first with diffidence, afterward with vain confidence; he entices others to accompany him in his sinful pleasures—this makes it more dangerous; they strengthen each other in wickedness, but "though hand join in hand, the wicked shall not go unpunished."

To show the influence of bad example, and the danger of presumption, Baxter has related the following anecdote: "A man was driving a flock of fat lambs, and something meeting them and hindering their passage, one of the lambs leaped upon the wall of the bridge, and his legs slipping from under him, he fell into the stream; the rest seeing him, did as he did, one after one leaped over the bridge into the stream, and were all, or almost all, drowned. Those that were behind did little know what was become of them that were gone before, but thought they might venture to follow their companions; but as soon as ever they were over the wall and falling headlong, the case was altered. Even so it is with unconverted carnal men; one dieth by them and drops into hell, and another follows the same way; and yet they will go after them because they think not where they are gone. O, but when death hath once opened their eyes, and they see what is on the other side of the wall, even in another world, then what would they give to be where they once were."

Last summer I noticed a little incident that may serve to illustrate our subject; the same thing, no doubt, is of frequent occurrence. An insect had entered the house and was upon the back of a chair; having walked to the end, it very circumspectly employed its feelers above, below, and all around. Ascertaining that the side was slippery and precipitous, it turned round and went back again; this it did several times, nor would it leave its position until it could do so with safety. And yet man—man, with the powers almost of an angel, rushes blindly on to ruin.

It is well known that the elephant, when about to cross a bridge, puts his foot down inquiringly to ascertain its strength, nor will he proceed unless he is satisfied the bridge is sufficiently strong to support him; but the transgressor ventures on the bridge of sin, beneath which rolls the river of eternal woe, bearing with him the weight of his immortal interests, the "vast concerns of an eternal state."

By the laws of motion, the boy sliding or skating on the ice cannot easily stop himself, and sometimes he rushes into the openings or air-holes, that are often found on the surface, and meets with an untimely end.

It is so with the laws of sin; the sinner increases his momentum as he advances; from hearkening to the counsel of the "ungodly," he proceeds to the way of open "sinners,"—a little further and he sits complacently in the seat of the "scornful." Now his doom is sealed!

Thus it was with Babylon's proud king; not content with having been an idolater all his life, against his better knowledge—for the judgment that befel his forefather, Nebuchadnezzar, must have instructed him—he would ridicule the true religion, he would insult the majesty of Heaven. He sends for the sacred vessels of the Sanctuary, that he and his companions may magnify themselves over the captive tribes of Israel. But behold! in the midst of his blasphemous revelry, the Hand—the terrible hand, appears, and the presumptuous monarch, after having seen his doom recorded on the wall of his own palace, is suddenly cut down, and his kingdom given to another.

RELIGIOUS ALLEGORIES.

My heart is fixed.—Ps. cviii. 1. *I press toward the mark, for the prize.*—Phil. iii, 14.

DECISION AND PERSEVERANCE.

See where the Alps rear up their grant crow!
King of the mounts, with coronet of snow;
Scorning all time, and change, his stalwart form,
Endures the peltings of eternal storm;
In awful pride, enthroned above the skies,
Peaks upon peaks in matchless grandeur rise:

'Mid frowning glaciers on whose icy crest,
The savage vulture builds its craggy nest,
The fathomless abyss extends beneath,
And leads the traveller to the realms of death:
Napoleon comes in quest of fame and power,
He scans the mounts that high above him tower.
Though " *barely possible*," he will " advance,"
And in Italia plant the flag of France ;
In vain the mountain, like a dreadful ghost,
Rises to frighten the advancing host.
O'er towering cliff and yawning gulf he speeds,
He means to pass nor aught of danger heeds ;
He scales the summit with his conquering train,
And like the vulture swoops upon the plain.

HERE the Alps lift up their snow-capped heads in awful sublimity ; their icy pinnacles tower above the clouds ; their colossal forms arise, mountain on mountain piled. To all save the bounding chamois or his intrepid pursuer, they appear inaccessible ; here vast overhanging precipices threaten destruction, and there the treacherous abyss lies concealed, ready to engulf the unwary traveller ; Winter reigns supreme upon his throne of desolation ; eternal tempests increase the horror of the scene. In vain does the famished traveller search for some stunted lichen, or the smallest animal, to save him from approaching death ; he sees nothing but boundless seas of ice— no signs of life are there—it seems the very tomb of nature ; the solemn solitude is broken only by the roar of the tempest or the thunder of the avalanche.

Yet over all these obstacles Napoleon would advance ; he inquires of the engineer Marescot, who has just explored the wild passes of the St. Bernard, if it is possible to pass. " *Barely possible*," answers the officer. " Very well," says Napoleon, " en avant," " advance," and at the head of his army of above 30,000 men, with their arms, horses, and artillery, he commences the arduous passage. The

mountains seem to bid defiance to the utmost eff.
of the martial host; but dangers and difficulties deter
him not; like the gale that wafts the vessel sooner
into port, they only urge him on toward the object of
his ambition; he conducts the army over slippery
glaciers, wide yawning ravines, and eternal snows;
he braves the fury of the tempest, and the crash of
the avalanche—and overcoming every obstacle, he
swoops upon Italy like the Alpine eagle upon his prey.

In the conduct of Napoleon in this instance, we
have a striking example of decision and perseverance.
If we can "out of the eater bring forth meat," and
"from the strong bring forth sweetness," it will be
well.

The importance of possessing a decided character
is best seen in its results, as the value of a tree is
best known by its fruits; by its aid Napoleon accomplished the objects of his ambition—fame, and
wealth, and glory, and power. With it, a man attains that which he sets his heart upon; without it,
he becomes easily discouraged and fails. With it,
he controls his own movements, and influences, also,
the conduct of others; without it, he loses his own
individuality, and becomes a creature of circumstances. In fine, man without decision, is like a rudderless vessel, tossed upon an uncertain sea; while
the decided character, like the genius of the storm,
commands the winds and the waves, and they obey
him.

The importance of decision being so apparent, it
becomes an interesting inquiry, "How can it be obtained?" After a proper object of pursuit is selected,
it seems essential that a fuller *knowledge* of the object should be secured; no pains ought to be spared
in order to obtain a perfect knowledge of the object
or profession, in all its parts; this is necessary to

the foundation of such a character. The traveller who knows his way, walks with a firm step, while he that is in doubt about his path, advances with hesitation.

Another thing deemed essential, is *Confidence* in the object of our choice, that it will yield us satisfaction; possessing a knowledge of our route, and a belief that at the end of our journey we shall be at home, the things that discourage others have no influence at all upon us. So it is with the decided character, in the path he has chosen. Does opposition present itself? he assumes the attitude of a gladiator, determined to conquer or die; does danger appear, as it did to Shadrach and his companions, when the burning fiery furnace stood in their path? he burns the more ardently to fulfill his mission. Is he ridiculed, as were the builders of the walls of Jerusalem? he heeds it not, he still goes forward. Finally, does he find himself forsaken? it throws him on his own resources, it makes him firmer in his purpose, as the tree that stands alone and braves the storm, strikes deeper its roots into the ground. If engaged in a good cause he is, like Milton's Abdiel,

"Among the faithless, faithful only he
"Among innumerable false, unmoved,
"Unbroken, unseduced, unterrife
"His loyalty he kept, his love, his zeal.
"Nor number, nor example, with him wrought,
"To swerve from truth or change his constant mind,
"Though single."

In the case of Napoleon the above points were exemplified; he selected, as the object of his choice, military warfare—he made himself acquainted with every thing belonging to it as a science. He had confidence in it, as a means of procuring him th highest objects of his ambition; hence his devotion to it—hence his perseverance; dangers and difficulties are seized as allies—he rises with the storm, and "barely possible," is to him an assurance of success.

To the Christian soldier, decision is of the highest importance; he has selected the Christian warfare as a means of procuring to him, "Glory, Honor, and Immortality." "If the righteous are scarcely saved," it behooves him to know what belongs to "his calling." He needs a knowledge of himself, of his duties, and of his privileges; a knowledge of the way, its dangers, and its difficulties; a knowledge of his enemies, their methods, and their power; a knowledge of his Almighty leader, of his Spirit, and of his word. He needs a living, practical faith, in religion, that it will secure to him "Eternal Life." Opposition, danger, and death, may stare him in the face, but if decided, he will say "none of these things move me," "my heart is fixed, I will sing and give praise," and having fought the good fight of faith, he will be enrolled among those who persevere to the end, and are saved:—

"Faith, mighty faith, the promise sees, and looks to that alone,
Laughs at *impossibilities,* and cries '*it shall be done!*'"

Decision of character may, however, belong to very different individuals; to the bad as well as the good, to Satan as well as to Abdiel. We may, like Enoch, "set ourselves" to walk with God; or be like the wicked whose "heart is fully set in them to do evil." We may say with pious Joshua, "choose you this day whom ye will serve, but as for me and my house we will serve the Lord;" or with ambitious Pizarro, we may draw the line with the sword, and say, "on this side lie poverty and Panama, on that, Peru and gold; as for me and the brave, we will cross the line." With the martyr Paul, we may exclaim "I go to Jerusalem, though bonds and afflictions await me there." Or with the patriot Pompey, "it is necessary for me to be at Rome, though it is not necessary for me to live."

The following anecdotes related by Foster, exhibit striking examples of decision and perseverance:

"An estimable old man, being on a jury, in a trial of life and death, was completely satisfied of the innocence of the prisoner; the other eleven were of the opposite opinion, but he was resolved the man should not be condemned. As the first effort for preventing it, he made application to the *minds* of his associates, but he found he made no impression; he then calmly told them that he would sooner die of famine than release them at the expense of the prisoner's life. The result was a verdict of acquittal." What follows is a less worthy instance:

"A young man having wasted, in two or three years, a large fortune, was reduced to absolute want. He went out, one day, with the intention of putting an end to his life; wandering along he came to the brow of an eminence that overlooked what were once his own estates; here he sat down and remained fixed in thought some hours. At length he sprang up with a vehement exulting emotion—he had formed the resolution that all these estates should be his own again; he had formed his plan also, which he began immediately to execute; he walked forward determined to seize the very first opportunity to gain money, and resolved not to spend a cent of it, if he could help it. The first thing was a heap of coals shot before a house; he offered to wheel them into their place—he received a few pence for his labor; he then asked for something to eat, which was given him. In this way he proceeded, always turning his gains to some advantage, till in the end he more than realized his lost possessions, and died a miser, worth more than a quarter of a million of dollars."

RELIGIOUS ALLEGORIES.

The fool rageth.—Prov. xiv. 16. *Let patience have her perfect work.*
James, i. 4.

PASSION AND PATIENCE.

Behold here! Passion, stamping, mad with rage;
He tries the knotted cord to disengage.
He twists and twirls, and fumes and frets in vain,
And all impatient cuts the cord in twain.
See! there is gold! that Providence has sent:
Favor abused—it feeds his discontent.

His soul a tempest—storms around him rise;
Thunder and lightning shake the trembling skies:
A troubled ocean—white with foaming spray,
Whose restless waters cast up mire and clay.
  But mark the contrast! Patience much at ease,
Th' intricate cord unravels by degrees.
No bags of gold has he. But what is more,
He has content—of this an ample store;
While the bright Rainbow, sparkling in the sky,
Is pledge to him of future joys on high:
His soul a calm—by mellow light caressed;
A placid lake—whose waters are at rest.

Two very different characters are here presented to our view: Passion, storming, wild with rage—Patience, calm and tranquil. For some time, Passion has been endeavoring to unravel a hank of entangled twine or cord, In his great hurry, he entangles it more and more. It is full of knots; he grows hot with rage; his face is miscreated; he wears the aspect of a fury. Stamping with anger, he tramples upon some toys that lay near him, and breaks them into pieces. A bag of gold is seen standing at his side. This only feeds his pride; it makes him more outrageous to think that *he* should have such work assigned him. A tempest is seen to arise behind him; the clouds gather blackness; thunders roll; fearful lightnings glare around. This is to show the state of his mind—wild, fiery and tempestuous. He is also fully represented by the troubled sea, seen in the back ground. Tumultuous it tosses its foaming billows; its restless water casts up mire and dirt. So his troubled spirit, agitated by the tumult of his passions gives utterance to oaths, blasphemies and imprecations. Miserable youth! The fire of hell is enkindled within him!

Patience, on the other hand, sits with unruffled composure. He, too, has had the same work assigned him. He has the knotted cord to unravel; but he goes about it in the spirit of duty; patiently he unties knot after knot, overcomes difficulty after difficulty, until the whole is cleared. He has finished his task; he is seen looking upward, to show that he seeks help and counsel from on high. A heavenly light descends and sheds its luster round about him. Help is afforded. In the back-ground is seen a placid lake: this denotes the composure of his mind. Not a wave of perplexity dashes across his peaceful breast. He has not riches; no gold is seen shining by his side; he is, however, contented with his condition; nor is he without hope of future good. The Bow of Promise, glittering in the distant sky, intimates to us that he looks forward to a future recompense.

Passion represents a man of the world: one who has his portion in this life. The Almighty Father has appointed a work to all men; yea, every thing living—moving—creeping—swimming—flying—has its work to do. Duty is incumbent upon all. It is a condition of existence; it is also a condition of happiness. Man is under this universal law. The man of the world, lacking the proper qualifications for duty, fails in discharging it aright. He works from wrong motives, and for wrong ends; he does all to the glory of self. No wonder he makes such bungling work of it.

By the knotted cord, may be understood those difficult passages of life through which man, as such, has to pass—afflictions, disappointments, etc. These are more than the worldly-minded man can bear. The reason seems clear enough. He has set his heart upon earthly objects; hence the removal of these objects from him, affects him very sensibly. These are thy gods, O man of the world! When trouble comes, of course he does not look upward; he has no business there. He looks down—down—continually

"He leans to his own understanding," instead of waiting for further developments. He becomes impatient, fretful, peevish, angry and passionate. He would curse God and die, if he was not afraid to die. He is

"Instantly, with wild demoniac rage,
"For breaking all the chains of Providence,
"And bursting his confinement, though fast barr'd
"By laws divine and human."

Providence may have lavished wealth upon him: he spurns the giver; he abuses his gifts. His pride becomes more inflamed; his table becomes a snare unto him; his riches add to his discontent. What he needs, though he may not know it, is a hope beyond the grave. He has title deeds enough on parchment, but none to the kingdom of Heaven—houses and lands, but no "hiding place" in which to enter when the great day of His wrath shall come. He has no anchor to enable his vessel to ride out the gales of adversity. Clouds and darkness surround him; a tempest is in his path; he is a cloud carried with the tempest, to whom is reserved the mist of darkness forever; a troubled sea, which cannot rest, whose waters cast up mire and dirt.

Patience represents the man of God—him who has chosen God and the world to come for his portion. In this world, he, too, has presented to him the knotted cord—trials, perplexities and afflictions. Man is born to trouble. He endures all things as seeing him who is invisible; in patience he possesseth his soul. He looks at the difficulty calmly; he considers what is best to be done, and which is the best way to do it. If it is beyond his power or skill, he looks to God for assistance. The composed state of his mind gives him a great advantage over the impatient one; but if he finds his own arm too short, he is intimate with *One* who is mighty to save, and who is a very present help in times of trouble. Soon the knot is untied, the difficulty is overcome, and the victory is gained. Hence a holy calm pervades him; he knows that all things are working together for his good. His soul is like a placid lake, reflecting the rosy light of heaven.

Earth to him may be a tempestuous ocean; but the eye of faith ever sees the beacon of Truth gleaming across its dark blue wave, pointing him to the haven of repose. Therefore, though cast down, he is not destroyed—perplexed, yet never in despair. He reckons that his light afflictions will work for him a far more exceeding and eternal weight of glory. He looks not at the things which are seen, but at those that are not seen. He has no gold—he is poor; but the Bow of Promise spans for him its glorious arch. "He is joyful in hope." He is reminded of his inheritance above. There he has a throne at the right hand of the King of Glory—a mansion in the skies—a bower in paradise—a rest in Abraham's bosom—a shelter from the storm—a city which has foundations. No wonder that he sets his affections on things that are above. There is his portion fair—there, too, is his heart—there is his eternal dwelling place. He would rather have the lot of Lazarus here, and his portion hereafter, than fare sumptuously every day with Dives, and be perplexed with him at last in the hell of torment. As he walks through the vale of poverty and distress, the heavenly light shines around him, and awakens the voice of song:

> "Although the fig tree shall not blossom,
> "Neither shall fruit be in the vines;
> "The labor of the olive shall fail,
> "And the fields shall yield no meat:

"The flocks shall be cut off from the fold,
"And there shall be no herd in the stalls:
"Yet I will rejoice in the Lord—
"I will joy in the God of my Salvation."

How greatly is Patience to be preferred before Passion. Passion is a fury, breathing out threatening and slaughter; Patience is a cherub, whispering words of love and joy. Passion is a tempest, charged with lightnings, hail and thunder; Patience is a holy calm, where peace reigns and stillness triumphs. The one is a troubled sea, casting up mire and dirt—the other, a placid lake illuumined by the mellow light of heaven. The one a foretaste of the fire of hell—the other, a pledge of everlasting repose.

"The man possess'd among the tombs,
    Cuts his own flesh and cries;
He foams and raves, till Jesus comes,
    And the foul spirit flies."

"Beloved self must be denied—
    The mind and will renew'd;
Passion oppress'd and patience try'd,
    And vain desires subdu'd."

"Lord, how secure and blest are they,
    Who feel the joys of pardon'd sin!
Should storms of wrath shake earth and sea,
    Their minds have heaven and peace within."

"How oft they look to heavenly hills,
    Where streams of living pleasures flow;
And longing hopes and cheerful smiles
    Sit undisturb'd upon their brow!"

Fight the good fight. 1 Tim. vi. 12—*taking the shield of Faith --- and the Sword of the Spirit.* Eph. vi. 16, 17.

THE CONQUERING CHRISTIAN.

A glorious Temple rises to our view,
The conquering Christian fights his passage through,
His dreadful foes who now attack him sore,
False Shame behind, fell Unbelief before,
And worldly Love—great idol here below,
Unites to aid in Christian's overthrow;
But he, courageous, takes at once the field.

Armed with his ancient, well-appointed shield;
A two-edged sword he wields, well known to fame,
And prostrates at one blow the dastard Shame;
On Worldly Love he falls with many a blow,
And soon he lays the usurping monster low.
Now Unbelief, the champion of the rest,
Enraged, bestirs him, and lays on his best;
A fearful thrust he makes at Christian's heart,
The Shield of Faith receives the murd'rous dart;
With his good sword brave Christian wounds him sore,
And out of combat he is seen no more;
Into the Temple now the Victor speeds,
And Angel Minstrels chant his valiant deeds.

The above represents a man fighting his way toward a beautiful Palace; it is his home. From various causes he has been long estranged from his paternal inheritance. He is by some means reminded of its endearing associations—of its ancient magnificence—of its voices of happiness and love; pleasant things to delight the eye; choral symphonies to enchant the ear; rich viands to gratify the taste, are there. He becomes anxious to return; he determines at once to regain possession of his mansion, or perish in the attempt. He meets with opposition; the odds is fearful, three to one. His enemies do not absolutely deny his rights, yet they are determined to oppose him to the uttermost. He gives battle, and by dint of skill and courage, he routs his foes, gains a complete victory, and enters his home in triumph.

This allegory represents a part of the Christian warfare. The temple or palace signifies that glorious inheritance which the Almighty Father has bequeathed to all of his children. It contains all tha can please, delight, or enchant the soul, and that forevermore. For it is an inheritance that is incorruptible, undefiled, and which fadeth not away. The Hero denotes a man who has decided to be a Christian. By the influence of the Holy Spirit on his heart, he is convinced of his outcast condition—of the impotency of created good to make him happy—of the insignificance of the things of time compared with those of eternity. Convinced of these, in the strength of grace, he says, "I will arise and go to my Father," and he goes accordingly. But he soon meets with enemies who powerfully oppose his progress, and among the first of these is

Shame. Our passions, or powers of feeling have been given to us by our benevolent Creator, to subserve our happiness, and shame among the rest.

> ".Art divine
> Thus made the body tutor to the soul—
> Heaven kindly gives our blood a moral flow
> And bids it ascend the glowing cheek."

Shame stands as a sentinel to warn us of danger, and so put us on our guard. But all of our passions are perverted from their proper uses, and sin has done it. Therefore as man loves darkness rather than light—calls evil good and good evil—puts bitter for sweet and sweet for bitter—so also he changes the proper uses of shame. Instead of being ashamed of the bad, he is ashamed of the good. Shame is an enemy hard to conquer. The convert finds it so. He feels ashamed at first to be seen by his old companions, in company with the truly pious; or going to a religious meeting—or on his knees praying—or in any way carrying the cross of Him whom he has now chosen to be his Master. Shame confronts him every where, and gives him to understand that for the most part, religious people are a poor, low, and ignorant set; that no person of character will associate with them, etc. Christian remembers that what is highly esteemed among men is had in abomination with God. That shame after all, is the promotion of fools only. Thus he vanquisheth shame by the sword of the Spirit even by the word of the Lord.

As soon as shame is disposed of, another foe appears—*Love of the world*. This consists in a greater attachment to this present world, than becomes one who is so soon to leave it and live forever in another. As the boy should learn what he may need when he shall become a man, so should the mortal acquire what it may need when it puts on immortality. The natural man is so strongly wedded to earthly objects, that to him the separation is impossible. Argument will not effect it. He may be convinced intellectually, that the things of earth are transitory and unsatisfying, yet he pursues them eagerly. His feelings may be lacerated by the death of some beloved relative, and his hopes blasted by the loss of property, still he cleaves to earth. The power of the Almighty alone can help him. He needs a new principle of feeling and of action; even that of faith that overcomes the world. Obtaining this principle, he looks not at the things that are seen, but at those which are unseen.

The genuine Christian convert has many conflicts ere he can set his affections on the things above. *Worldly Love* opposes him perseveringly; in his religious experience; in his self-denying duties; in his ·····givings, and in his sufferings. The Christian, however, knows that he must conquer that foe, or perish—therefore he sets himself to meditate upon his duty—he searches the Scriptures—he finds that God's enemies are those who mind earthly things—he wishes not to join them—that the love of the world is hatred to God—if any man love the world, the love of the Father is not in him; and animated by the example of Christ his Lord, who left heaven for man, he renounces earth for God. He dies to the world and lives to Christ. As a soldier of Jesus he fights under his banners, and comes off more than a conqueror through Him who has loved him.

Unbelief is a gigantic foe. He is indeed the champion of all the rest, peculiarly skillful and bold in his attacks. He knows how to shift his ground adroitly. Sometimes he assails vehemently, denying Christianity itself; nay, the very existence of the Almighty, declaring that "God is nature, and that there is no other god," and that "death is an eternal sleep." Thus by one stroke he would sweep away the being and attributes of the Eternal; the doctrines, promises and commandments of the word of God, man's responsibilities, and consequent duties. Were this stroke successful, it would deprive man of all happiness in this life, and of the consolations of hope in the life that is after death. It expels him a second time from paradise into a desert where not even thorns and briars spring up for his support.

Unbelief, however, does not always act so boldly. Sometimes he admits the existence of God, and the subject of religion in general, but denies that man owes duties to the former, or that he is interested in the latter. He will even approve of the form of religion, provided there is no power, no faith, no Holy Spirit in it. Unbelief in this form destroys thousands of immortal souls who profess Christ, yet not having true faith, in works deny him. He that believeth not shall be damned.

Sometimes unbelief attacks the Christian under the garb of benevolence. He pities and deplores most feelingly, the present evils that flesh is heir to. He promises you a terrestrial heaven. But, first, the present order of things must be abolished. All institutions, political and religious, must be abrogated. The foundations of society must be broken up—its frame-work dissolved—that is to say, a perfect chaos must be made, out of which shall arise a perfect paradise. You must first pass through a vast howling wilderness where no water is, and then (if indeed your carcass does not fall in the wilderness) you will be conducted into the promised land.

In these ways does unbelief make his onsets, suiting his methods to the dispositions of the age, or to the circumstances of individuals. The Christian repels them with the shield of faith, and the sword of the spirit, which is the word of God. He possesses the divine word which is full of promises, and that faith which is a deep conviction of things not seen, and the substance or foundation of things hoped for. Therefore he gives no quarter to unbelief; God hath spoken, it is enough. There is a mansion for him; he will possess it. His Saviour has conquered and reigns. He will conquer and reign also. He beholds by faith, a glorious mansion, a palm of victory, a song of triumph, a crown of life. Animated by the prospect, he fights his way through all his foes, and as he fights he sings—

> "The glorious crown of Righteousness,
> To me reached out, I view,
> Conqueror through Christ I soon shall rise,
> And wear it as my due."

Who gave himself a ransom for all.—1 Tim. ii. 6.

THE IMPERIAL PHILANTHROPIST.

The hapless crew upon the reef are cast;
And round them rages wild the furious blast;
Deep calls to deep with wide-mouthed thundering roar,
Loud beat the billows on the rock-bound shore;
Crash after crash is heard with fearful shock,
As the boat dashes on the craggy rock.
The affrighted crew nor skill nor courage have,
To save their bark from the devouring wave;

Russia's great Czar beholds them on the reef
And nobly hastens to afford relief:
Boldly he plunges in the boiling waves;
And all the fury of the tempest braves,
He leaps on board, and with a skillful hand,
Through rocks and breakers, brings them safe to land.

WE have here a picture of danger and of deliverance. Peter the Great, Emperor of all the Russias, had been sailing in one of his yachts as far as the Ladoga Lake; finding himself refreshed by the seabreeze, instead of landing at St. Petersburg, he sailed down the Neva toward the open sea of the gulph of Finland. The day had been very fine; toward evening, however, the weather suddenly changed; the Emperor resolved to land, but he had scarcely reached the shore, when the storm burst forth in all its fury. The waves rose and beat against the craggy rocks of the coast, and the wind roared from the wild sky with a thundering voice; in a few minutes a black cloud, let down like a curtain, hid the scene from view. Still, however, the Emperor looked and listened; he thought he heard the voice of distress mingling with the yell of the storm; his penetrating glance soon discovered a boat struggling against the rolling surge, that was driving it towards the furious breakers. The men, most of them being soldiers, are evidently at a loss what to do; presently the boat is dashed upon a reef; the sea breaks over it mountains high. The Emperor immediately sends a vessel to their aid, but in vain; the men on board want both skill and courage to execute the dangerous task. The poor men on the reef, seeing themselves deserted by their companions, rend the air with their piteous cries for help; the Emperor can contain himself no longer,—he springs into his own boat, calling on all who have hearts to dare for their brethren, to follow him. By great exertions he reaches as near to the sufferers as the breakers will allow—he perceives that he is yet too far off to aid them—what they need is a skillful pilot—he plunges into the raging billows, bravely he buffets the mountain surge, now floating on the topmost wave, now sinking in the depths beneath; soon he gains the boat,—he springs on board like a delivering angel. The men, resouled at sight of the Emperor risking his life to save them, renew their efforts—they soon get off the shoal into deep water, and the Emperor guides them skillfully through the rocks and shoals, and brings them safe to land.

Now he is overwhelmed with the grateful demonstrations of those whom he has saved from the jaws of destruction, and of those happy wives and children, who but for him would now have been orphans and widows; he enjoys the luxury of doing good—he feels most truly that "it is more blessed to give than to receive."

"The quality of mercy is not strained;
"It droppeth as the gentle rain from heaven
"Upon the place beneath. It is twice blessed;
"It blesseth him who gives, and him who takes,
"'Tis mightiest in the mightiest; it becomes
"The throned monarch better than his crown."

We admire, and very justly too, the surprising condescension, the tender compassion, the heroic courage, and the consummate skill of the Emperor of all the Russias, in risking his life for the sake of a few poor men—but what is this compared with the grace of our Lord and Saviour, "*Jesus?*" The Emperor lost nothing of his dignity in doing what he did; he laid aside none of his titles; he assumed not a lower rank; in the boat, among the waves, and on the shoal, he was still an Emperor. But Jesus laid his glory by; the glory that he had with the Father before the world was; the glory resulting from creative power; the glory of guiding the armies of earth and heaven; the glory of eternity. "He emptied himself," "he made himself of no reputation." The master becomes a slave; the king becomes a subject; the maker of worlds becomes a creature, the God becomes a worm! How surprising this condescension; how wonderful this humility:

"Bound every heart and every bosom burn."

And O, with what tender compassion Jesus pitied us, as he saw us exposed to the gulph of eternal death! In the depths of our misery he exclaimed, "Behold! I come," and immediately hastened to our relief. O how he weeps, groans, prays, and dies for us, and for our salvation! He pities our ignorance—he groans for our unbelief—he weeps for the hardness of our heart—he dies for our guilt.

What heroic courage *He* displays in working out our deliverance! How he grapples with the powers of darkness! How he triumphs over temptation, poverty, and shame! How he conquers principalities and thrones, making a show of them openly! He wrests from death his dreadful sting, proves victorious over the grave, and opens the gates of Paradise to all believers. What divine wisdom, also, *He* manifests in the work of redemption; in securing to man his liberty, and to God his glory. How skillfully the Saviour confutes all the sophistry of the devil; how wonderfully he answers all the cavils of his adversaries. How, by his questions, does he take the wise in their own craftiness! His laws fill with admiration the hearts of his worshippers. How skillfully he guides his followers through the rocks and shoals of temptation and sin, and lands them safely on the banks of deliverance. "Verily he hath done all things well." Hallelujah!

But for whom did the Saviour labor and suffer? Peter risked his life for mortals like himself; Jesus gave his for beings infinitely beneath him. Peter for his own soldiers, Jesus for those who were arrayed under the banner of his great foe; Peter for his own subjects, Jesus for the subjects of another kingdom; Peter rescued merely his friends, Jesus died for the salvation of his enemies. Herein is love, "God commendeth *His* love toward us in that while we were yet sinners," consequently enemies, "Christ died for us."

In the case before us—one rather of contrast than comparison—we see the men, re-spirited by the presence of their Emperor, come to save them, labor with all their might; had they not done so, they could not have been saved, notwithstanding all the skill, power, and good will of their Prince. But we, alas! stupid and ignorant as we are, when our Deliverer comes to our aid, are found questioning his skill, denying his power, and disbelieving his kind intentions; instead of working "out our own salvation," with fear and trembling, while he works in us, helping us both to will and to do of his good pleasure.

Those who were saved from death by the philanthropic Emperor, showered upon him every demonstration of gratitude; they invoked eternal blessings on his head, and devoted their lives to his service; and shall not we be grateful to our Spiritual deliverer? His name ought to be to us above every name. His name Salvation is; to the man that believes, Christ is precious—he meditates upon his wondrous love, upon his unparalleled condescension, upon his heroic courage, upon his tender compassion, and upon his divine wisdom, until the fire of grateful emotion burns within him, and he presents himself a living sacrifice, holy and acceptable before the Lord, saying—

> "Were the whole realm of nature mine,
> That were an offering far too small;
> Love so amazing! so divine!
> Demands my life, my soul, my all."

And he devotes himself accordingly to the service of his King and Saviour. As a good subject, he will obey His laws, and seek to promote the peace and prosperity of his kingdom; as a good soldier, he will follow his Captain through every danger, and every death, and having gained the victory, he will ground his arms at Jesus' feet, and so be ever with the Lord.

The following is a noble instance of genuine philanthropy, where a person risked and actually lost his life for the salvation of others:—A Dutch East Indiaman was wrecked in a terrible tempest off the Cape of Good Hope; the sailors were every instant perishing for want of assistance. An old man, named Woltemad, by birth an European, and who was at this time a resident of an island off the coast, heard the lamentations of the distressed crew and hastened to their relief. The noble Dutchman borrowed a horse and proceeded to the wreck, with a view of saving at least some of their number; he returned safe with two of the unfortunate sufferers, and repeated this dangerous trip six times, each time bringing with him two men, and thus saved in all fourteen persons. The horse was by this time so much exhausted, that the man did not think it prudent to venture out again; but the entreaties of the poor sufferers increasing, he ventured one trip more, which proved so unfortunate that he lost his own life; for on this occasion too many rushed upon him at once, some catching hold of the horse's tail, and others of the bridle, by which means the horse, wearied out, and too heavily laden, was overwhelmed by the billows, and all drowned together. The East India Company impressed with so noble an instance of philanthropy, ordered a monument to be erected to his memory.

Therefore let us not sleep, as do others; but let us watch and be sober.
1 Thess. v. 6.

THE WINTRY ATMOSPHERE.

    The icy mountains here lift up on high
    Their barren peaks, toward the arctic sky;
    Terrific regions, where grim Winter reigns,
    And bends the whirlwind in his frosty chains.
    All life has fled, save where the shaggy beast
    Prowls with intent on human blood to feast;

'T is nature's tomb; no living voice is heard,
Of murmuring brook, nor cheerful warbling bird
No leafy tree, nor smiling fields of green,
Nor corn luxuriant waving, here is seen.
In this cold clime some mariners are found,—
Two, froze to death, lie stretched upon the ground;
Others, more wise, to keep themselves awake,
They leap and shout, and strive their friends to wake.
One plies the rod—yet from all anger free—
To rouse his neighbor from his lethargy;
Death of his prey, while thus engaged, he cheats,
And finds himself revive the more he beats.
These work and live, although the conflict's sore,
The rest they slumber and awake no more.

HERE we have a picture of the Polar regions; the accumulating masses of ice raise to the sky their snowy summits. The formation, perhaps, of future icebergs. Here Winter sits securely upon his throne of desolation. Unmolested by the Solar King, he sways his icy scepter. The very winds are hushed to silence by his power; a desolate and terrible region. It is the sheeted sepulcher of Nature deceased. No signs of life are seen, except the Polar beast, fitted for his dreary abode. No sound of rippling brook, nor voice of joyous bird echoes through the icy cliffs. To bless the eye, no leafy forests wave to the breeze. No cheerful fields of living green appear. To bless the heart, no rising corn, the all-sustaining food of man, bends with its weight of wealth. In this inhospitable climate, man, if he possess not a stout heart, soon dies. A drowsiness steals over him. He feels a very great inclination to lay down, then cold chills, throughout his life's blood, slowly creep. He sinks into a lethargy from which he never more awakes.

In the picture are seen a few mariners who are thrown into this unfriendly climate. Two of them, in consequence of giving way to their drowsy feelings, have fallen asleep. It is the slumber of the grave. The others, aware of the deadly influence of intense cold, exert themselves to keep it off. They leap about and cry aloud. They are alarmed for their companions. They strive to arouse them from their dangerous sleep. One perceiving his friend to have some signs of life in him, procures a rod; he lays it on unsparingly; he finds himself benefitted by the exercise; he continues it; he is successful; he saves the life of his friend; they continue actively employed until deliverance appears. Thus, their lives are preserved. The rest, cast into the deep sleep of death, are left to the beasts of prey.

The wintry atmosphere represents that spiritual declension that too frequently happens. Piety is in danger of freezing to death. The church has gone too far north. The thermometer of holiness has sunk almost to zero. The sun of righteousness casts but a few feeble flickering rays athwart the gloom profound. Fearful state indeed! The stillness of spiritual death prevails. The shaggy one alone is alive and active. "He goeth about as a roaring lion seeking whom he may devour." The voice of prayer is hushed. No joyful hallelujahs break the monotony of the awful solitude. Doctrine and discipline are neglected. Even the all-sustaining word of God is forsaken. Melancholy position! She will soon become a mere iceberg, dashing herself and others into oblivion. It has sometimes occurred, that by the faithful prayers and active labors of *one* saint, the church has been brought out of the wintry atmosphere, and been saved. This *one* living disciple brings the whole church to Jesus, the Sun of Righteousness, and keeps her there by faith, until the whole tide of *His* rays fall full upon her. Her frozen heart now begins to thaw; soor it melts into penisence and love; now the voice of prayer breaks forth as the morning; the song of praise again mounts upwards; God's house is filled with worshippers; ministers are clothed with salvation; converts are multiplied, and the sons of God shout aloud for joy.

The wintry atmosphere may furthermore denote the condition of individual Christians when thrown into he society of the wicked, when compelled in the order of providence to dwell in the "tents of Kedar." In the absence of the genial influences of religious ordinances, the freezing influences of ungodly principles and practices prevail. Infidelity itself may perhaps lift up its daring front, and defy the God of the armies of Israel; deny the inspiration of the sacred page, and laugh the Christian to scorn as a weak enthusiast. If unwatchful, the professor will at first fall a prey to the stupor of indifference. Then the chilling influence of sin will creep over him; the life's blood of his piety is arrested in its course; heart and intellect are benumbed; Faith, Hope and Love are now but indistinct images of the past. He is in danger of spiritual death.

As in the engraving, we see one arousing his companions with a rod or stick, so the Christian should endeavor to awaken his brother when he sees him falling beneath the influence of a wicked atmosphere. He may possess more Christian experience, or more spiritual understanding; he has a stronger faith, or is better acquainted with the wiles of the devil; these are so many gifts or graces, that he is in duty bound to exert for the salvation of his brother; hence he is to exhort and admonish him with all long-suffering and faithfulness. If this fails, he is to reprove, nay, to "rebuke him sharply," and in no wise to suffer sin upon his brother. Though it may seem harsh, yet he is to persevere as long as any signs of life remain, lest he perish for whom Christ died; he will tell him of the danger to which he exposes his immortal soul, of the reproach he will bring upon religion if he falls into sin, of the wounds he will again inflict upon the sacred heart of Jesus; that he will cover heaven with sackcloth, and make hell echo with exultations of fiendish delight—he will not spare in order to arouse him from his slumber. With the hammer of God's word he will strike him, with the sword of God's Spirit he will pierce him, and with the fuel of God's love, he will enkindle a fire round about him. He is successful—soon the sleeper moves—he melts—he weeps—he prays; in his gratitude he exclaims, "Let the righteous smite me, it is an excellent oil unto me," faithful are the wounds of a friend! Thus the active Christian, by his perseverance, under God, saves a soul from death, and hides a multitude of sins.

Most beneficial, also, has the exercise been to himself; it has proved the means of his own safety; by it he has been kept watchful and prayerful; his gifts and graces have been strengthened; the more he labored for his brother, the more he was blessed in his own soul. So true is the promise, "He that watereth others, shall be watered also himself."

The Wintry Atmosphere is such a dangerous region that the Almighty himself becomes, as it were, alarmed for the safety of his children, when he sees them exposed to its influence; he uses the rod of correction in order to keep them awake—he uses it in love—whom he loveth he chasteneth. Woe! woe! unto us, when He commands the ministers of affliction to "let us alone." Poverty, reproach, sickness and death, are employed by our heavenly Father as instruments of correction—yet they are blessings in disguise. He gives us *poverty* in time, that we may be invested with the riches of eternity:—reproach, that we may receive the plaudits of the King Eternal:—sickness of body that the soul may flourish in immortal health:—*Death*, to usher us into Life, into his immediate presence, that where *He* is there we may be also. God's children have borne witness in time, and they will bear witness to all eternity, "That it was good for them to have been afflicted."

> "Long unafflicted, undismayed,
> In pleasure's path secure I strayed;
> Thou mad'st me feel the chastening rod,
> And straight I turned unto my God,
> What though it pierced my fainting heart,
> I blessed the hand that caused the smart,
> I taught my tears awhile to flow,
> But saved me from eternal woe."

> "In sable cincture, shadows vast,
> Deep-tinged and damp, and congregated clouds,
> And all the vapory turbulence of heaven,
> Involve the face of things. Thus winter falls,
> A heavy gloom oppressive o'er the world,
> Through Nature shedding influence malign."
> "Ocean itself no longer can resist
> The binding fury; but, in all its rage
> Of tempest taken by the boundless frost,
> Is many a fathom to the bottom chained,
> And bid to roar no more:— a bleak expanse,
> Shagged o'er with wavy rocks, cheerless and void
> Of every life, that from the dreary months
> Flies conscious southward. Miserable they!
> Who, here entangled in the gathering ice,
> Take their last look of the descending sun;
> While, full of death, and fierce with ten-fold frost,
> The long long night, incumbent o'er their heads,
> Falls horrible."—*Thompson.*

For I saith the Lord will be . . . . a wall of fire round about. Zec. ii. 5

THE PROTECTED TRAVELER.

'T is night,—the Traveler with labor spent,
Beneath the forest's shade has pitched his tent;
He and his household soon are fast asleep,
Their toilsome journey makes their slumbers deep;
Above their heads the stars are glowing bright,
Like diamonds sparkling on the breast of night;
This is the signal for the savage beast
To roam the forest for his bloody feast;

Leopards and lions round the tent now prowl,
And wake the woodland with their fearful howl;
The Traveler, startled at the dreadful sound,
A blazing fire soon kindles all around;
The monsters see it, and with horrid roar,
Rush through the thicket and appear no more.

As when Elisha, 'mid the Syrian band,
Saw sword and spear arrayed on every hand,
In gracious answer to the prophet's prayer,
Angelic banners flashed upon the air;
Jehovah's armies round about him came
With burning chariots and steeds of flame;
The fiery seraphs circled all his path,
And kept him safely from the Syrian's wrath.

In these days of emigration, multitudes are continually leaving the homes of their fathers for distant climes. The populous cities of the old world are traversed; the broad blue ocean is traversed; the vast forests of the new world are traversed, in order to find a home of peace and plenty. The engraving shows a family tended and guarded for the night. The travelers, weary with the day's journey, seek a commodious place whereon to pitch their tent. The sun already begins to sink below the horizon; the shadows lengthen, and night, silent and majestic, assumes her empire over the earth. Stars of glittering beauty bespangle her bosom and reflect their brilliancy on the broad leaves of the forest. The travelers retire to rest; wooed by fatigue, "balmy sleep" soon lights upon their eyelids; their slumbers are deep; but they are soon to be disturbed; night gives the signal for the beasts of prey to come forth from their dens; hungry and thirsty for blood they come; roaming, ravening, and roaring they come; the woods echo their fearful howlings; they scent out the travelers; they surround the tent; they clamor loudly for its inmates; dreadful is the confusion; the beasts growl and fight with each other, that each might have the prey to himself—the travelers awake in trembling distress. One of them has heard of the effect of fire upon wild beasts; while they are quarrelling, he quickly lights his brand, puts it to some dry leaves, and kindles a blaze; to this he adds more fuel, nor ceases heaping it on till he has encircled the tent with flames. His efforts are successful; the wild beasts are now affrighted, and roaring dreadfully with fear and rage, they rush impetuously through the trees, and come near the tent no more.

The preservation of the traveler from the fury of the wild beasts by means of fire, represents the preservation of the Christian from the attacks of Satan and his helpers, by the Almighty. Among the Jews, and many other ancient nations, fire was regarded as emblematical of the Deity, and indeed not without reason, for on several well authenticated instances did the Almighty manifest himself under the appearance of fire. Moses was summoned before a court of fire to receive his commission as deliverer of Israel. God was in the fire. In their flight from Egypt, and after travels in the desert, the Israelites were guided by a column of fire. Their salvation and the Egyptians' overthrow, for Jehovah was there. In his reception of the sacrifices and prayers of his people, God answered by fire. When He gave his law upon the terrible Mount, he spake out of the midst of the fire. And when long after he would re-publish his law to all nations, the commission of the Apostles as the deliverers of the world, was crowned with fire, God was with them, and to be with them to the end of the world.

The Christian is a traveler; he is traveling through the wilderness of this world; he will pass through it only once; in whatever part of the wilderness he pitches his tent, he is safe from all the open attacks of his foes; his faith, love and obedience, secure to him the protection of the Almighty. He is holy in heart and life; holiness tends to God's glory, and upon "the glory there is a defence;" this is the glory that dwells in the midst of him, and where this is, there will be also "the wall of fire round about." The celestial fire burning between the Cherubim in the Jewish temple, but shadowed forth him in whose heart Christ dwells by faith,—the living "temple of the Holy Spirit."

Since his expulsion from the realms of light, the Devil has hated with perfect hatred every symbol of Jehovah's presence and glory; he hates the light—he is the prince of darkness—he is the great extinguisher, putting out the light of truth and holiness as often as he can effect it; he thought to extinguish the "Light of the World," by nailing it to a tree, but in so doing he only broke into pieces the vase that contained it, causing it to shine forth with brilliancy, and to fill the whole earth with glory.

The great adversary is spoken of as "going about" the world as a roaring lion "seeking whom he may devour;" once, when prowling about on this wise, he met with one of the saints of God, whom he desired to worry and devour, but behold! there was a hedge of burning bushes all around him. In vain he tried to get at him; though used to fire, he could not stand the fire of love and holiness—he knew very well too, that no one could put out this fire, demolish this burner, except the man himself. Satan is permitted to tempt; he lays his plots with hellish ingenuity; h executes them with cruelty worthy of a devil; to de stroy this man of God, he called into his service the pestilence, the sword, the tornado, and the lightning. The lightning came and did its work—the sword came and did its work—the pestilence came and did its work—the tornado came and did its work,—yet the man of God is safe; he lives in his integrity; the hedge of fire around him burns higher and brighter, and becomes a beacon of hope to all the children of men. The devil, discomfited, leaves him, and flees away to his own place, because "Job sinned not nor charged God foolishly."

In like manner every child of God is surrounded by a divine protection; the servants of Satan are just like their master, they hate the light, and him that brings it; but were they to beset him, as the Assyrian army beset the prophet Elisha, he would be safe. The chariots of fire, and the horses of fire, with Seraphim and Cherubim, would encompass him. He may lay him down in peace—a wall of fire protects him, high as heaven, deeper than hell, wide as eternity—fire! fire! fire! formless, impetuous, mysterious, and devouring fire, is his safeguard and trust.

As the traveler by building a fire protects not himself only, but all who are in the tent, so the Christian, by his faith, love and obedience, secures the protection and blessing of God upon all his household. "I will show mercy," saith the Holy One of Israel, "unto thousands of generations of those that love me and keep my commandments;" and one who had lived long in the world, and had seen much of it, declared, "I have never seen the righteous forsaken, nor his posterity begging bread."

The traveler may put out his fire without water— he can do it by omitting to supply it with fuel, or by casting earth upon it, thereby smothering it, and thus expose himself and others with him to all the dangers of the forest. So the Christian may extinguish the fire of Almighty protection, the light of the Holy Spirit; he may do so, too, without employing the waters of transgression—he may do it by withholding the proper fuel, by "leaving off to do good," by neglecting the means of grace. He may do it by casting earth upon it, by letting the world gain the ascendancy in his heart and affections—the love of the world will put out the fire, "quench the Spirit," and leave the man again exposed to the malice of the evil one.

In the Book of the Prophets we read of some who "kindle a fire" and walk in the light thereof, who yet "lie down in sorrow," they are not safe; these may be the self-righteous—the mere nominal professor, who builds a fire with the wood, hay, and stubble, of his own performances; it lacks the heat of love and holiness—God is not in it. Satan heeds it not—he breaks through it as easily as a lion through a cobweb, and seizes upon the defenceless sinner for a prey.

Of others it is said that they "encompass themselves about with sparks" merely; this may mean those who esteem themselves good enough already, good naturally—hence they have no need of performances of any kind. The man of this class neglects, as useless, the light of truth, and faith, and the fire of love; he can dispense with Bible, Priest and Temple; he lies down in peril—the devil don't mind a few sparks.

It was a custom among the ancient highlanders of Scotland, when they would arouse the people for any great purpose, to send throughout the land a cross dipped in blood; wherever the cross was received, there the people immediately kindled a blazing fire, hence it was called "the Fire Cross." The blood-stained Cross of Christ has been sent and is now going throughout the world; the purpose for which it is sent, the greatest of all achievements; wherever it is received, a fire is kindled amid the surrounding darkness. The fire of a Saviour's love, the fire of Almighty power,

"Jesus' love the nation's fires,
"Sets the kingdoms in a blaze."

Hasten! O hasten! ye who bear the cross, ye ministers of his that do his pleasure! carry round "*the Cross*," until a fire shall be kindled every where, and the whole earth be filled with the glory of God.

For ye are bought with a price.—1 Cor. vi. 20. *Those that seek me early shall find me.*—Prov. viii. 17.

THE PEARL OF GREAT PRICE.

Behold, the slave with joyful beaming eyes,
Holds up to view his glorious glittering prize;
A pearl, more precious than its weight in gold;
The price of Freedom, and of bliss untold:
The prince who promised the auspicious meed,
From his rich palace hastens down with speed;

With his own hand—unrolled that all may see—
The title-deed presents of Liberty.
The slave may enter now that mansion fair,
A slave no longer, but a rightful heir.
  So when the sinner by Apollyon bound,
The priceless pearl of Gospel grace has found;
He breaks his chains, and into Freedom springs,
No more a slave, he ranks with priests and kings;
By the great Lord of All, to him 't is given,
To be his child on earth, and heir in heaven.

A CERTAIN Prince, desirous of adorning his coronet with a pearl of the greatest value, promises Liberty to any one of his slaves who shall find one of a certain number of carats; the Prince owns, upon his manor, a "Fishery," where the slaves, at proper seasons of the year, dive for pearls. The usual mode of operation is as follows: The divers, throwing off their clothes, dress themselves in complete suits of white cotton; this is to protect their bodies from the contact of the medusae, or sea-nettles; then, each diver letting himself over the side of the boat, places his feet upon a stone, which is held by the seibor, or puller up. On his left arm he carries a small basket to hold the oysters he may collect—(the pearl is found in the fleshy part, near the joint of the shell)—then closing his nostrils with a piece of elastic horn, he gives the signal with his arm, and is immediately lowered down; the stone enables him to sink without difficulty. Here, in a period varying from thirty to a hundred seconds, he employs himself in filling his basket; as soon as this is done, or if he wants breath, he jerks the rope, and is immediately hauled to the surface.

In the engraving is seen the fortunate slave, who has secured the prize; as soon as he discovers his good fortune, forsaking boat and basket, he leaps overboard and makes toward the shore, exclaiming

"I've found it! I've found it!" Others shout with him; the Prince, his master, hears the tumult, and learning the cause, repairs without delay to the bank of the river, to receive the pearl, and to bestow on the finder the promised reward—where, in the presence of all, he reads his deed of manumission, and proclaims him *free*. And he is free—his head, and heart, and hands, are now his own, he is now free.

Happy man; Liberty, fair sister of Piety, has stooped upon the wing to bless him; nor is this all— he is free to call his former master *Abba*, that is, father, and his mistress, *Imma*, that is, mother; he is, according to custom, adopted as a son—his future path is irradiated with knowledge, wisdom, and happiness.

By the slave finding the costly pearl, and obtaining thereby his liberty, is signified the sinner, who finds "the Kingdom of Heaven," or who, in other words, experiences religion; this puts him into possession of a liberty more precious than gold, and more to be desired than fine gold:—

> A liberty unsung
> By Poets, and by Senators unpraised;
> Which monarchs cannot grant, nor all the powers
> Of earth and hell confederate, take away:
> A liberty which persecution, fraud,
> Oppression, prisons, have no power to bind;
> Which, who so tastes, will be enslaved no more.

This is the liberty of Gospel salvation; a sinner is a slave—a slave not to one master, but to many, who exercise over him a cruel despotism. Satan takes the lead in tyrannizing over him; it is true he is a willing slave, but not the less a slave for that, for let him but try to free himself from his power, and he at once feels that he is bound; Satan is his lord and master, he says to him "go, and he goeth, come, and he cometh, do this, and he doeth it." He is a captive, led about just as the devil pleases. Miserable bondage! *Sin* has dominion over him, forbidden objects control his passions, and his passions control his will; he is enslaved to the law of sin, he is chained to "this body of death." Sin wields over him its scepter with despotic sway, "he is sold under sin;" even when he would do good, evil is present with him. Again, he is a slave to the terrors of the law; mount Sinai still stands, giving forth its dreadful voice of many thunders, and emitting its flashes of devouring fire; he stands quaking and trembling beneath its fearful brow. He is also "subject to bondage through fear of death;" although he may make a show of courage, when among his guilty companions, over the bottle, or in the battle-field, yet he dreads his approach; his very image embitters his sweetest pleasure, and makes him miserable. These are some of the lords that exercise dominion over the poor sinner; verily he is bound!

The King of Holiness offers liberty to the sinner, on condition that he exercise "repentance toward God, and faith in Jesus Christ;" thus runs the proclamation. The slave who found the pearl was obedient; what did he know at first about pearls? he might have argued, with himself at least, that it was impossible that such uncouth, muddy oysters, could contain such priceless gems, and so have given up the idea, and with it freedom; but he sought in the manner prescribed, and found—thus his obedience secured an ample reward.

Salvation is found only by those who seek aright. That the sinner might not lose his labor, the Almighty Lord tells him *where* it may be found; he tells him to look for it in *His* word, in *his* house and ordinances; he tells him *how* he is to conduct the search—he is to lay aside his self-righteousness and put on sackcloth; he is to descend into the depths of humility, and there, by earnest, persevering prayer, and living faith, to seek until he finds—and the promise is, "If thou seekest her as silver, and searchest for her as for hid treasure, then shalt thou understand the fear of the Lord, and find the knowledge of God."

But who shall describe the glorious liberty of the children of God. Satan reigns and tyrannizes over them no longer; his chain is broken, his allegiance is renounced; he is no longer the proud conqueror, leading his captive in chains; he lies bruised beneath the Christian's feet—he may threaten, but he cannot harm; he may tempt, but he cannot compel.

He who finds gospel freedom is delivered from the dominion of sin; his understanding is now enlightened, the darkness of ignorance has passed, the true light now shines; his mind is now free—free to do good. He takes pleasure in righteousness. "O," he exclaims, "how I love thy law!" Henceforth the testimonies of Jehovah are the songs of his rejoicing in the house of his pilgrimage; in him the promise is fulfilled, "Sin shall not have dominion over you."

From the curse of the law, moreover, he is free Jesus has been made a curse for him—there is, therefore, now no condemnation; for him the fires of Sinai no longer burn; Jesus has quenched them with his blood—for him its voice of many thunders is for ever hushed—Jesus has whispered, "peace, be still." Death has now for him no more terrors—Death is a vanquished enemy, he is numbered among his gains. Why should he fear who has beheld "the burst gates—the demolished throne—the crushed sting—the last gasp of vanquished death?" Thanks be unto God, who giveth us the victory through our Lord Jesus Christ.

O, the glorious liberty of the children of God! The slave has become a son; he may now call God Abba, Father, and the church Imma, Mother; he is now an heir of God and fellow-heir with Jesus Christ—he receives a clear title-deed to mansions in the skies. Heaven for him

>Opens wide
>Her ever-during gates, harmonious sound
>On golden hinges turning.

He is now free to see the king in his beauty, to see *Him* as he *is* who loved him and gave himself for him—to hold converse with angels and archangels, with all the holy, and the wise. "Glorious liberty" indeed! wondrous freedom! he is free to explore the regions of immortality and love; and as the years of interminable duration roll onward, he will live yet more free.

>"All hail, triumphant Lord,
>Who sav'st us with thy blood;
>Wide be thy name ador'd,
>Thou rising, reigning God,
>>With thee we rise,
>>With thee we reign,
>>And empires gain
>>Beyond the skies."

Blessed are your eyes for they see. Matt. xiii. 16. *And to know the love of Christ which passeth knowledge.* Eph. iii. 19.

THE GREAT DISCOVERY.

When brave Balboa gained the mountain's height,
A glorious prospect burst upon his sight;
The great Pacific stretched before him lies,
And fills with new delight his ravished eyes;
O sight sublime! It meets the distant sky,
The splendid image of eternity.
He gazes on that sea, his hope of old.

Whose waters wander by the realms of gold;
Visions of wealth and glory fill his mind,
And he forgets the toils he left behind.
The dream is realized! that dream sublime,
That bore him onward through each deadly clime
O'er burning mountains and o'er stormy main,
Through death and danger, far from ancient Spain,
His bursting heart adores that mighty Power
That brought him safely to behold this hour;
He prostrate falls, his grateful homage pays,
And to the God of heaven devoutly prays.

Above is portrayed the great discovery of the Pacific Ocean, made by Balboa, a Spanish Cavalier. Balboa had for some time settled down in Hispaniola. Here he cultivated a farm, but hearing of an expedition that was about to set out for the west, he determined to join it. He was greatly in debt, and the governor had issued a proclamation forbidding debtors to leave the Island. Balboa, however, was resolved to go. He caused himself to be rolled on board of one of the vessels in a cask. He did not make his appearance until the ship was far out to sea. The commander at first threatens to send him back—but the ship pursued her way. He quickly rose into favor; became governor of the colony planted at the Isthmus, and distinguished himself by the talents of command. Rumors of the golden country still farther westward continued to inflame the minds of the Spaniards. Distance, disease, mountains covered with eternal snows, and oceans tossed by perpetual storms, could no longer restrain them. Balboa took the lead of the expedition and pushed on to conquest. Many of the Indian tribes are to be conquered. These brave but defenseless warriors soon fall before the arms of the Spaniards, who, the more blood they shed, the more they thirst for gold. An alliance is formed with a powerful Cacique, who sends Balboa a rich present in gold and slaves. On the daring Spaniard leads his soldiers. Indian tribes are conquered, mountain difficulties are passed, and burning, sickly regions traversed. Now the moment is at hand when he is to be more than recompensed for all his labors. The misty summits of the hills rise before him. One of these is pointed out to him as the object of his search. He commands his troops to halt. He himself ascends alone, with his drawn sword. Having reached the top, he casts his eyes round; the Pacific spreads out before him; imbued with the religion of his country, he falls on his knees weeping, and offers thanks to God for permitting him to see this glorious sight. On his return to Darien, the whole population poured forth to meet him. They hailed him as the glory of Spain; as the gift of heaven sent to guide them into the possession of honors and riches incalculable.

. The *Pacific Ocean*, and its discovery by the bold Spaniard, may serve to illustrate the ocean of God's love, and the joyful feelings of him who, for the first time, discovers it. The sinner is settled down in his sins; he is employed in cultivating Satan's husbandry; "he is sowing to the flesh." He hears of a revival of religion, of an expedition heavenward; he is determined to join it; he is in debt; dead in trespasses and in sins. Satan, his governor, will not permit him to quit. He hedges up his way round about him. He is however resolved to join the expedition that is bound for Heaven. By a violent effort he escapes and joins the converts. He is decided; he seeks earnestly the salvation of his soul; his way is now beset with difficulties; enemies appear on every hand to impede his progress; his old companions come to entice him; his old sins come to tempt him, and his old master strides before him the whole breadth of the way

He now strengthens his alliances with the children of God. He receives sometimes some gracious tokens of the divine favor; he is encouraged to persevere; on he goes, weeping—praying—wrestling—fighting. His old companions are silenced; his sins no longer have dominion over him, and Satan falls like lightning from heaven. Now the time of triumph is near, when he will be more than paid for all he has endured. His heavenly guide directs him to the object of his inquiries. He ascends alone the mount—the sacred mount of Calvary. He casts his eyes around; the peaceful ocean of Almighty love spreads out before him; there it lays, covering all time and extending to eternity; immense—boundless—overwhelming.

> When this Almighty sea of love
> His rising soul surveys,
> Transported with the view, he's lost
> In wonder, love, and praise.

All is *peaceful*, above—below—within—around. He has *peace* with God through our Lord Jesus Christ. A peace which passeth all understanding fills his breast. He is at peace with man and beast. It is as the opening of the gate of heaven to his soul. An immense region of truth, divine truth, is laid bare to his view. A new and heavenly light flashes over his mind. Old things have passed away, and all things have become new.

On this mount of vision he discovers that God is Love; not only lovely and loving, but *Love;* nothing but love. In his nature and operations love; pure unexampled love. Here he beholds the Son of God; the maker of earth; the well beloved of heaven, suffering and dying for him—for all—for a world of sinners. For the foulest of the foul, *He* dies. He beholds with astonishment the tokens of his love.

Earth is suddenly arrested in her retrograde motion, and rolled back again to God. Strange darkness covers the world, that all might henceforth be light forever; the opened sepulchres proclaim life and immortality. Here he beholds a new and living way cast up; a high way from earth to heaven, and countless multitudes leaving behind them the badges of their guilt, pollution, and wretchedness, and washed and clothed in the robes of salvation, ascend thereon. Forward they go, each one walking in his uprightness. A cloud overshadows them for a little while,— that is death. Soon they ascend toward the gates of the heavenly city. Now the golden portals are lifted up, and the children of glory enter in. A multitude that none can number are thus ransomed from hell and the grave, and all through the love of God in Christ Jesus. Behold what manner of love is this, that the Father has bestowed on us, that we should be called the sons of God. Well might the rapt poet sing—

> I rode on the sky,
> Freely justified I,
> Nor envied Elijah his seat;
> My soul mounted higher,
> In a chariot of fire,
> And the moon it was under my feet.

An indifferent spectator walking far beneath Balboa, seeing him prostrate on the mount, and with uplifted hands offering his thanksgiving, might have laughed him to scorn for a madman, or have pitied him for his weakness. He may not have been so high.. He knows not that the ocean exists. He perhaps denies its existence altogether. Thus it often happens to the man of the world when he sees converts having tasted that the Lord is gracious, give vent to their feelings in a lively manner; or when he hears experienced Christians discourse on the love of God, it is foolishness to him. He considers the persons so acting, to be "beside themselves," or very weak minded. He may perhaps deny altogether the existence of vital godliness and religious experience, yet if the skeptic would but "come and see" for himself, he would confess that "the half was not told him."

In order to make his great discovery, Balboa had to rise above the world. So it behooves him who would discover the great pacific of eternal love, to rise above sublunary things; especially must he surmount the fogs of prejudice, the mists of ignorance, and the clouds of unbelief which surround the surface of the earth.

Having made his discovery, the Spaniard was at once rewarded with honor and glory. He looked upon the past with contempt, as not worthy to be compared with the splendor that awaited him. So he feels who realizes that God is love. He is clad with the "*Best Robe.*" He looks with disgust on the past. He hates the vain pomps and glories of the earth; is astonished at his infatuation, in being so taken up with them; and yet what he now possesses is but as the drop to the teeming shower. The wealth of eternity awaits him.

Balboa could not explore his vast prize. Had he traversed the ocean till this time, he would have gone over only a small portion of it; much of it he would never see. Realms of gold lay glittering upon its placid margin. Mines of wealth lay hidden beneath its purple wave. He had but found the key of this magazine of wealth. So the discoverer of Almighty love can know but little of his precious prize while here below. Boundless—fathomless—endless, it spreads out before him, and will ever spread. Here he merely sips of its overflowings. He has but discovered the key of this treasure-house of love. O the depth of the riches, both of the wisdom and goodness of God!

They wandered in deserts.—Heb. xi. 38. *For here we have no continuing city, but seek one to come.*—Heb. xiii. 14.

PASSAGE THROUGH THE DESERT.

Amid the arid desert's burning sands,
The Caravan proceeds, in various bands;
Jew, Frank, and Mussulman, in search of gain,
Unite to traverse the destructive plain.
The desert drear, more terrible to brave,
Than furious tempest, on the ocean wave:

RELIGIOUS ALLEGORIES. 275

The sky a molten dome of quiv'ring heat ;
The earth a furnace, glows beneath the feet;
The wild waste echoes as they move along,
With laugh of humorous tale, or voice of song.
Armed, and united, they no danger fear
From lion prowling, nor from robber's spear;
But other foes oft-times 'gainst them advance,
More to be dreaded than the Arab's lance :
The sandy column, and sirocco's blast,
Laden with certain death, come rushing past.
Down straight they fall, flat on their faces lie,
While the destroying angel passes by ;
Through varied dangers, thus their way they wend,
Until at length they reach their journey's end.

HERE is represented the passage of a caravan through the great and terrible desert of Africa. Merchants being desirous of visiting the interior parts of Africa, for the sake of trading with the natives, form themselves into companies for this purpose. Here may be seen Arabs, Jews, Franks, and others, uniting for a common end, regardless of the differences of country and of creed ; they hire a certain number of camels, with their drivers—they lay in their stock of goods, provisions, etc. ; they furnish themselves with a compass, and with arms for defense. When all is prepared, the signal for departure is given, and the caravan moves onward ; by degrees they leave all traces of the living world behind them—soon they come in sight of the desert—evening now casts its shadows round them—they find a stopping place ; here they rest for the night. In the morning they commence the perilous route : in a short time, nothing is beheld by the travelers but one vast ocean of sand, bounded only by the horizon ; as they move on the heat becomes intense—the sky appears like a dome of molten fire—the earth glows like a furnace beneath their feet ; a momentary gloom overspreads the faces of the travelers as they see scattered here and there upon the sand, skeletons, the remains of former travelers. They shorten the distance by rehearsing tales of wit and humor. Sometimes the desert rings with the sound of their merry songs,—they trust to the guides for direction, and to the guards for safety; being well armed they fear nothing. Sometimes, while yet on the border, the lion of the desert appears; he sees them united and watchful—he dare not attack them—he lashes his sides with his furious tail, and with a dreadful roar he bounds out of sight. Sometimes the Arab robbers, who think they have an hereditary right to plunder travelers, attack the caravan—they meet with a stout resistance, and finding themselves worsted, they quickly disappear amid clouds of dust and sand.

Other enemies, however, frequently appear, that laugh to scorn their might of union, and hold in derision the shaking of the glittering spear; the pestilential simoom, with the speed of thought, comes rushing on towards them, and unless they fall instantly upon their faces and hold their breath, they are all dead men. Sometimes they behold huge pillars of sand before them, the sun gleaming through them, giving them the appearance of pyramids on fire— each one is large enough to bury the caravan; now they move towards them with fearful rapidity—now they take another direction. The wind shifts, and dashing against each other, they vanish in a storm of sand. Sometimes the caravan is refreshed by meeting with a fertile spot called an oasis—here is seen the grassy plain, the flowing fountain;—here is heard the voice of singing birds; here the palm, the vine, and the olive tree abound. New spirited, the caravan resumes its journey, and in good time reaches the place of its destination.

The passage through the desert may be considered as an allegorical representation of the passage of the church of Christ through the moral desert of this world. The church is in quest of eternal gain. She seeks a city which is out of sight; "the New Jerusalem." The way thereto is through a moral desert, which is destitute of every heavenly plant. No living stream flows through the midst thereof. No food for the soul is there; no provision for immortality. Above, around, beneath, the elements are, in themselves considered, unfriendly to spiritual life and spiritual progress. Hence the church furnishes herself with provisions,—Christ, and the word of Christ; her compass, the law of Jehovah; her weapons, the whole armor of God; her watchmen and guides, the ministers of Jesus.

The caravan was exposed to danger and death from the lion—the robber—the moving sands, and the fell simoom. The church, too, has her dangers to contend against. No sooner does she commence her march, than Abaddon, the destroyer, comes out against her. If he sees her united, moving on firmly, and watchful withal, she is safe, and he knows it. He gnashes his teeth with rage, and looks about for more defenseless prey. Woe, woe to the straggler he may meet with in his wrath,—to him who through indolence has lingered behind, or through pride thinks he can take care of himself,—he falls a victim to his temerity. His fate becomes a monument of warning unto others. Next she is assailed by the disciples of ancient heresies. These come forth against her with their rights of prescription and of proscription. They advance "damnable doctrines," and seek to plunder her of her heaven-born treasures. But the church is armed, thoroughly armed. The efficient panoply, "the whole armor of God" is round about her. The sword of the Lord and of Gideon prevails, and the spoilers vanquished, retire amid the dust of their own confusion. But other foes sometimes appear, more dangerous than Satan undisguised. Splendid images of idolatry present themselves, glittering with the gilded pageantry of pompous ceremonies; impositions of unrighteous prerogative. Their tops reach the very heavens. They move to and fro, threatening to overwhelm the church beneath their crushing weight. She looks on awhile in astonishment at such heaven-daring impiety. She stands firm; she is girt about with truth. With a loud voice she gives utterance to her faith,—" Jehovah, he is the God! Jehovah, he is the God!" The sandy fabrics disappear like the moving columns of the desert.

Sometimes, as a last resort of fiendish malice, the simoom of persecution is let loose upon her. Earth and hell combine. The kings of the earth set themselves, and the rulers take counsel together, saying, "Let us break their bands asunder, and cast away their cords from us." The watchword is, "destroy, destroy," and the whole power of the enemy is hurled against the Lord's anointed. Her ordinary weapons of defense are here of no avail. She has recourse to "*all prayer*." She falls down low in the dust. In God is all her trust. He is her help and her shield. She hides herself in Him until this "calamity be overpast." In every conflict she comes off victorious, as long as she continues united and watchful.

Sometimes the church is favored with extraordinary manifestations of divine power and love; these are to her as an oasis in the desert. The river that makes glad the city of God pours its full streams into the midst of her. She enjoys a glorious revival; it is a foretaste of heaven. She arises and puts on strength. Multitudes are added unto her. Clothed with salvation, she again moves onward in all the power of truth, and in the majesty of holiness, clear as the sun, fair as the moon, and glorious as an army with banners. Above her waves triumphant the banner of Redemption. Taking up the song o' prophecy as she advances, she sings—

> In the wilderness shall burst forth waters,
> And torrents in the desert;
> And the glowing sand shall become a pool;
> The desert and the waste shall be glad,
> And the wilderness shall rejoice and flourish,
> Like the rose shall it beautifully flourish.

Thus she goes forward from strength to strength, scattering in her path a new creation, until mercy's triumphs are complete, and God is all in all.

> Lord, what a wretched land is this,
>   That yields us no supply;
> No cheering fruits, no wholesome trees,
>   Nor streams of living joy!
>
> Yet the dear path to thine abode
>   Lies through this weary land;
> Lord! we would keep that heavenly road,
>   And run at thy command.
>
> Our souls shall tread the desert through
>   With undiverted feet;
> And faith and flaming zeal subdue
>   The terrors that we meet.
>
> A thousand savage beasts of prey
>   Around the desert roam;
> But Judah's lion guards the way,
>   And guides the pilgrims home.
>
> Through simoom blasts, with gloomy fears
>   We trace the sacred road;
> Through lonely wastes and dangerous snares
>   We make our way to God.

He heapeth up riches and knoweth not who shall gather them.—Ps. xxxix. 6. *The covetous, whom the Lord abhorreth.*—Ps. x. 3.

SELFISHNESS.

Look at the selfish man! See how he locks
Tight in his arms his *mortgages* and *stocks!*
While *deeds* and *titles* in his hands he grasps,
And *gold* and *silver* close around him clasps.
But not content with this, behind he drags
A *cart* well laden with the ponderous bags;
The *orphans'* wailings and the *widow's* woe,

From mercy's fountain cause no tears to flow;
He pours no cordial in the wounds of pain,
Unlocks no prison, and unclasps no chain;
His heart is like the rock where sun nor dew
Can rear one plant or flower of heavenly hue.
No thought of mercy there may have its birth,
For helpless misery or suffering worth;
The end of all his life is paltry pelf,
And all his thoughts are centered on—*himself*,
The *wretch* of both worlds; for so mean a sum,
" *First starved in this, then damned in that to come.*"

HERE is a poor fool "crouching beneath" more than "two burdens." Look at him! see how he pants, and heaves, and groans beneath his load. With his right hand he grasps a large bag of gold and silver, together with bonds, titles, deeds and mortgages. In his left he clutches fast, stocks and pledges, while suspended to his left shoulder dangles interest upon interest. Around his waist is buckled a leathern girdle, to which a wagon is attached by means of traces. This is loaded with bags and bales of rich annuities. He appears to have made " a clean sweep" wherever he has been; desolation follows in his train. On the left hand of this receiver-general, stands a female, accompanied by two children. Look at them. They have come through the peltings of a winter's storm, poorly clad as they are, to lighten the poor man's load. They have nothing to carry. See! they are beseeching him to allow them to bear part of his burden. It would help them somewhat; it would circulate the blood, and keep them warm; it would benefit him, however, a great deal more,—perhaps save his life. He looks angry; he growls at them; he curses them in the name of his god, and spurns them from his presence. The man cannot be in his right mind, surely. Refusing assistance, on he goes again, lamenting very much the time he has lost, for "time" with him "is money." On he goes, puffing and sweating and dragging. At length, still followed by the woman and children, he comes to a bridge thrown across a river rolling rapidly. It looks quite safe; as he proceeds, it bends and cracks with the weight, and just when he arrives at the middle, it gives way and down he goes, bags and all; he sinks to the bottom like a stone. The dark wave rolls over him; he dieth as a fool dieth; his memory has perished.

The above engraving represents Selfishness refusing the claims of distressed humanity. Perhaps all the manifestations of sin in man may be traced to selfishness as their source. The warrior in his pursuit of glory; the politician in hunting for power; the covetous in scheming for wealth; the scholar in his aspirations for fame; all act from the principle of selfishness. Here the selfish principle manifests itself in the acquisition of money; in keeping it, and of course fixing the heart upon it as an object worthy to be adored. The most High, looking down from the height of his holiness, pronounces the man, "*fool*." Fool in so mistaking the true ends of life,—in so mistaking the nature of things as to think the soul could be satisfied with dust and corruption; in employing the noble powers of the mind about things so base, mean, and contemptible,—in loving that which cannot return our love. Fool, in substituting the body for the soul,—time for eternity,—the world for God. Fool, to be "bit by rage canine of dying rich, *guilt's blunder, and the loudest laugh of hell.*" Fool, in heaping up riches and knowing not who shall gather them.

"High built abundance heap on heap, for what?
To breed new wants and beggar us the more,
Then make a richer scramble for the throng.

> Soon as this feeble pulse which leaps so long,
> Almost by miracle is tired with play;
> Like rubbish from disploded engines thrown,
> Our magazines of hoarded trifles fly;
> Fly diverse, fly to foreigners, to foes;
> New masters court, and call the former fools,—
> How justly, for dependence on their stay,
> Wide scatter first our playthings, then our dust.

This is bad enough, but what is worse, the man of selfishness is a man of *guilt*, often of deep, double-dyed, damnable guilt; even in its most innocent form, selfishness dethrones the blessed God from his proper place in the human heart. Selfishness is a rank idolator—he worships the creature more than the Creator. "Thou shalt have no other gods before me." Like the horse-leech, he is continually crying, give, give; he covets his neighbor's possessions—he is determined to obtain them if he can, either by fair means or by foul—to this end he often bears false witness against his neighbor—nay, he will destroy his reputation, sometimes take his life.

He is a devourer of widow's houses; he forestalls and forecloses whenever he can gain by so doing. Selfishness is a thief—first, in withholding what belongs to God and the poor; secondly, in actually seizing upon the property of others. See him go forth to take possession of his neighbor's farm or house—in the face of day he goes; the sun is looking at him, and God is looking at him, and the prophet of God within his breast—conscience—remonstrates, as did the prophet Elijah, when Ahab had gone down to the vineyard of Naboth, to take possession thereof. But selfishness is deaf to the voice of the prophet, and the helpless family is turned out into the streets, and another inheritance is added to his rent-roll.

How great is the guilt of selfishness; by him the

commandments of God are all set at nought; nay, standing on the mountain of his ill-gotten wealth, he takes the two tables of the law, and breaks them to pieces, trampling the remnants beneath his feet. His heart is ossified, callous, hard as the nether millstone; the ministers of religion plead for help—he regards it not; the daughters of benevolence plead for objects of charity all in vain; the weeping widow and the wailing orphan stand before him, begging only what will support life a day—he spurns them from his presence. He has more than he needs, or ever will need, yet—dog in the manger like—he snarls and keeps it all.

In the map of Palestine may be seen the Dead Sea; several rivers pour their streams into the midst thereof, and among them the Jordan. Here they are all swallowed up; the Dead Sea gives nothing back but bitterness and dearth. It was formerly said that birds in their passage over it dropped down dead;—selfishness is a *dead sea*, receiving all, giving nothing, save misery, and want, and death.

In the engraving, the house in the back ground looks ruined and desolate—selfishness has been there. It is related of the locusts that "the noise they make in browsing the plants and trees may be heard at a distance, like an army plundering in secret; wherever they march the verdure disappears from the country, like a curtain drawn aside. The trees' and plants, despoiled of their leaves, make the hideous appearance of winter instantly succeed the bright scenes of spring—fire seems to follow their tracks." Selfishness may look behind him if he will, and see in his rear the same marks of desolation.

Selfishness is a great advocate for the *protection* of his own interests; he has become rich, yet he is not rich God-ward. He has mortgages, but he him self, alas! is mortgaged to the devil, and when the time expires, *he* will foreclose, and take possession. He has pledges enough on earth, but no pledge of a future inheritance in heaven. And where! where is the hope of the *wretch*, though he hath gained, when God taketh away his soul!

"How shocking must thy summons be, O Death!
To him that is at ease in his possessions;
Who, counting on long years of pleasures here,
Is quite unfurnished for that world to come!
In that dread moment how the frantic soul
Raves round the walls of her clay tenement;
Runs to each avenue, and shrieks for help,
But shrieks in vain! How wishfully she looks
On all she's leaving, now no longer hers!
A little longer, yet a *little* longer,
Oh, might she stay, to wash away her stains,
And fit her for her passage! Mournful sight!
Her very eyes weep blood; and every groan
She heaves is big with horror. But the foe,
Like a staunch murderer, steady to his purpose,
Pursues her close, through every lane of life,
Nor misses once the track, but presses on;
Till forced at last to the tremendous verge,
At once she sinks to everlasting ruin."

Fear not, for I am with thee.—Gen. xxvi. 24. *I will fear no ill* * *
art with me.—Ps. xxiii. 4.

THE IMPERIAL PASSENGER.

When the great Cæsar, bent on high emprise.
Beheld the winds and waves against him rise,
The sea and skies in wild commotion roll,
To damp the ardor of his mighty soul ;
But winds and waves in vain 'gainst him engage,
And waste upon themselves their empty rage ;
He nothing fears, he deems himself a God,

And furious tempests but await his nod.
Not so the mariners,—in sore dismay
They dare not venture from the sheltered bay,
To whom the chief their craven souls to cheer,
" Who carries Cæsar, need no danger fear."
Awed into courage, soon they're on the wave,
And all the fury of the ocean brave.

THE above engraving represents Julius Cæsar in a violent storm. He is encouraging the boatmen to pull away. Cæsar and Pompey at this time were about to dispute the empire of the world. The legions of Pompey were at Macedonia. Those of Cæsar lay at Brundusium, on the other side of the river Apsus. Cæsar judging his presence to be absolutely necessary for the safety of his army, determined to cross the river, notwithstanding it was guarded by the ships of Pompey. A furious tempest raged also at the same time. Depending upon his good fortune, he disguised himself, and secured a small fishing boat. His mind occupied with the importance of his mission, thinks not of danger. He has had so many hairbreadth escapes on flood and field, that he deems himself under the immediate protection of the gods; nay, that he himself possesses the power of controlling fortune. The boatmen think, however, very differently. Though accustomed to danger, they will not put to sea in the present gale. Cæsar thinking all would be lost, assumes a commanding attitude, throws off his disguise, and addressing the pilot, exclaims, *Quid times? Cæsarem vehis.* " What do you fear? you carry Cæsar." The effect is electrical. Struck by his courageous bearing, the sailors, ashamed of their fears, immediately put to sea with the intrepid chieftain. They exert themselves to the utmost; brave fearlessly the peltings of the storm, and land their noble passenger safely on the other side.

The above instance of profane history may serve

to illustrate the presence of God with his people, and the confidence they should have in him. The presence and consequent power of God exists, of course, every where. We cannot tell where God is not. We see him in the embattled host that nightly shines in the blue vault of heaven; in the queen of night, as sailing through the sky, she gives to the shadowed earth a look of kindred affection.—When rosy morn lifts up the curtain of darkness and gives to our view the glorious orb of day coming forth from his chambers, rejoicing as a strong man to run a race; in the vast mountain, towering to meet the skies; the immense ocean, rising in the greatness of its strength; the embowered forest, bending to the breeze; the deep blush of the verdant mead; the smiles of the luscious corn, and in the laughing flowers, we see the power and presence of the Omnipotent. The thunder proclaims him in the heavens; the woodland minstrels among the trees; the mountain torrent, and the rippling brook, bespeak his power; insects sporting in the sun beams, and leviathan in the depths of the sea, alike show forth his praise. Magnitude cannot o'erpower him, minuteness escape him, or intricacy bewilder him. He guides and preserves all by his presence and power.

> "The rolling year
> Is full of Thee. Forth in the pleasing spring
> Thy beauty walks, thy tenderness and love;
> Then comes thy glory in the summer months,
> With light and heat refulgent. Then thy sun
> Shoots full perfection through the swelling year.
> Thy bounty shines in autumn unconfined,
> And spreads a common feast for all that lives.
> In winter, awful Thou! with clouds and storms
> Around thee thrown, tempest o'er tempest rolled
> Majestic darkness! on the whirlwind's wing,
> Riding sublime. Thou bid'st the world adore,
> And humblest nature with thy northern blast."

The presence of God with his people is, however, manifested in a different manner. Nature is managed by subordinate agents; the church by his immediate presence. Natural objects wax old and perish, as doth a garment; yea, the elements will melt with fervent heat; the earth also, and the works that are therein, shall be burned up; but of the church it is declared, that the gates of hell shall not prevail against it; and of Christ's kingdom, which is the church, it is said, thy kingdom is an everlasting kingdom, and thy dominion without end. Hence to perpetuate the church, the presence of God has been manifested in a peculiar manner. In the march of the church through the ages of time on toward eternity, how plainly has he shown his powerful presence.

Is the world through sin, covered with a flood of waters, as with a garment?—God himself superintends the building of an ARK, for the salvation of his infant church. Does famine threaten her with destruction?—He opens to her wants the granaries of Egypt. Does the sea oppose her when she would go and "sacrifice to the Lord her God?"—He divides for her a passage through the midst thereof, and she goes through dry shod. Does she suffer hunger in the desert?—He unlocks the store-house of heaven and feeds her with angels' food. Is she thirsty?—The very rocks are made to yield streams of living water. By his presence her foes fall before her; Jordan's waves roll backward, and Canaan spreads for her repast its stores of milk and honey. "Happy art thou, O Israel! Who is like unto thee, O people saved by the Lord, who is the sword of thy excellency and the shield of thy help?"

Nor has the church been less favored with the divine presence, since Jesus paid in full the price of her redemption, re-modelled his temple, and adorned the sanctuary with the beauty of holiness. When we see the Savior in the storm, on the sea of Tiberias, chiding the fears of his disciples, and stilling the winds and the waves, we see a type and a promise of his future presence with his people. Emmanuel, "God with us;" this is his name; how full of consolation! with us in his own proper person. The government is still upon his shoulders. "He will not give his glory to another." He does not rule by proxy. He needs no "vicar" on the earth. His real presence is with his people. He is fulfilling his own gracious promise, "lo, I am with you alway, even to the end of the world."

The fact of being engaged in an important enterprise, and a consciousness that great results will follow a certain course of conduct, nerves up the soul to action, and enables it to do and suffer. When the boatmen knew who it was that said unto them, "Fear not," knowing too that the fate of nations depended upon their conduct, they were inspired with energy and courage, and determined to sink or swim with Cæsar. But behold a greater than Cæsar is here.

Jesus, the Almighty conqueror, says to his people, "*Fear not, for I am with you.*" In the furious tempest that sometimes meets them in the path of duty when their hearts quail, and all appears to be lost, His glorious presence shines amid the darkness. "*Fear not,*" he exclaims, "*you carry Jesus.*" The church, emboldened at the sight, dismiss their fears, receive a new inspiration, and in the strength of a living faith respond: "Therefore will we not fear though the earth be removed out of its place, and th mountains be cast into the depths of the sea, for the Lord of hosts is with us, the God of Jacob is our refuge."

"*Fear not, you carry Jesus.*" Thou desponding

one, fear not. Does not Christ dwell in thy heart by faith? Is not "Christ in you" the life of faith—the life of love—"the hope of glory?" Is he not working in you both to will and to do? Then be strong in the Lord and in the power of his might. Fear not, He is thy *shield*, and thy exceeding great reward.

Of Cyrus it is said, that he knew his soldiers, every one by name. But by the Captain of your salvation, the very hairs of your head are all numbered. Unbelief dims the eye so that it cannot see Jesus. Faith opens it, and the glorious presence of the Savior is revealed. Where the king is, there also is the court; and where the Savior is, there also is his court. His attendants are all there. Power —majesty—riches and glory, encircle his throne. Stormy winds, lightning and thunder, are ministers of his that do his pleasure.

God is with his people. He is their covenant God. Hence all his attributes are employed for their good. He cares for them. As a father pitieth his children, so he pities them that fear him. He has purchased them by his own blood." They are his "peculiar treasure;" "the lot of his inheritance." Therefore no weapon that is formed against them can prosper. To banish distrust forever from their hearts, he pledges himself never to leave them, never to forsake them.

> When thou passest through the waters I will be with thee
> And through the rivers they shall not overflow thee;
> When thou walkest through the fire thou shalt not be burned,
> Neither shall the flame kindle upon thee,
> For I am the Lord thy God, the Holy One of Israel,
> Thy Savior.

I will trust in thee.—Ps. lvi. 3.   *According to your Faith be it unto you.*—Matt. ix. 29.

VENTURING BY FAITH.

Behold the flames in all their fury roll,
Raging and spreading, spurning all control;
Upward they shoot in many a gleaming spire,
And then rush downward in a flood of fire.
With fiercer heat the burning columns glow,
And soon the building totters to and fro.

But whence that scream that rings upon our ears?
In the high casement see, a child appears!
With outstretched arms, imploring for relief—
The crackling timbers only mock his grief.
"O Father, save!" in piteous tones he cries,
At length his father hears him and replies,
"Fly to my arms, my son, without delay—
Fly ere the flames devour their helpless prey."
Death hastes behind, *Hope* beckons from before;
He ventures freely, and his danger's o'er.

"THE soul of an awakened sinner," says Dr. Coke, "before he ventures on Christ for salvation, may be compared to a person who is in some of the upper stories of his house when he learns that it has taken fire, and that all its nether parts are so far involved in flame as to cut off his retreat." The engraving shows a young person who has been roused from his midnight slumbers by the raging flames which burst into the place where he was reposing, or perhaps he was awakened by the voice of some friend, who raised a warning cry from without. The child, thoroughly awakened, sees that if he stays where he is, he will perish in the flames; he hears the voice of his father—he flies to the window—he sees the outstretched arms—he is invited to leap or cast himself from the burning house; the attempt seems perilous indeed, but having *faith* in the word of his father, he takes the perilous leap—he ventures all—he falls into the hands of his father, unharmed; he is saved from death.

This is a good illustration of the act of justifying Faith. The child in the burning house, perhaps made several efforts to escape from the approaching ruin; he attempts to gain the door, but finding the flames increase upon him, he is obliged to give up his hope of escaping this way, and to ascend the stairs before the pursuing fire. His friends without, who know his condition and danger, (particularly his father,) entreat him to cast himself from the upper window, as the only means by which his life can be preserved.

The child hears the earnest entreaties of his friends—hesitates, attempts, retires, approaches the window, calculates upon the fearful height, and dreads to make the effort. His understanding is convinced that the fire will soon overtake and destroy him, yet while the danger appears somewhat remote, he strangely lingers; possibly thinking there may be some other way to escape, besides casting himself from the window.

His friends again encourage him to venture from the window, assuring him that they have provided for his safety by spreading on the ground the softest materials, to break the violence of his fall; full of hesitation, he asks for sensible evidence; they desire him to look—he makes an effort, but the darkness of the night, and the injury his sight has sustained, only permit him to view the object of his wishes obscurely and indistinctly. Belief and doubt contend for the empire of his mind, and by keeping it in an equipoise, prevent it from making any decisive choice.

Thus far the situation of the child resembles that of the soul who feels his need of salvation. The understandings of both are enlightened; the judgments of both are convinced by the force of evidence; they appear to assent to the truths which are proposed for their belief, and still neither of them has escaped to the place of safety, or city of refuge, which lies before him. Both, however, have found the way to escape the impending ruin; and to him who thus spiritually seeks after Christ, it may be said, thou art not far from the kingdom of God; but still one thing is lacking, that is, to *venture* on the Savior for salvation.

Thus far, in the allegory, the child has made no effectual effort to escape from within the burning walls; while lingering in his room, in a state of indecision, agonizing for deliverance, without using the means of obtaining it, feeling a measure of confidence in his friends below, but not enough to venture, the flames burst into his apartment and scorch him in his last retreat. Alarmed at the immediate prospect of death, he concludes—if I remain here I shall surely die, and if I cast myself down from the building, I shall but die.

Fully impressed with this truth, he once more repairs to the window; he pays more attention to the call of his friends, particularly to that of his father the difficulty now appears somewhat less, and the prospect of safety greater, than what he before imagined. Encouraged by these favorable appearances, as well as driven by terror, he commits his soul to God—he casts himself into the arms of his father below. In a moment, in the twinkling of an eye, he falls! he is caught and embraced by his father; he finds every thing prepared for his reception, as he had been promised, and he now feels himself in a state of safety. With tears of grateful joy, and a heart overflowing with thankfulness for his deliverance, he gives glory to God, and finds his bosom filled with peace.

This is the case of every soul who, by faith, *ventures* his all on Christ. But who can find words to express all that is conveyed by this simile? Every one who has cast himself into the arms of his heavenly father through the atoning sacrifice, can feel it, but adequate expressions are not to be found. Human language is too poor to unfold in all their branches, the things of God, and we are often under the necessity of resorting to such expedients in order to find a medium to communicate our thoughts.

We see by the allegory that no one is in a state of safety till they have actually ventured on Christ for salvation. The soul may be convinced that there is no other way of salvation, but by venturing on Christ, but unless it acts, and puts forth an effort, there is no salvation. The youth in the burning house may be convinced he must leave it if he would save his life, but he may, perhaps, think there is no immediate danger if he stays in the house a little longer; it will take some time, he thinks, for the fire to consume the foundation on which the floor of his apartment rests. The very reverse of this may be true—the fire has almost reached him, and he knows it not; all that supports the platform on which he stands is well nigh consumed, and he may be precipitated in a moment into the burning flames below. So the soul may be rationally convinced that if it remains in its present state it must be forever lost, yet thinking that there is time enough yet to attend to the subject of the soul's salvation in earnest, and wishing to remain in its present state a little longer, "a little more sleep, and a little more slumber, and folding of the arms to sleep," sudden destruction may come in a moment—the cords of life may be snapped asunder, without a moment's warning, and sink into the flaming billows to rise no more.

We will suppose that the youth in the burning house, instead of trying to get out of it as soon as possible, should stop to ascertain by what means the house took fire—who set it on fire—this man or the other, or whether it took fire accidentally or not—would not every spectator call him a fool for troubling himself about such questions while his life was in such danger. Would not the cry be, escape for thy life—tarry not—look not behind thee—leave the burning house instantly? Equally foolish would that soul be who is convinced of his guilt and danger, instead of flying to Christ for salvation, should spend its time in trying to find out the reason why sin was suffered to lay waste the works of God—could it not have been prevented—and many other subjects of the like kind, equally unfathomable by the human mind.

It must be observed that the Faith exercised by the youth in the burning house, caused him to act, and venture his life on the issue. Perhaps he might reason, that his being at such a distance from his father and his friends, who stood on the ground below, it would be impossible for them to save him from being dashed to pieces should he cast himself down; there may be a strong conflict between belief and unbelief, but genuine faith will conquer. The soul that is truly and savingly in earnest about its salvation, not only believes in a general manner that the Bible is the voice of God to man, but his belief must induce him to hearken to that voice, and consider its threatenings as denounced against his disobedience; he must, in order to obtain salvation, fly to Christ, cast himself upon his mercy, and claim the promises which are made to the soul that puts its trust in his mercy and power.

The youth in the burning house discovers that there are no back stairs by which he can reach a place of safety, for they are already entirely destroyed by the fire, or else nothing but a burning mass, so that escape by them is utterly impossible. In like manner the truly awakened soul will see that there is no other way of escape but to leave the state of sin and death, as there can be no salvation while remaining in it. But if the soul will go forward and cast itself into the everlasting arms of love and compassion, he who cannot lie, promises salvation.

* * *

"Come, humble sinner, in whose breast
  A thousand thoughts revolve,
Come, with your guilt and fear oppressed,
  And make this last resolve:

I'll go to Jesus, though my sin
  Like mountains round me close;
I know his courts, I'll enter in,
  Whatever may oppose."

Broad is the way that leadeth to destruction, and many there be that go in thereat. . . . Narrow is the way which leadeth unto life, and few there be that find it.—Matt. vii. 13, 14.

THE PATH OF LIFE, AND WAY OF DEATH.

The Path of Life, and Death's frequented way,
Who can describe? what pencil can portray?
The way of Death is broad, with downward slide,
Easy and pleasant to man's lust and pride;
'T is thronged with multitudes who glide along
With gold, and drink, and dance, and wanton song:

RELIGIOUS ALLEGORIES. 299

> Nor these alone—but some of decent mien,
> "Harmless" and "useless" on the way are seen;
> In ruin's gulph it ends. See! rising there,
> Thick clouds of blackness, and of dark despair.
>   The Path of Life lifts up its narrow breadth,
> High o'er the realms of darkness and of death;
> Sky-rising, still, laborious and straight,
> Leading directly up to heaven's gate;
> 'T is wondrous strange, and yet, alas! 't is true,
> The Path of Life is traveled but by few,
> Though ending where the shades of night ne'er fall,
> But one eternal Light encircles all.

HERE is depicted the path of life, and the way of death. The way of death is exceeding broad, and on an inclined plane. It has a downward tendency; it is occupied by a vast multitude. Some are seen throwing themselves off the way headlong, others are bearing aloft the terrible banners of war. They are elated with victory. Here the man of pleasure revels in delight. The drunkard is dancing with wild delirious joy, and the miser groans beneath his bags of gold. There are, however, some sober, respectable people on the way. These appear to look grave and thoughtful. The way ends, you perceive, in total darkness. Thick clouds of curling blackness rising from a pit or gulph, cover the extremity of the way. The travelers enter the dismal shades, and we see them no more.

From the way of death you see another way, or path rather, stretching up, as it were, into the clouds. This is called the path of life. It is extremely narrow. It is moreover difficult on account of its upward tendency. Few persons are seen walking on it; these scattered here and there. This path appears to end well. We can see where it does end. A beautiful palace opens its golden gates to receive the wearied travelers. From its opened portals bursts forth a dazzling light that illuminates the pathway beneath,

By the way of death, is signified the way of sin that leads to death eternal. "The wages of sin is death." Its downward tendency denotes, that it is much easier to go wrong than to go right. The way of sin is easy and pleasant to man's corrupt nature. He delights in it after the inner man. Were it not so, surely so many in all ages would not be found walking therein. The Creator himself gives us the reason. "The thoughts of the imaginations of his heart are evil, only evil, and that continually." Hence man follows the bent of his inclination. He goes with the stream; "every one in his own way." To do otherwise, would require self-denial, and vigorous, persevering effort.

In the engraving, some are seen casting themselves off the way. By this is meant, not that sinners grow tired of the way of sin exactly, but that they are tired of themselves; they are tired of life. Their substance is expended in gambling and profligacy. The means of indulging their depraved appetite no longer exists; hence they commit suicide; plunge into eternity, and add to the number of those who die without hope, for "Except ye repent, ye shall all likewise perish." Others, by their excesses in riotous living and debaucheries, break down their constitution, and destroy life, and thus perish with those who "live not out half their days."

Warriors are also in the way of death, raising to the breeze the flag of triumph. These denote the men "who delight in war,"—who, for wealth and glory, "sink, burn, and destroy," and slaughter their fellow-creatures. These violate the law of Jehovah, "Thou shalt not kill." Drunkards too are in this way, carousing with strong drink, dancing with maniac madness, and yet, on the way to ruin, drowning the cares of time, but planting thorns for eternity.

These belong to the class of whom it is said, "such shall not inherit the kingdom of God." The one with the bag of gold represents that very large class who worship Mammon on the earth; who never think even of heaven, except when they remember that it is paved with gold. These are idolaters; the meanest of the Devil's drudges, the vilest of the slave of sin. Others enjoy the pleasures of sin; but he sweats and groans beneath his load; he takes place with the breakers of God's law, "Thou shalt have no other gods before me."

Some pass the time in wanton dalliance; these designate the adulterer, fornicator, and the impure. These take pleasure in unrighteousness; give up their affections to the control of lust; indulge in mere animal delights; imbrute their manhood; quench their intellect, and barter the glories of heaven for a "portion in the lake which burneth with fire and brimstone; this is the second death." Others of staid and respectable appearance are in this way. Men of dignity and of consequence; men of morals and philosophy, all honorable men; men who are harmless in their generation, honest in their dealings. They "render to Cæsar the things which are Cæsar's," but alas for them, they do not "render unto God the things which are God's." One thing only is wanting. "One thing thou lackest." The heart is unsurrendered; hence there is no repentance—no living faith—no homage—no love—no obedience—no salvation. These, alas, all take rank with the "unprofitable servant," who was cast into outer darkness, where there is weeping, and wailing, and gnashing of teeth.

But time would fail to describe the various characters that throng the way of death. The gross sensualist, the haughty Pharisee, and the specious hypocrite, are all here. But is it possible some one may say, that so many are in the way to eternal death? God himself has answered the question; we have heard his voice. It is not only true that they *are* going, but that they go of their own accord. The sinner is threatened, admonished, and warned, and yet he goes on. He is persuaded, entreated, and invited to turn and live, and yet he goes on.

If you see a man traveling a road that you know to be frequented with robbers, you tell him of his danger; he persists in going on; the robbers strip him and leave him for dead; who is to blame? The sinner is warned of his danger, and yet he persists in sin. Numbers control not the sword of justice. The antideluvians were faithfully warned; they went on and perished in the flood. The men of Sodom were warned; they persisted, and perished in the rain of fire. The Jews were warned also, even by the Son of God, and yet they went on in rebellion, until of their city not one stone was left standing upon another, and themselves scattered and peeled among the nations.

The sinner neglects a great salvation. Neglecting only to get into the Ark will expose him to the flood of fire. Neglecting salvation, he contemns the "love of God." He "tramples upon the blood of the covenant. He does "despite to the Spirit of grace." How shall he escape if he neglects so great salvation. "These shall go away into everlasting punishment."

"I saw the lake of quenchless fires,
  And souls on its billows tost;
Despair, remorse which ne'er expires,
  The worm of the deathless lost.

Grief filled my bursting heart,—I cried,
  Shall this distress end never?"
The shrieks of millions loud replied,
  "These pangs endure—forever!"

By the path of life is designated the path of holiness, that leads to life eternal. "Blessed are the pure in heart, for they shall see God." It is narrow and steep; it requires care and effort. The pilgrim must deny himself; take up his cross daily, and watch unto prayer. It is difficult only to flesh and blood; to the carnal mind, not to the spiritual; to the unregenerate, not to him that is born again. To the righteous its ways are ways of pleasantness, and all its paths are paths of peace. Narrow is the way that leads to life, and few there are that find it. Fewer still endure to the end thereof. The few were once in the way of death. They were among the many that were called. They obeyed the heavenly call, forsook the broad way, and entered upon the path of life.

The Path of Life ends well; God delights in holiness. He did not overlook Noah in the overflowing of the ungodly, nor Lot in Sodom. The faithful few are God's jewels; his hidden ones, while tribulation and "angush are assigned to the disobedient." The patient continuance of the righteous in well doing "will be rewarded with glory, and honor, and immortality," for the ransomed of the Lord shall return and come to Zion with songs and everlasting joy upon their heads. They shall obtain joy and gladness, and sorrow and sighing shall flee away.

> "I saw the countless, happy throng
> In the blissful regions high;
> White robes—gold crowns—and lofty song,
> With their harps in harmony.
> Hope brightened at the dazzling sight,
> 'Shall aught from heaven sever ?'
> And myriads sung—' Our peace, joy, light,
> And glory, last forever."

The world passeth away.—1 John, ii, 17. *Now is the day of salvation.*—2 Cor. vi. 2. *Ye know not what shall be on the morrow.*—James iv. 14.

PAST, PRESENT, AND FUTURE.

Look on the *Past*. Behold! wide scattered round,
Time's fragments—every where they strew the ground:
The Dead are there—once blooming, young and gay,
'Mid putrefaction, lo! they waste away.
The aged oak, once tall, and strong, and green,
Decayed and withered in the past is seen;
The lordly mansion, once the owner's trust,
Its glory gone, see crumbling into dust.

E'en Egypt's boast, the pyramids of yore,
Shall fall to ruin, and be known no more.
The *Past* is gone ; the *Future*, black as night,
By clouds lies hidden from all mortal sight ;
The *Present's* here—see there with angel brow,
Wisdom lifts up her voice of mercy. *Now*—
Now—the accepted time, the gracious day,
When man repentant, wipes his stains away ;
Inspires new life, through the atoning blood,
And writes his name among the sons of God.

THIS picture is emblematical of the Past, Future, and Present, as these divisions of time appear to us, who are now on the stage of human life. Behold the Past ! see there the fragments that time has left behind : there is the burying place, filled with the records of the past—what a volume of Biography is the grave-yard ; there they lay, the blooming and the beautiful—the strong and the active—all mouldering into dust. The laughing eye—the noble brow—the dimpled cheek—the teeth of pearl—the musical tongue—the brain creative—and the cunning hand—all, all, are silent in the tomb, and melting into earth.

There too, is the oak, that once towered in strength and beauty, now withered and decayed ; once it gave shelter to the beasts of the field, the fowls of heaven lodged in its branches—now it needs a prop to prevent its falling to the ground.

The splendid mansion is seen crumbling into dust. Architecture, and sculpture, and painting, had bestowed upon it their highest efforts ; the artist looked with pride upon it, the owner delighted in it ; but it is gone—its glory has departed—it is among the things that have been.

In the distance are seen the huge forms of the pyramids ; Egypt's renown and the wonder of the world—memorials of the past, telling us of the folly, cruelty, despotism, and ambition of kings—telling us, too, doubtless, of the sweat, and groans, and tears, and blood, of thousands of the men like ourselves, who slaved and labored to build those gigantic monuments—but these also, will pass away; if not before, they must when the earth shall reel to and fro, and totter ike a drunken man. Then, at least, all physical reminiscences of the past, sinking into the deep sea of oblivion, will be recognized no more.

The *Future* is represented by clouds of darkness that rise upon the path, and shut out from mortal vision all prospect of what is before. *Religion*, the daughter of the skies, who descended from heaven, and who is hastening back again to her blest abode, is seen on the circular path of time. It is time *Present* wherever she appears; she holds in her hand a scroll, see its burden! She is in earnest—she looks benignly and compassionately as she passes by—she makes known to man his highest good; above her head is seen a crown of glory—this she promises to all who will obey her voice, and improve the present time.

The past is gone. The castles—the mansions—the green oaks—and the towers—and let them go! The monuments of the pride and ambition, and wickedness, of kings and conquerors, are crumbling into dust, and let them crumble! The glory, splendor and renown of heroes, are fast fading away, and le them fade. But the dead shall live again—they that sleep in the dust shall awake—that which is sown in dishonor shall be raised in glory.

The past is gone—time once lost, is lost for ever. Past opportunities for doing good and for getting good, are gone, and gone for ever. " 'Tis greatly wise to talk with our past hours, and ask them what report they bore to heaven." Happy he,

"Whose work is done; who triumphs in the past,
Whose yesterdays look backward with a smile;
Nor like the Parthian wound him as they fly:
That common but opprobrious lot. Past hours,
If not by guilt, yet wound us by their flight,
If folly bounds our prospect by the grave.

Yet there is a sense in which the past never dies. It haunts us like the ghost of the murdered—it is ever present—an angel of light casting upon us a look of heavenly love, or a demon of darkness scowling with malignity and hate—the memory will exist for ever. The remembrance of past actions will, therefore, live forever. "O, for yesterdays to come."

The *Future* is concealed—clouds and darkness hide it from our view. We know not what a day may bring forth, nor what an hour; we know, however, that Death is there—and after death the Judgment—and after the judgment the issues thereof—"*Eternal life*," or "*Eternal death*." But this is all we know, and this is enough, if we are wise; how much of joy or sorrow there may be for us in the future, we know not; whether our path will be strewed with roses or with thorns, we cannot tell—most likely they will be mixed. What opportunities for improvement in religious duties and privileges, or what hindrances, we may have, we know not—how much of life—who can tell? A man may plant, and build, and lay up goods for many years, and yet to-day may be his last day—to-night his soul may be required of him.

If then, the past is gone, and if the future may never come to us in life, it behooves us to improve the present. God, in his mercy offers salvation *now*. *Now* is the accepted time, *now* is the day of salvation. What is it that is offered? Salvation. Thou cans't not do without salvation; without it thou art lost and lost forever. Seize then, O seize the angel as she passes, nor suffer her to go until she bless thee. The present time, how important! it includes the vast concerns of the eternal state. Destroy it not, there is a blessing in it. "Throw years away? throw empires, and be blameless." The *present* seize,

> . . . "O what heaps of slain
> Cry out for vengeance on us! Time destroyed,
> Is suicide, where more than blood is spilt;
> Time flies—death urges—knells call—heaven invites—
> Hell threatens—all exerts; in effort all;
> More than creation labors!—labors more!
> Man sleeps, and man alone; and man for whom
> All else is in alarm; man the sole cause
> Of this surrounding storm; and yet *he sleeps*,
> As the storm rocked to rest."

Now is the accepted time; God will accept thee now; he no where promises to accept thee to-morrow. Think, O think, of thy soul, and its value; think of Jehovah and his love; think of Christ and his precious blood; think of heaven and its eternal blessedness; of hell and its terrible torments. Upon thy present conduct rests thy eternal destiny. What art thou sowing? What art thou working? What art thou treasuring up? Let conscience answer. Think of the past, and all its guilt—of the future and its great uncertainty—of the *present* as thine. To-morrow may be too late; now is the day of salvation—now thou may'st wash away thy sins, calling upon the name of the Lord—inspire a new life—rejoice in glorious hope—enroll your name among the children of God, and become a glorious citizen of immortality in heaven.

Improve the present. See! look on that beach; there is a boat high and dry, with a man in it—he is asleep. The ship to which he belongs is in the offing; she will sail the next tide. The tide rises—the man sleeps on—the tide ebbs—he awakes—the water is gone, the ship is gone, and he is left to perish on a desolate island. There is a tide in man's spiritual affairs, which, when taken at the rise, leads on to heaven;— omitted, he may be left to perish. My spirit, saith the Lord, shall not always strive with man.

Now is the accepted time. Behold that rail-road car; it has just started—look again—there is a person with his hands upraised, exclaiming, " alas, too late!" He is left behind his friends are all on board, and is not with them—great is his grief. Man is a stranger here—God sends the chariot of his love to bear him home; again and again it comes—it is here now—O sinner, step on board. The Saviour is there—he invites thee to leave thy sins, and sinful companions, and get on board of the heavenly car—the car of mercy. It is ready to start—all things are now ready—some of thy friends are there. Hesitate not—delay not—or, like the passenger, thou may'st find thyself in a more mournful sense "*too late,*" and, " a moment you may wish when worlds want wealth to buy."

O God, our help in ages past,
  Our hope for years to come,
Our shelter from the stormy blast,
  And our eternal home.

Before the hills in order stood,
  Or earth received her frame,
From everlasting thou art God,
  To endless years the same.

Thy word commands our flesh to dust,
  " Return, ye sons of men ;"
All nations rose from earth at first,
  And turn to earth again.

A thousand ages in thy sight,
  Are like an evening gone ;
Short as the watch that ends the night,
  Before the rising sun.

The busy tribes of flesh and blood,
  With all their lives and cares,
Are carried downward by the flood,
  And lost in following years.—*Watts.*

For of him, and through him, and to him, are all things.—Rom. xi. 36
Time is short.—1 Cor. vii. 29. *Which is, and which was, and which is to come.*—Rev. i. 8.

PROVIDENCE, TIME, ETERNITY.

Upon a narrow isle, 'mid waters vast,
By stress of tide the voyagers are cast;
Beneath—around—a dark and boundless sea;
Above, thick clouds wrap all in mystery
The Ocean wears the shore on every side,

As Time decreases 'neath the Eternal tide,
Yet one—deluded man! strives much to reach
The shells and pebbles on the crumbling beach;
The waves dash on—another pondering stands,
And sees destruction come with folded hands.
Not so the third—he turns his longing eyes,
And views a chain descending from the skies,
The *Providential* chain with links of love,
Watched by an eye that never sleeps above;
He grasps the chain—from all his fears it saves,
While his companions perish 'neath the waves.

In the engraving is seen a representation of the all-seeing eye. It is placed above every thing else, to show that the eye of God's Providence watches over all creation, taking notice of every event throughout all time and space. Though to human vision there may be clouds and darkness about the throne of the Eternal, yet to his all-seeing eye, darkness is as noonday. All things are before him, and nothing is too minute for his inspection. He sees the rise and fall of empires, and with equal attention sees the sparrow fall to the ground, for in a certain sense nothing is great or small before him. Throughout all time and space, the eye of Providence penetrates; yea more, it reaches farther; eternity itself, to the human mind dark, fathomless, boundless, endless, is penetrated and comprehended.

A chain is seen descending from above, of which we can neither see the beginning or the ending; but as far as we can discover, is but a small part of a mighty whole. It is true a man may see a few of the links of the chain before him, their connection with each other, but how far they may extend above or below his vision, he has no knowledge. This shows us that the great chain of God's Providential dispensations in the universe is but partially seen or comprehended. It is true while on these mortal shores.

we may see a few of the connecting links of this chain, but to what heights it reaches, or to what depths it penetrates, we have no adequate conception.

"In what manner, indeed," says a celebrated writer, "Providence interposes in human affairs, by what means it influences the thoughts and counsels of men, and, notwithstanding the influence it exerts, leaves to them the freedom of choice, are subjects of a dark and mysterious nature, and which have given occasion to many an intricate controversy. Let us remember that the manner in which God influences the motion of all the heavenly bodies, the nature of that secret power by which he is ever directing the sun and the moon, the planets, stars, and comets, in their course through the heavens, while they appear to move themselves in a free course, are matters no less inexplicable to us, than the manner in which he influences the counsels of men. But though the mode of divine operation remains unknown, the fact of an over-ruling influence is equally certain, in the moral, as it is in the natural world."

"In cases where the fact is clearly authenticated, we are not at liberty to call its truth in question, merely because we understand not the manner in which it is brought about. Nothing can be more clear, from the testimony of Scripture, than that God takes part in all that happens among mankind, directing and over-ruling the whole course of events, so as to make every one of them answer the designs of his wise and righteous government."

"We cannot, indeed, conceive God acting as the governor of the world at all, unless his government were to extend to all the events that can happen. It is upon the supposition of a particular providence, that our worship and prayers to him are founded. All his perfections would be utterly insignificant to us, if they were not exercised on every occasion, according as the circumstances of his creatures required. The Almighty would then be no more than an unconcerned spectator of the behavior of his subjects, regarding the obedient and rebellious with an equal eye."

In the lower part of the engraving is seen a little spot of earth in the vast ocean by which it is surrounded, on which is seen three persons. This small place may represent *Time*, which has arisen out of the eternity of the past. Though now visible, it is destined soon to sink into oblivion in the midst of the mighty waters. One of the figures on this little spot of time is seen very busy in collecting the little pebbles or particles of shining dust around him. How foolish this, when he must know that the rolling tide will soon overflow all around him. Equally foolish is he, who, in this transitory life, instead of looking upward and using the means Providence has placed within his reach for his escape from overflowing destruction, spends his precious moments in collecting the little baubles and toys of earth.

On the left is seen one who appears to be gravely philosophizing upon the scene he beholds around him. He realizes that he is standing on a speck of earth, in the midst of a mighty ocean, of which he can neither see the bottom or the shore. He looks backward ; all is dark to his vision ; he looks around him ; all is mysterious and incomprehensible ; forward ; all, all, is thick darkness. He is sensible that the tide of death will soon overflow him and all with whom he is connected ; but will eternal oblivion and forgetfulness be his portion ? Perhaps he thinks so ; but at times the immortal spirit will stir within him and "startle back" at the thought of annihilation. Ah, poor fool ! he turns his back and will not look at the bright chain of God's Providence which so manifestly appears. Perhaps he may try to persuade himself that the chain hangs there by *chance*. He has been told that earth and heaven are connected by it. He professes to see no necessary connection; he cannot see its beginning, how it is supported on high. He has heard that by it man can be elevated to a heavenly life. This may appear foolishness to him. Perhaps he may think that if man were destined to live hereafter, he would not have been placed on these mortal shores; or if immortal, it will be in some other mode than that pointed out in the Bible. He is wise in his own conceit. He turns himself from Gods' method of salvation; refuses to look upward; continues to reason " in endless mazes lost ;" will not lay hold of the only hope set before him; he "wonders and perishes" in the overflowing of the mighty waters.

One of the persons on the little island is seen with his eyes turned upward his hands are uplifted in thankfulness and adoration. He beholds the bright chain of God's Providential mercy; he lays hold of the only hope set before him. It is true he can see but a few of the connecting links of the golden chain above, but he fully believes that it is connected with, and sustained by, an Almighty Power above. He has occasional glimpses of the all-seeing eye; he feels that he is under its supervision. He feels himself encircled, upheld and sustained by Infinite power and love, and rejoices that all things are under the control of a kind Providence.

It is true the Christian may see clouds and darkness above, around, and below him. He may not know why sin, and consequently misery, is suffered to exist in the universe of God. He may not know why he is placed here in the circumstances by which he is surrounded. He weeps often; it may be to see how sin has laid waste the works of God; how the wicked often triumph, and the good are crushed into the dust. He may not know the beginning, or origin of God's Providential dealings, how far they reach into this, or other worlds. But notwithstanding the Christian may not be able to fathom these and many other subjects, yet he confides in the Almighty power above. He lays hold of salvation; he is elevated to the regions of eternal light and glory, while his unbelieving companions perish amid the dark rolling waters of the ocean.

The ocean has sometimes been considered as an emblem of eternity, on account of its vast extent, its fathomless depths, and its appearance to human vision oftentimes, as without a bottom or shore. "Eternity," says one, "with respect to God is a duration without beginning or end. With regard to created beings, it is a duration that has a beginning, but will never have an end. It is a duration that excludes all number and computation; days, months, and years, yea and ages, are lost in it like drops in the ocean. Millions of millions of years, as many years as there are sands on the sea-shore, or particles of dust in the globe of the earth, and these multiplied to the highest reach of number, all these are nothing to eternity. They do not bear the imaginable proportion to it, for these will come to an end as certainly as a day; but eternity will never, never, never, come to an end! It is a time without an end! it is an ocean without a shore! Alas! what shall I say of it! it is an infinite, unknown something, that neither human thought can grasp, nor human language describe!" * * *

Alleluia! for the Lord God omnipotent reigneth.—Rev. xix. 6.

THE TRIUMPH OF CHRISTIANITY.

'T is come! 't is come! The long expected day;
When sin no longer o'er the earth bears sway;
But Truth, triumphant, sheds its mellow light,
And all below is clear, and pure, and bright.
See Christianity! the gift of Grace!
Receives in form the homage of our race;

Europa fair, her princely tribute brings,
A grateful offering, to the King of kings;
Asia rejects the *Shasters* and the *Sword*,
Throws by the *Koran*, and receives the *Word;*
Lo! Afric breaks her chains of crime and blood,
And lowly bending, lifts her hands to God.
No more she wages wars for white man's gold—
No more she mourns her children bought and sold.
See, too, America, with pipe of peace!
Comes now to sue for love and heavenly grace;
The tomahawk, and bow, and cruel knife,
T' exchange for records of eternal life:
'T is come! 't is come! the long expected day!
Lo! God has triumphed, Truth divine bears sway;
Loud alleluias heavenly angels sing,
For earth, renewed with joy, receives her king.

THE above engraving represents Christianity receiving the homage of the world. In her right hand she holds the crown of immortality; in her left, the Word of God; her looks and bearing bespeak grace, dignity, majesty, empire, triumph, and matchless love. Behold *Europe* brings her crown—emblem of power—and lays it meekly at the feet of Christianity. *Asia*, represented by a follower of Mahomet, laying aside the cimeter and the Koran, receives with humble adoration, instead thereof, the revelations of God's word. *Africa* is represented by a figure in a kneeling posture; she has broken off her chains, and is lifting her hands to heaven. *America* is represented by an Indian; he holds in his hand the calumet or pipe of peace; he has laid aside the murderous tomahawk, the bow that sprang the arrow of death, and the scalping knife. He buries the hatchet for ever and offers the emblem of *peace*.

The above is a representation of the final triumph of Christianity over the world—a day long expected by the faithful, even from the time of the first promise, "he shall bruise thy head." That this earth—

this blood-stained earth—should become the scene of triumph, has ever been the hope of the righteous, that here, where was the first defeat, renewed conflict, and continued struggle—here would be, and ought to be, the arena of victory. Exulting in this hope, the prophet touched the sacred harp of prophecy, and sang of "the sufferings of Christ, and of the glory that should follow," when he would see of the travail of his soul and be satisfied. In this hope Israel's king prayed, "that thy way may be known upon the earth, and thy saving health among all nations." Inspired by this hope, martyrs have kissed the stake, embraced the flames, and gone triumphantly home to God; yea, the general assembly of the Church of the first-born—the whole body of the faithful upon earth—in this hope rejoicing, have sent up their prayers continually, which, like intercessory angels surrounding the throne of the Eternal, have prayed, O "let thy kingdom come."

And now it has come. *Europe* is the Lord's—she consecrates to God her dominion—her kings and queens are subject to Messiah, and labor to promote the best interests of their people; her people are all righteous—her philosophers having proved all things, hold fast now that which is good; her rich men deposit their wealth in the bank of heaven—her statesmen, studying the politics of both worlds, regard also the interests of both—the poor are raised to competency, to knowledge, and to virtue, and consequent happiness. Her arts and sciences are consecrated to God; her ships of war now sail in the service of the prince of peace—ships of commerce are floating Bethels. The songs of Jesus have succeeded to the songs of Satan, and blasphemies are turned to praise.

"The abundance of the sea is converted to God," railroads, steamboats, and telegraphs, are all em ployed in promoting God's glory, and in benefiting mankind. The Anglo-American race, and others, partake of this triumph; they have labored for it—they rejoice in it, and say, lo! this is our God! we have waited for him, we will rejoice in his salvation.

Asia too, is the Lord's; here, where the conflict first began with sin and death—here the victory is gained. The lion of the, tribe of Judah has prevailed—the inhabitants, so long enslaved by despotic creeds, now exercise faith in the Lord Jesus Christ—so long oppressed by systems of superstition and blood, now rejoice under the mild yoke of the Savior,—the Koran and Shasters are exchanged for the Bible—*Juggernaut* for Calvary—*Kalee* for Jesus—*Mahomet* for God. Here now is seen "China without its wall of selfishness—India without its castes—and earth without its curse." The people are elevated, the nations are united, Jehovah is their King.

Africa throws off her load, and breaks her chains, and comes to Jesus—so long crushed and degraded, she has at length arisen—she takes her place again with the nations of the earth, with the redeemed. Ignorance, superstition and slavery, are now no more. Her warfare is past—her mourning is o'er—her long captivity is at an end. Jehovah has triumphed—his children are free.

> "No more Coomassie offers human blood,
> But takes for sacrifice the Lamb of God,
> And on Siberia's long contested ground,
> A living army of the cross is found.
> The gospel tree so ample and so pure,
> Bears precious fruit; its leaves the nations cure;
> Its healing influence to Loango spreads;
> Angola feels it, and health's blossoms sheds,
> And where Cimbebas no fresh water brings,
> Life's fountains bubble in a thousand springs.
> Korana's shepherds now Christ's flock become,
> And Bosheman's Kraals are changed to home, sweet home.

Good Hope has added Faith and humble Love;
The Cross has triumphed! praise to God above."

America, the whole of the western world, rejoices in the light of the glorious Sun of Righteousness—the islands of the sea wait for Jehovah's law—the Indian tribes obey his word, and hail him their Almighty Lord. The tomahawk, and scalping knife, and other weapons of war and blood, are exchanged for the olive branch—for the war-whoop is now heard the sound of the "church-going bell," greeting the Sabbath morning—the disciple of the Pope has become the disciple of Jesus, and laying aside all superstition, he worships the Lord his God, and him *only* does he serve. The dispersed of the seed of Abraham, the "scattered and peeled" among the nations, have looked upon him "they pierced." The winds of heaven have blown upon the valley of dry bones—they have revived—they have come forth out of their graves, and seizing every one the banner of his tribe, have hastened to join the army of Messiah.

Hail! happy day! Jesus the Conqueror reigns—the song of triumph resounds—island answers to island—continent to continent—world to world;—earth, with all its voices—heaven, with all its harps, resound, "the kingdoms of this world are become the kingdoms of our Lord and of his anointed, and he shall reign for ever and ever; alleluia! alleluia! the Lord God Omnipotent reigneth"—"he that sat upon the throne said, Behold, I make all things new!"

Even now, the Spirit is moving on the face of the human chaos—fiat after fiat goes forth, and what light breaks in on the darkness of ages—what mighty masses of humanity are uplifting themselves in solemn majesty, like primitive mountains rising from the deep—what more than verdant beauty clothes the moral landscape; how gloriously dawns the Sabbath of the world! Where is now the midnight gloom of darkness and idolatry?—The desolation and misery attendant on sin? We look and listen, but no reign of darkness, no habitation of cruelty, no sound of anguish remains. The will of God *is* done on earth, as it is done in heaven!—the nations own no other law, and hence their aspect is that of a happy family. The Church aims at no other end, and hence all her members are invested with the garments of salvation, and with the robes of praise. The world is bathed in the light of peace and purity, and love.

Inanimate nature itself partakes of the general joy. To the eye of the renewed man it exhibits a beauty unknown before, and to his ear it brings lessons of surpassing wisdom. The trees wave with gladness, and the floods clap their hands; the light of the moon is as the light of the sun, and the light of the sun is seven fold. Over the scene, the morning stars sing together, and the sons of God shout for joy, while the divine Creator himself complacently beholds it, and proclaims it GOOD.

THE END.

CONTENTS OF ALLEGORIES.

LOOKING UNTO JESUS, ... 166
WALKING BY FAITH, ... 172
THE SURE GUIDE, ... 178
CHARITY, OR LOVE, ... 184
PRIDE AND HUMILITY, ... 190
THE SACRIFICE, ... 196
NO CROSS, NO CROWN, ... 202
THE LIFE-BOAT, ... 208
OBEDIENCE AND WISDOM, ... 214
DANGER OF PRESUMPTION, ... 220
DECISION AND PERSEVERANCE, ... 226
PASSION AND PATIENCE, ... 232
THE CONQUERING CHRISTIAN, ... 238
THE IMPERIAL PHILANTHROPIST, ... 244
THE WINTRY ATMOSPHERE, ... 250
THE PROTECTED TRAVELER, ... 256
THE PEARL OF GREAT PRICE, ... 262
THE GREAT DISCOVERY, ... 268
PASSAGE THROUGH THE DESERT, ... 278
SELFISHNESS, ... 280
THE IMPERIAL PASSENGER, ... 286
VENTURING BY FAITH, ... 292
PATH OF LIFE AND WAY OF DEATH, ... 298
PAST, PRESENT, FUTURE, ... 304
PROVIDENCE, TIME, ETERNITY, ... 310
TRIUMPH OF CHRISTIANITY, ... 316

DIRECTIONS

FOR

GETTING AND KEEPING

SPIRITUAL PEACE AND COMFORT.

ABRIDGED FROM

RICHARD BAXTER,
AUTHOR OF "THE SAINTS' EVERLASTING REST;" "CALL TO THE UNCONVERTED," ETC.

CINCINNATI:
HENRY HOWE, PUBLISHER.

BAXTER'S

SPIRITUAL PEACE AND COMFORT.

It must be understood, that the case here to be resolved is not, How an unhumbled, profane sinner, that never was convinced of sin and misery, should be brought to a settled peace of conscience. But the case in hand is, 'How a sinner may attain to a settled peace of conscience, and some competent measure of the joy of the Holy Ghost, who hath been convinced of sin and misery, and long made a profession of holiness, but liveth in continual doubtings of their sincerity, and fears of God's wrath, because of an exceeding deadness of spirit, and a want of that love to God, and delight in him, and sweetness in duty, and witness of the Spirit, and communion with God, and the other like evidences which are found in the saints.'

Of my directions, the first shall be only general, and the rest more particular. And all of them I must entreat you, 1. To observe the order and method, as well as the matter; and that you would practice them in the same order as I place them. 2. And to remember that it is not only comfortable words, but it is directions for your own practice, which here I prescribe you; and therefore that it is not the bare reading of them that will cure you; but if you mean to have the benefit of them, you must bestow more time in practicing them, than I have done in penning them: yea, you must make it the work of your life.

Direction I. 'Get as clear a discovery as you can of the true cause of your doubts and troubles; for if you should mistake in the cause, it would much frustrate the most excellent means for the cure.' Sometimes the cause begins in the body, and thence proceedeth to the mind; sometimes it begins in the mind, and thence distempereth the body. Sometimes in the mind, it is most, or first from worldly crosses, and thence proceedeth to spiritual things. And of spiritual matters, sometimes it begins upon scruples or differences in religion, or points of doctrine; sometimes and most commonly, from the sense of our own infirmities; sometimes it is only from ordinary infirmities; sometimes from some extraordinary decays of inward grace; sometimes from the neglect of some weighty duty; and sometimes from the deep wounds of some heinous, secret, or scandalous sin; and sometimes it is merely from the fresh discovery of that which before we never did discern; and sometimes from the violent assault of extraordinary temptations. Which of these is your own case, you must be careful to find out, and to apply the means for cure accordingly. Even of true Christians, the same means will not fit all. The difference of natures, as well as of actual cases, must be considered. One hath need of that tender handling, which would undo another; and he again hath need of that rousing which another cannot bear.

Direct. II. 'Make as full a discovery as you can,

how much of the trouble of your mind doth arise from your melancholy and bodily distempers, and how much from discontenting afflictions in your worldly estate, or friends, or name, and according to your discovery make use of the remedy.'

For melancholy, I have by long experience found it to have so great and common a hand in the fears and troubles of mind, that I meet with not one of many, that live in great troubles and fears for any long time together; but melancholy is the main seat of them; though they feel nothing in their body, but all in their mind. Where this is the cause, usually the party is fearful of almost every thing; a word, or a sudden thought will disquiet them. Sometimes they are sad, and scarce know why : all comforts are of no continuance with them; but as soon as you have done comforting them, and they be never so well satisfied, yet the trouble returns in a few days or hours, as soon as the dark and troubled spirits return to their former force : they are still addicted to musing and solitariness, and thoughts will run in their minds, that they cannot lay them by : if it go anything far, they are almost always assaulted with temptations to blasphemy, to doubt whether there be a God, or a Christ, or the scriptures be true ; or whether there be a heaven or a hell ; and oft tempted to speak some blasphemous words against God ; and this with such importunity, that they can hardly forbear; and ofttimes they are tempted to make away themselves. Now to those that find that melancholy is the cause of their troubles, I would give this advice. Expect not that rational, spiritual remedies, should suffice for this cure : for you may as well expect that a good sermon, or comfortable words, should cure the falling sickness, or palsy, or a broken head, as to be a sufficient cure to your melancholy fears; for this is as real a bodily disease as the other. Do not therefore, lay the blame on your books, friends, counsels, instructions if these troubles be not cured by words: but labor to discern truly how much of your trouble comes this way, and then fix in your mind in all your inquiries, reading, and hearing, that it is the other part of your trouble which is truly rational, and not this part of it which is from melancholy, that these means were ordained to remove. Only constant importunate prayer is a fit and special means for the curing of all.

If you would have these fears and troubles removed, apply yourself to the proper cure of melancholy. Avoid all passion of sorow, fear, and anger, as much as you can; and all occasions, and discontents and grief. Avoid much solitariness, and be most commonly in some cheerful company. Not that I would have you do as the foolish sinners of the world do, to drink away melancholy, and keep company with sensual, vain, and unprofitable persons, that will draw you deeper into sin, and so make your wound greater instead of healing it, and multiply your troubles when forced to look back on your sinful loss of time. But keep company with the more cheerful sort of the godly. There is no mirth like the mirth of believers, which faith doth fetch from the blood of Christ, and from the promises of the word, and from experiences of mercy, and from the serious fore-apprehensions of our everlasting blessedness. Yet sometimes it may not be amiss to confer with some that are in your own case, that you may see that your condition is not singular. For melancholy people, in such distresses, are ready to think, that never any was in the case as they are in; or at least, never any

that were truly godly. When you hear people of
the most upright lives, and that truly fear God, to
have the same complaints as you have yourself, it
may give you some hopes that it is not so bad as
you before did imagine. However, be sure that
you avoid solitariness as much as you well can.
Also take heed of too deep, fixed, musing thoughts;
studying and serious meditating be not duties for
the deeply melancholy; you must let those alone
till you are better able to perform them, lest by
attempting those duties which you cannot perform,
you shall utterly disable yourself from all: therefore I would advise you by all means, to shake and
rouse yourself out of such musings, and suddenly
to turn your thoughts away to something else. To
this end, be sure that you avoid idleness and want
of employment; which as it is a life not pleasing
to God, so it is the opportunity for melancholy
thoughts to be working, and the chiefest season
for Satan to tempt you. Never let the devil find
you unemployed, but see that you go cheerfully
about the works of your calling, and follow it with
diligence; and that time which you redeem for
spiritual exercises, let it be most spent in thanksgiving, and praises, and heavenly conference.

The second part of this direction was, that you
take notice how much of your disquietness may
proceed from outward crosses; for it is ordinary
for these to lie at the root, and bring the heart into
disquiet and discontent, and then trouble for sin
doth follow after. Alas, how oft have I seen verified that of the apostle; 2 Cor, vii. 10. "The
sorrow of the world worketh death." How many,
even godly people have I known, that through
crosses in children, or in friends, or losses in
estates, or wrongs from men, or perplexities that

through some unadvisedness they were cast into, or the like, have fallen into mortal disease, or into such a fixed melancholy, that some of them have gone beside themselves; and others have lived in fears and doubting ever after, by the removal of the disquietness to their consciences? How sad a thing is it, that we should thus add to our own afflictions? And the heavier we judge the burden, the more we lay on! As if God had not done enough, or would not sufficiently afflict us. We may more comfortably bear that which God layeth on us, than that which we immediately lay upon ourselves! Crosses are not great or small, according to the bulk of the matter, but according chiefly to the mind of the sufferer. Or else, how could holy men "rejoice in tribulation, and be exceeding glad that they are accounted worthy to suffer for Christ?" Reproaches, wrongs, losses, are all without you; unless you open them the door willfully yourself, they cannot come into the heart. God hath not put the joy or grief of your heart in any other man's power, but in your own. It is you therefore that do yourselves the greatest mischief.

Direct. III. 'Be sure that you first lay sound apprehensions of God's nature in your understanding, and lay them deeply.'

This is the first article of your creed, and the first part of "life eternal, to know God!" His substance is quite past human understanding; therefore never make any attempt to reach to the knowledge of it, or to have any positive conceivings of it, for they will be all but idols, or false conceptions; but his attributes are manifested to our understandings. Well consider, that even under the law, when God proclaims to Moses his own name, and therein his nature, Exod. xxxiv, 6, 7, the first and greatest part is, " The Lord God, merciful and gracious, long-suffering, and abundant in goodness and truth, keeping mercy for thousands, forgiving iniquity, transgression, and sin." And he hath sworn, " That he hath no pleasure in the death of a sinner, but rather that he return and live."— Think not therefore of God's mercifulness, with diminishing, extenuating thoughts, nor limit it by the bounds of our frail understandings ; for the heavens are not so far above the earth, as his thoughts and ways are above ours. Still remember that you must have no low thoughts of God's goodness, but apprehend it as bearing proportion with his power. This will make God appear more amiable in your eyes, and then you will love him more readily and abundantly. If you think of God as one that is glad of all advantages against you, and delighteth in his creatures' misery, it is impossible you should love him. The love of yourselves is so deeply rooted in nature, that we cannot lay it by, nor love anything that is absolutely and directly against us. We conceive of the devil as an absolute enemy to God and man, and one that seeks our destruction, and therefore we cannot love him. And the great cause why troubled souls do love God no more, is because they represent him to themselves in an ugly, odious shape. To think of God as one that seeks and delighteth in man's ruin, is to make him as the devil. And then what wonder if instead of loving him, and delighting in him, you tremble at the thoughts of him, and fly from him. As I have observed children, when they have seen the devil painted on the wall, in an ugly shape, they have partly feared, and partly hated it. If you do so by God in your fancy, it is not putting the name of God on him when you have done, that will reconcile your affections to him as long as you strip him of his divine nature.

God hath given no command for duty, but what most perfectly agreeth with the nature of the object. He hath therefore bid us love God and delight in him above all, because he is above all in goodness; even infinitely and inconceivably good; else we could not love him above all, nor would he ever command us so to do. How gladly, and freely, and frequently do you think of your dearest friends. And if you did firmly conceive of God, as one that is ten thousand times more gracious, loving and amiable than any friend you have in the world, it would make you not only to love him above all friends, but also more freely, delightfully, and unweariedly to think of him. The fixed apprehension of God's goodness and merciful nature, would cause a fixed apprehension of the probability of your happiness, as long as you are willing to be happy in God's way. For reason will tell you, that he who is love itself, and whose goodness is equal to his almightiness, and who hath sworn, that he hath no pleasure in the death of a sinner, but rather that he repent and live, will not destroy a poor soul that lieth in submission at his feet, and is so far from resolved rebellion against him, that he grieveth that it is no better, and can please him no more.

These right apprehensions of God would overcome those terrors which are raised only by false apprehensions of him. And doubtless a very great part of men's causeless troubles, are raised from such misapprehensions of God. For Satan knows, that if he can bring you to think of God as a cruel tyrant and bloodthirsty man-hater, then he can drive you from him in terror, and turn all your love and cheerful obedience into hatred and slavish fear. I say therefore again, do not only get, but also fix deep in your understanding, the highest thoughts of God's natural goodness and graciousness that you possibly can raise. For when they are at the highest, they come short ten thousand fold.

Direct. IV. 'Be sure that you deeply apprehend the gracious nature, disposition, and office, of the Mediator Jesus Christ.'

Our thoughts of God are necessarily more strange, because of our infinite distance from the Godhead; and therefore our apprehensions of God's goodness will be the less working, because less familiar. But in Christ, God is come down into our nature, and so Infinite goodness and mercy is incarnate. The man Christ Jesus is able now to save to the utmost all that come to God by him. We have a merciful High-Priest that is acquainted with our infirmities. Herein we see the will of God putting forth itself for our help in the most astonishing way that could be imagined. Here is more than merely a gracious inclination. It is an office of saving and showing mercy also that Christ hath undertaken; even "to seek and to save that which was lost;" to bring home straying souls to God; to be the great Peacemaker between God and man, to reconcile God to man, and man to God; and so to be the Head and Husband of his people. Certainly the devil strangely wrongeth poor, troubled souls in this point, that he can bring them to have such hard, suspicious thoughts of Christ, and so much to overlook the glory of mercy which so shineth in the face of the Son of Mercy itself. How can we more contradict the nature of Christ, and the Gospel description of him, than to think him a destroying hater of his creatures, and one that watcheth for our halting, and hath more mind to hurt us than to help us? How could he have manifested more willingness to save, and more tender compassion to the souls of men, than he hath fully manifested? If twenty were ready to drown in the sea, and if one that were able to swim and fetch all out, should cast himself into the water, and offer them his help, were it not foolish ingratitude for any to say, 'I know not yet whether he be willing to help me or not;' and so to have jealous thoughts of his good-will, and so perish in refusing his help? How tenderly did Christ deal with all sorts of sinners. He professed that he "came not into the world to condemn the world, but that the world through him might be saved." "How oft would he have gathered them as a hen gathereth her chickens under her wings (mark, that he would have done this for them that he cast off) and they would not?" When his disciples would have had "fire come down from heaven to consume those that refused him," he reproves them, and tells them, "They knew not what spirit they were of." Yea, he prayeth for his crucifiers, and that on the cross, not forgetting them in the heat of his sufferings. Thus he doth by the wicked; but to those that follow him, his tenderness is unspeakable, as you would have said yourself, if you had but stood by and seen him washing his disciples' feet, and wiping them; or bidding Thomas put his finger into his side, " and be not faithless, but believing." Alas! that the Lord Jesus should come from heaven to earth, from glory into human flesh, and pass through a life of misery to a cross, and from the cross to the grave, to manifest openly to the world the abundance of his love, and the tenderness of his heart to sinners; and that after all this we should suspect him of cruelty, or hard-heartedness or unwillingness to show mercy; and that the devil can so far delude us as to make us think of the Lamb of God as if he were a tiger or devourer!

Direct. V. The next step in right order to comfort is this: 'You must believe and consider the full sufficiency of Christ's sacrifice and ransom for all.'

If Satan would persuade you either that no ransom or sacrifice was ever given for you, or that, therefore, you have no Redeemer to trust in, and no Saviour to believe in, and no sanctuary to fly to from the wrath of God, he must first prove you either to be no lost sinner, or to be a final, impenitent unbeliever; that is, that you are dead already; or else he must delude your understanding, to make you think that Christ died not for all; and then I confess he hath a sore advantage against your faith and comfort.

Direct. VI. The next thing in order to be done is this: 'Get clear apprehensions of the freeness, fullness, and universality of the new covenant or law of grace.'

I mean the promise of remission, justification, adoption, and salvation to all, so they will believe. No man on earth is excluded in the tenor of this covenant. And therefore certainly you are not excluded; and if not excluded, then you must needs be included. Show where you are excluded if you can! You will say, 'But for all this, all men are not justified and saved.' *Ans.* True, because they will not be persuaded to accept the mercy that is freely given them.

Direct. VII. 'You must get the right understanding of the difference between general grace and special. And between the possibility, probability, conditional certainty, and absolute certainty of your salvation. And so between the comfort on the former ground and on the latter.'

Do not begin the way to your spiritual peace by inquiring after the sincerity of your graces, and trying yourselves by signs. Let the first thing you do, be to obey the voice of the Gospel, which calleth you to accept of Christ and special mercy. "This is the record, that God hath given us eternal life, and this life is in his Son. He that hath the Son hath life." Fix this deep in your mind, that the nature of the Gospel is first to declare to our understandings the most gracious nature, undertakings, and performances of Christ for us, which must be believed to be true : and secondly to offer this Christ with all his special mercy to every man to whom this Gospel comes, and to entreat them to accept Christ and life, which is freely given and offered to them. Remember then you are a lost sinner. For certain Christ and life in him is given and offered to you. Now your first work is, presently to accept it; not to make an unseasonable inquiry, whether Christ be yours, but to take him that he may be yours. If you were condemned, and a pardon were freely given you, on condition you would thankfully take it, and it were offered to you, and you entreated to take it, what would you do in this case ? Would you spend your time and thoughts in searching whether this pardon be already yours ? Or would you not presently take it that it may be yours ? Or if you were ready to famish, and food were offered you, would you stand asking first, 'How shall I know that it is mine?' Or rather take and eat it, when you are sure it may be yours if you will. Remember, That your first work is to believe, or accept an offered Saviour. You must learn to receive the comforts of universal or general grace, before you search after the comforts of special grace. I here suppose you so far sound in the doctrine of the Gospel, as neither with some on one hand, to look so much at special grace, as to deny that general grace, which is the ground of it, or presupposed to it. Nor with others, so far to look at universal mercy, as to deny special.

Suppose you are yet graceless, is it nothing to you that it is a God of infinite mercy that you have to do with, whose compassions are ten thousand times greater than your dearest friends'? is it not an exceeding comfort, that there is one of such infinite compassion as the Lord Christ, who hath assumed our nature, and is come down to seek and save that which was lost; and is more tender-hearted to poor sinners than we can possibly conceive? Yea, who hath made it his office to heal, and relieve, and restore, and reconcile. Yea, that hath himself endured such temptations as many of ours; for we have not a High-priest which cannot be touched with the feelings of our infirmities; but was in all points tempted like as we are, without sin. "For that he himself hath suffered being tempted, he is able to succor them that are tempted."—Heb. ii, 14–18. Have you discountenance from men? Christ had much more. Doth God seem to forsake you? So he did by Christ. Are you fain to lie on your knees crying for mercy? Why Christ, in the days of his flesh was fain to offer up "strong cries and tears, to him that was able to save him. And was heard in that he feared." It seems that Christ had distressing fears as well as you, though not sinful fears. Have you horrid temptations? Why Christ was tempted to cast himself headlong, and to worship the devil, for worldly preferment; yea, the devil had power to carry his body up and down to the pinnacle of the temple, and the top of a mountain. If he had such power of you, would you not think yourself certainly his slave? Also, suppose that you are graceless, is it nothing that a sufficient sacrifice and ransom is given for you? This is the very foundation of all solid peace. Also, suppose you are graceless, is it nothing that God hath, under his hand and seal, made a full and free deed of gift to you and all sinners, of Christ, and with him of pardon and salvation! Almost all that I have hitherto said to you is comprised in that one text, John iii, 16: "God so loved the world, that he gave his only begotten Son, that whosoever believeth in him, should not perish, but have everlasting life." Though you were yet graceless, you have now this comfort, that your salvation is probable as well as possible. You are very fair for it. The terms are not hard in themselves, on which it is tendered. For Christ's yoke is easy, and his burden is light, and his commands are not grievous. Yea, this exceeding comfort there is, even for them that are graceless, that their salvation is conditionally certain, and the condition is but their own willingness. They may all have Christ and life if they will. Now I desire you in all your doubts, that you will well consider and improve this one truth and ground of comfort. Would you, in the midst of your groans and complaints and fears, take it for a small mercy, to be certain that you shall have Christ if you will? Would it not revive you and overcome your fears?

Direct. VIII. The next thing that you have to do, for building up a stable comfort, and settling your conscience in a solid peace, is this, 'Be sure to get and keep a right understanding of the nature of saving faith.'

The Scripture is so full and plain in assuring pardon and salvation to all true believers, that if you can be sure you are a believer, you need not make any doubt of your interest in Christ, and your salvation. Seeing therefore that all the question will be, Whether you have true faith? Whether you do perform the condition of the new covenant? (for all other doubts God hath given you sufficient ground to resolve, as is said,) how much then doth it concern you to have a right understanding of the nature of this faith. It is first, a believing that the Gospel is true; and then an accepting of Christ therein offered to us, with his benefits; or a consenting that he be ours, and we be his; which is nothing but a true willingness to have an offered Christ. Remember this well, that you may make use of it, when you are in doubt of the truth of your faith. Thousands of poor souls have been in the dark, and unable to see themselves to be believers, merely for want of knowing what saving faith is. It is the understanding's belief of the truth of the Gospel, and the will's acceptance of Christ and life offered to us therein; which acceptance is but the hearty consent or willingness that he be yours, and you his. This is the faith which must justify and save you.

Wicked men are willing to have remission, justification, and freedom from hell, (for no man can be willing to be unpardoned, or to be damned;) but they are not willing to have Christ himself in that nature and office which he must be accepted; that is, as an holy head and husband to save both from the guilt and power, and all defilement and abode of sin, and to rule them by his law, and guide them by his Spirit, and to make them happy by bringing them to God, that being without sin, they may be perfectly pleasing and amiable in his sight, and enjoy him forever. Thus is Christ offered, and thus to be accepted of all that will be saved, and thus no wicked man will accept him, (but when he ceaseth to be wicked). To cut all the rest short in a word, I say, that in this foredescribed willingness or acceptance, repentance, love, thankfulness, resolution to obey, are all contained, or nearly implied, so that the heart of saving faith is this acceptance of Christ, or willingness to have him to justify, sanctify, guide, and govern you. Find but this willingness, and you find all the rest, whether you expressly see them or not. So much for that direction.

Direct. IX. Having thus far proceeded in discovering and improving the general grounds of comfort, and then in discovering the nature of faith, which gives you right to the special mercies of the covenant following it; your next work must be 'To perform this condition by actual believing.'

Your soul stands in extreme need of a Saviour. God offereth you a Saviour in the Gospel. What then have you next to do but to accept him?

When God, in the Gospel, bids you take Jesus Christ, and beseecheth you to be reconciled to him, what will you say to him? If your heart answer, 'Lord, I am willing, I will accept of Christ and be thankful,' why then the match is made between Christ and you, and the marriage-covenant is truly entered, which none can dissolve. If Christ were not first willing, he would not be the suitor and make the motion; and if he be willing, and you be willing, what can break the match? And here I would not leave you at that loss as some do, as if there were nothing for you to do for the getting of faith; for certainly God hath prescribed you means for that end, "Faith cometh by hearing, and hearing by the word of God preached." Rom. x, 17. Therefore see that you wait diligently on this ordinance of God. Read the Scriptures daily, and search them to see whether you may not there find that holiness is better than sin. And however some seducers may tell you, that wicked men ought not to pray, yet be sure that you lie on your knees before God, and importunately beg that he would open your eyes, and change your heart, and show you so far the evil of sin, and the want and worth of Christ and holiness, that you may be unfeignedly glad to accept his offer.

Let such also see that they avoid wicked, seducing company, and occasions of sin; and be sure that they keep company with men fearing God, especially joining with them in their holy duties. Let such be sure that they use that reason which God hath given them, to consider frequently, retiredly, seriously, of the vanity of all those things that steal away their hearts from Christ; and of the excellency of holiness, and how blessed a hope it is to have nothing in us of heart or life that is displeasing to God, but to be such as he taketh full delight in; and of the certainty and inconceivable greatness of believers' everlasting happiness.

Direct. X. When you have gone thus far, your soul is safe, and you are past your greatest dangers, though yet you are not past your fears; your next work therefore for peace and comfort is this; 'To review and take notice of your own faith and thence to gather assurance of the certainty of your justification, and adoption, and right to glory.'

See that you do not content yourself with the forementioned general comforts, without looking after assurance and special comforts. See that you dream not of finding assurance and special comfort from mere general grounds. For men to conclude that they shall certainly be saved, merely because God is merciful, or Christ is tender-hearted to sinners, and would not that any should perish, but all should come to repentance; or because God delights not in the death of him that dieth, but rather that he repent and live; or because Christ died for them; or because God hath given Christ and life in the Gospel to all, on condition of believing; these are all but mere delusions. It is the Spirit dwelling in us that is the witness or proof that we are God's sons; for he that hath not his Spirit is none of his. And the Spirit is not discerned by us in its essence, but in its workings; and therefore to discern these workings, is to discern the Spirit, and these workings are marks that we speak of: so that the Spirit witnesseth our sonship, as a reasonable soul witnesseth that you are a man and not a beast. You find by the acts of reason, that you have a reasonable soul, and then you know, that having a reasonable soul, you certainly are a man. So you find by the works or fruits of the Spirit, that you have the Spirit (that is, by marks; and Paul enumerates the fruits of the Spirit to that end,) and then by finding that you have the Spirit you may certainly know that you are the child of God. Or (to speak more plainly,) the spirit witnesses first and principally, by giving us those graces and workings which are our marks; and then, secondly by helping us to find and feel those workings or marks in ourselves; and then, lastly, by raising comforts in the soul upon that discovery.

Direct. XI. In the trial of your state, 'Be sure that you make use of infallible signs of sincerity, and take not those for certain which are not.'

Are you heartily willing to take God for your portion? And had you rather live with him in glory in his favor and fullest love, with a soul perfectly cleansed from all sin, and never more to offend him, rejoicing with his saints in his everlasting praises, than to enjoy the delights of the flesh on earth, in a way of sin and without the favor of God? Are you heartily willing to take Jesus Christ as he is offered in the Gospel; that is, to be your only Saviour, and Lord, to give you pardon by his bloodshed, and to sanctify you by his word and Spirit, and to govern you by his laws?

You must know that his laws reach both to heart and outward actions. That they command a holy, spiritual, heavenly life. That they command things so cross and unpleasing to the flesh, that the flesh will be still murmuring and starving against obedience. Particularly, they command things quite cross to the inclinations of the flesh; as to forgive wrongs, to love enemies, to forbear malice and revenge, to restrain and mortify lust and passion, to abhor and mortify pride, and be low in our own eyes, and humble and meek in spirit. They command things that cross the interest of the flesh and its inclination both together; I mean, which will deprive it of its enjoyments, and bring it to some suffering? As to perform duties even when they lay us open to disgrace and shame, and reproach in the world; and to deny our credit, rather than forsake Christ or our duty. To obey Christ in doing what he commandeth us, though it would hazard or certainly lose our wealth, friends, liberty and life itself; forsaking all rather than to forsake him; to give to the poor, and other good uses, and that liberally, according to our abilities. To deny the flesh all forbidden pleasures, and make not provisions to satisfy its lusts, but to crucify the flesh, with the affections and lusts thereof; and in this combat to hold on to the end, and to overcome. These are the laws of Christ, which you must know, before you can determine whether you are indeed unfeignedly willing to obey them. Put therefore these further questions to yourself, for the trial of your willingness to be ruled by Christ according to his laws.

Are you heartily willing to live in the performance of those holy and spiritual duties of heart and life, which God hath absolutely commanded you? and are you heartily sorry that you perform them no better? with no more cheerfulness, delight, success, and constancy?

Are you so thoroughly convinced of the worth of everlasting happiness, and the intolerableness of everlasting misery, and the truth of both; and of the sovereignty of God the Father, and Christ the Redeemer, and your many engagements to him; and of the necessity and good of obeying, and the evil of sinning, that you are truly willing, that is, have a settled resolution to cleave to Christ, and obey him in the dearest, most disgraceful, painful, hazardous, flesh-displeasing duties; even though it should cost you the loss of all your worldly enjoyments, and your life? Doth this willingness or resolution already so far prevail in your heart and life, against all the interest and temptations of the world, the devil, and your flesh, that you do ordinarily practice the most strict and holy, the most self-denying, costly, and hazardous duties that you know God requireth of you, and do heartily strive against all known sin, and overcome all gross sins and when you fall under any prevailing temptation, do rise again by repentance, and begging pardon of God, through the blood of Christ, do resolve to watch and resist more carefully for the time to come? In these five marks is expressed the Gospel-description of a true Christian.

Among all duties, I think the soul is naturally most backward to these following: To secret prayer, because it is spiritual, and requires great reverence, and hath nothing of external pomp or form to take us up with, and consisteth not much in the exercise of common gifts, but in the exercise of special grace, and the breathings of the Spirit, and searchings, pantings, and strivings of a gracious soul toward God. To serious meditation also is the soul very backward; also to the duty of faithful dealing with each other's souls, in secret reproof and exhortation, plainly (though lovingly) to tell each other of our sins and danger, to this the heart is usually very backward; partly through a sinful bashfulness, partly for want of more believing, lively apprehensions of our duty, and our brother's danger, and partly because we are loth to displease men and lose their favor, it being grown so common for men to fall out with those (if not hate them) that deal plainly and faithfully with them. Also to take reproof, as well as to give it, the heart is very backward. Even godly men, through the sad remainders of their sinfulness, do too commonly frown, and snarl, and retort our reproofs, and study presently how to excuse themselves, and put it by, or how to charge us with something that may stop our mouths, and make the reprover seem as bad as themselves. Though they dare not tread our reproofs under feet, and turn again, and all to rend us, yet they oft show the remnants of a dogged nature, though when they review their ways it costs them sorrow. We must sugar and butter our words, and make them liker to stroking than striking, liker an approving than a reproving them, liker a flattery than faithful dealing, and yet when we have all done, they go down very hardly, and that but half way, even with many godly people when they are under a temptation. The like may be said of all those duties which do pinch upon our credit or profit, or tend to disgrace us, or impoverish us in the world; as the confessing of a disgraceful fault; the free giving to the poor or sacred uses, according to our estates; the parting with our own right or gain for peace; the patient suffering of wrong, and forgiving it heartily, and loving bitter, abusive enemies, especially the running upon the stream of men's displeasure, and incurring the danger of being utterly undone in our worldly state (especially if men be rich, who do therefore as hardly get to heaven as a camel through a needle's eye): and above all, the laying down of our lives for Christ. It cannot be expected, that godly men should perform all these with perfect willingness; the flesh will play its part, in pleading its own cause, and will strive hard to maintain its own interests. O the shifts, the subtle arguments, or at least the clamorous and importunate contradictions that all these duties will meet with in the best, so far as they are renewed, and their graces weak! So that you may well hence conclude that you are a sinner, but you may not conclude that you are graceless, because of a backwardness and some unwillingness to duty.

Observe further, that I add your actual performance of duty; because true hearty willingness will show itself in actions and endeavors. It is but dissembling, if I should say I am willing to perform the strictest, holiest duties, and yet do not perform them; to say I am willing to pray, and pray not; or to give to the poor, and yet give not; or to perform the most self-denying costly duties, and yet when it should come to the practice, I will not be persuaded or drawn to them; I will not confess a disgraceful sin, nor further a good cause to my danger, cost or trouble; nor reprove, nor submit to reproof, nor turn from the way of temptations or the like. Action must discover true willingness. The son that said to his father, "I go, sir," but went not to labor in the vineyard, was not accepted or justified. If therefore you are in doubt whether your willingness be sincere, inquire into your practice, and performance. God commandeth you to pray, to instruct your family, to be merciful to the poor, to forgive those that wrong you, etc. The flesh and the devil persuade you from these. Do you perform them, or do you not? Though you may do it with backwardness and dullness, and weakness, yet do you do it? And desire you could do it better, and lament your misdoing it? And endeavor to do it better than you have formerly done? This shows then that the Spirit prevaileth, though the flesh do contradict it.

If your resolution at present be hearty, you ought not to vex and disquiet your mind, with doubtful tormenting fears what you should do, if you be put to it to forsake all, and suffer death for Christ, for he hath promised to lay no more on us than we can bear, but with the temptation will make us a way to come forth. Much less is it lawful for men to feign and suppose such calamities to themselves, as God doth never try men by, and then to ask themselves, 'Can I bear these for Christ?' And so to try themselves on false and dangerous grounds. Some use to be troubled, lest if they were put to long and exquisite torments for Christ, they should renounce him. One saith, 'I cannot endure the torments of hell for Christ;' another saith, 'Could I endure to be roasted or torn in pieces so many weeks or days together?' Or, 'Could I endure to die so many times over?' These are foolish, sinful questions, which Christ never desired you to put to yourselves. He never tries men's faith in this manner. Tormentors cannot go beyond his will Nay, it is but very few he tries by death, and fewer by an extreme, tormenting death.

Are you not unfeignedly willing to have Christ on the terms that he is offered? Are you not willing to be more holy? And beg of him to make you so? Would you not be glad if your soul were more perfectly sanctified, and rid of that body of sin, though it were to the smart and displeasing of your flesh? Are you not willing to wait on God, in the use of his ordinances, in that poor weak measure as you are able to perform them? Durst you, or would you quit your part in God, heaven, Christ, and forsake the way of holiness, and do as the profane world doth, though it were to please your flesh, or save your state or life? Do you not daily strive against the flesh, and keep it under, and deny its desires? Do you not deny the world when it would hinder you from works of mercy, or public good, according to your ability? Is it not the grief of your soul when you fall, and your greatest trouble that you cannot walk more obediently, innocently and fruitfully? And do you not after sinning resolve to be more watchful for the time to come? Are you not resolved to stick to Christ and his holy laws and ways, whatever changes or dangers come, and rather to forsake friends and all that you have, than to forsake him? Yet in a godly jealousy and distrust of your own heart, do renounce your own strength, and resolve to do this only in the strength of Christ, and therefore daily beg it of him? Is it not your daily care and business to please God and do his will, and avoid sinning in your weak measure? I hope that all this is so, and your own case; which, if it be, you have infallible evidences, and want but the sight and comfort of them; you have the true grounds for assurance, though you want assurance itself; your chief danger is over, though your trouble remain.

Direct. XII. The next rule for your direction for the right settling of your peace is this. 'You must know, that assurance of justification, adoption and right of salvation cannot be gathered from the smallest degree of saving grace.'

Understand, that I speak of God's ordinary working by means, not denying but God may, by a voice from heaven, or an angel, or other supernatural revelation, bestow assurance on whom he pleaseth. By the smallest degree of grace, I mean of faith, love, obedience, and those saving graces whose acts are the condition of our salvation. This much I can tell, that the least degree of grace that is saving, doth determine the soul for God and Christ, against the world and flesh that stand as competitors, and so where Christ's interest prevaileth in the least measure, there is the least measure of saving grace. As when you are weighing two things in the balance, and at last make it so near even weight, that one end is turned, and no more. so when you are considering, whether to be for Christ, or for the flesh and the world, and your will is but even a very little determined to Christ, and preferreth him; this is the least measure of saving grace. But then how a poor soul should discern this prevalent choice and determination of itself is all the question. For there is nothing more easy and common than for men to think verily, that they prefer Christ above the creature, as long as no temptation doth assault them, nor sensual objects stand up in any considerable strength to entice them. Nay, wicked men do truly, ofttimes, purpose to obey Christ before the flesh, and to take him for their Lord, merely in the general, when they do not know or consider the quality of his laws; that they are so strict and spiritual, and contrary to the flesh, and hazardous to their worldly hopes and seeming happiness. But when it comes to particulars, and God saith, Now deny thyself, and thy friend, and thy goods, and thy life for my sake; alas, it was never his resolution to do it; nor will he be persuaded to it. So that it is evident that it is no true, saving resolution or willingness, which prevaileth not for actual obedience. Now here comes in the unresolvable doubt, What is the least measure of obedience, that will prove a man truly willing and resolved, or to have truly accepted of Christ for his Lord? This obedience lieth in performing what is commanded, and avoiding what is forbidden. Now it is too certain, that every true believer is guilty of a frequent neglect of duty, yea, of known duty. We know we should love God more abundantly, and delight in him, and meditate more on him, and pray more oft and earnestly than we do, and instruct our families more diligently and speak against sin more boldly, and admonish our neighbors more faithfully, with many the like. Nay, many a true Christian, in time of temptation, hath been drawn to omit secret prayer or family duties, almost wholly for a certain space of time; yea, and perhaps to be so corrupted in his judgment for a time as to think he doth well in it, as also in forbearing praising God by psalms, receiving the sacraments, and communicating with the Church, hearing the word publicly, etc., and perhaps may not only omit relieving the poor for a time, but excuse it. Now what man can punctually determine just how often a true Christian may be guilty of any such omission? and just how long he may continue it? and what the duties be which he may possibly so omit, and what not? So also in sins of commission. Alas, what sins did Noah, Lot, David, Solomon, Asa, Peter, etc. commit!

Direct. XIII. From the last mentioned observation, there is one plain consectary arising, which I think you may do well to note by the way, viz: ' That according to God's ordinary way of giving grace, it cannot be expected that Christians should be able to know the very time of their first receiving or acting true saving grace, or just when they were pardoned, justified, adopted, and put into a state of salvation.'

Christ likeneth God's kingdom of grace to a grain of mustard-seed, which is at the first, the least of all seeds, but after cometh to a tree: and to a little leaven, which leaveneth the whole lump. The scripture oft calleth such young beginners, babes, children, novices, etc. We are all commanded to grow in grace; which implieth, that we have our smallest measure at the first. Heb. v, 12, showeth that strength of grace should be according to time and means. Common experience is an invincible argument for this. Men are at a distance from Christ, when he first calleth them to come to him; and many steps they have toward him before they reach to him. I here speak only of God's ordinary way of giving grace; for I doubt not but in some, God may give a higher degree of grace at the first day of conversion, than some others do attain in many years.

But this is not the ordinary course. Ordinarily convictions lie long on the soul before they come to a true conversion. Conscience is wounded, and smarting long, and long grudging against our sinful and negligent courses, and telling us of the necessity of Christ and a holy life, before we sincerely obey conscience, and give ourselves up to Christ. We seldom yield to the first conviction or persuasion. The flesh hath usually too long time given it to plead its own cause, and to say to the soul, 'Wilt thou forsake all thy pleasure and merry company, and courses? Wilt thou beggar thyself? or make thyself a scorn or mocking-stock to the world? Art thou ever able to hold out in so strict a course? and to be undone? and to forsake all, and lay down thy life for Christ? Is it not better to venture thyself in the same way as thou hast gone in, as well as others do, and as so many of thy forefathers have done before thee?' Under such sinful deliberations as these we usually continue long before we fully resolve; and many demurs and delays we make before we conclude to take Christ on the terms that he is offered to us. Now I make no doubt but most or many christians can remember how and when God stirred their consciences, and wakened them from their security, and made them look about them, and roused them out of their natural lethargy. Some can tell what sermon first did it; others can remember by what degrees and steps God was doing it long. The ordinary way appointed by God for the doing of it first, is the instruction of parents. And if this be God's first great means, then doubtless he will ordinarily bless his own means here, as well as in the preaching of the word.

From all this I would have you learn this lesson, That you ought not trouble yourself with fears and doubts, lest you are not truly regenerate, because you know not the sermon or the very time and manner of your conversion; but find that you have grace, and then, though you know not just the time or manner of your receiving it, yet you may nevertheless be assured of salvation by it. Search therefore what you are, and how your will is disposed, and resolved, and how your life is ordered, rather than to know how you became such.

Direct. XIV. Yet further I would have you to understand this: 'That as the least measure of saving grace is ordinarily undiscernible from the greatest measure of common grace, (notwithstanding the greatness of the change that it makes) so a measure somewhat greater is so hardly discernible, that it seldom brings assurance: and therefore it is only the stronger Christians that attain assurance ordinarily; even those who have a great degree of faith and love, and keep them much in exercise, and are very watchful and careful in obedience: and consequently (most Christians being of the weaker sort) it is but few that do attain to assurance of their justification and salvation.'

Here are two or three points which I would have

you distinctly to observe, 1. That it is only a greater measure of grace that will ordinarily afford assurance. 2. That therefore it is only the stronger, and holier, and more obedient sort of Christians that usually reach to a certainty of salvation. 3. That few Christians do reach to a strong or high degree of grace. 4. And therefore it is but few Christians that reach to assurance.

He that will attain to a certainty of salvation, must have a large measure of grace to be discerned. He must have that grace much in action, and lively action; for it is not mere habits that are discernible. He must have a clear understanding to be acquainted with the nature of spiritual things; to know what is a sound evidence, and how to follow the search, and how to repel particular temptations. He must have a good acquaintance and familiarity with his own heart, and to that end must be much at home, and be used sometimes to a diligent observation of his heart and ways. He must be in a good measure acquainted with, and a conqueror of contradicting temptations. He must have some competent cure of the deceitfulness of the heart, and it must be brought to an open, plain, ingenuous frame, willing to know the worst of itself. He must have some cure of that ordinary confusion and tumultuous disorder that is in the thought and affections of men, and get things into an order in his mind. He must be a man of diligence, resolution, and unwearied patience, that will resolvedly set on the work of self-examination, and painfully watch in it, and constantly follow it from time to time till he attain a certainty. He must be one that is very fearful of sinning, and careful in close obedient walking with God, and much in sincere and spiritual duty, that he keep not conscience still in accusing and condemning him, and God still offended with him, and his wounds fresh bleeding, and his soul still smarting. He must be a man of much fixedness and constancy of mind, and not of the ordinary mutability of mankind; that so he may not by remitting his zeal and diligence, lose the sight of his evidences, nor by leaving open his soul to an alteration by every new intruding thought and temptation, let go his assurance as soon as he attaineth it.

And then do I need to say any more to the confirmation of the third point, That few Christians reach this measure of grace? Oh! that it were not as clear as the light, and as discernible as the earth under our feet, that most true Christians are weaklings, and of the lower forms in the school of Christ? Alas, how ignorant are most of the best, how little love, or faith, or zeal, or heavenly-mindedness, or delight in God have they? How unacquainted with the way of self-examination? And how backward to it? And how dull and careless in it? Doing it by the halves, as Laban searched Rachel's tent? How easily put off with an excuse? How little acquainted with their own hearts? Or with satan's temptations and ways of deceiving? How much deceitfulness remaineth in their hearts? How confused are their minds? And what distractions and tumults are there in their thoughts? How bold are they in sinning? And how little tenderness of conscience, and care of obeying have they? How frequently do they wound conscience, provoke God, and obscure their evidences? And how mutable their apprehensions? And how soon do they lose that assurance which they once attained? And upon every occasion quite lose the sight of their evidences? Yea, and remit their actual resolutions, and so lose much of the evidence itself? Is not this the common case of godly people? Oh! that we could truly deny it. Let their lives be witness, let the visible neglects, worldliness, pride, impatiency of plain reproof, remissness of zeal, dullness and customariness in duty, strangeness to God, unwillingness to secret prayer and meditation, unacquaintedness with the Spirit's operations and joys, their unpeaceableness one with another, and their too frequent blemishing the glory of their holy profession by the unevenness of their walking, let all these witness, whether the school of Christ have not most children in it: and how few of those are fit to begin here the works of their priestly office, which they must live in forever, in the high and joyful praises of God, and of the Lamb, who hath redeemed them by his blood, and made them kings and priests to God, that they may reign with him forever. I am content to stand the judgment of all humble, self-knowing Christians, whether this be not true of most of themselves; and for those that deny it, I will stand to the judgment of their godly neighbors, who perhaps know them better than they know themselves.

And then this being all so, the fourth is undeniable, That it is but very few Christians that reach to assurance of salvation. The constant experience of the greatest part of believers tells us that certainty of salvation is very rare. Even of those that live comfortably and in peace of conscience, yet very few of them do attain to a certainty. For my part, it is known that God in undeserved mercy hath given me long the society of a great number of godly people, and great interest in them, and privacy with them, and opportunity to know their minds, and this in many places (my station by providence having been oft removed); and I must needs profess, that of all these I have met with few, yea very few indeed, that if I seriously and privately asked them, 'Are you certain that you are a true believer, and so are justified, and shall be saved,' durst say to me, 'I am certain of it.'

Now what is the use that I would have you make of this? Why it is this. If assurance of sincerity and justification (much more of salvation) be so rare among true Christians, then you have no cause to think that the want of it proveth you to be no Christian. You see then that you need not be always in disquiet when you want assurance. For else how disquiet a life should most Christians live!

Direct. XV. Yea thus much more I would here inform you of, 'That many holy, watchful and obedient Christians are yet uncertain of their salvation, even then when they are certain of their justification and sanctification; and that because they are uncertain of their perseverance and overcoming; for a man's certainty of his salvation can be no stronger than is his certainty of enduring to the end and overcoming.'

If a man have the fullest certainty in the world that he is God's child, yet if he be uncertain whether he shall so continue to the end, it is impossible that he should have a certainty of his salvation, for it is he only that endureth to the end that shall be saved.

Now that many eminent Christians of great knowledge, and much zeal and obedience, are uncertain of their perseverance is proved by two infallible arguments. 1. By experience: if any should be so censorious as to think that none of all those nations and churches abroad, that deny the doctrine of certain perseverance of all believers have any strong Christians among them, yet we have had the knowledge of such at home. 2. Beside the difficulty of the subject is a clear argument that a strong Christian may be uncertain of it. God hath made all those points plain in Scripture, which must be believed as of necessity to salvation; but the certainty of all believers' perseverance, is not a point of flat necessity to salvation to be believed. Otherwise it would be a hard matter to prove that any considerable number were ever saved till of late; or are yet saved, but in a very few countries. It is a point that the churches never did put into their creed, where they summed up those points that they held necessary to salvation. There are a great number of texts of Scripture, which seeming to intimate the contrary, do make the point of great difficulty to many of the wisest; and those texts that are for it, are not so express as fully to satisfy them.

Direct. XVI. The next thing which I would have you learn is this, 'That there are several grounds of the great probability of our salvation, beside the general grounds mentioned in the beginning: and by the knowledge of these, without any further assurance, a Christian may live in much peace and comfort, and in delightful, desirous thoughts of the glory to come. And therefore the next work which you have to do, is to discover those probabilities of your sincerity and your salvation, and then to receive the peace and comfort which they may afford you, before you can expect assurance in itself.'

Some kind of probability you may gather by comparing yourself with others. Though this way be but delusory to unregenerate men, whose confidence is plainly contradicted by the Scriptures, yet may it be lawful and useful to a humble soul that is willing to obey and wait on God: I mean to consider, that if such as you should perish how few people would God have in the world? Consider first in how narrow a compass the church was confined before Christ's coming in the flesh; how carnal and corrupt even that visible church then was; and even at this day the most learned do compute, that if you divide the world into thirty parts, nineteen of them are heathenish idolaters, six of them are Mahometans, and only five of them are Christians. And of these five that are Christians, how great a part are of the Ethiopian, Greek and Popish churches? So ignorant, rude, and superstitious, and erroneous that salvation cannot be imagined to be near so easy or ordinary with them as with us: and of the reformed churches, commonly called Protestants, how small is the number? And even among these, what a number are grossly ignorant and profane? And of those that profess more knowledge and zeal, how many are grossly erroneous, schismatical and scandalous? How exceeding small a number is left, then, that are such as you? I know this is no assuring argument, but I know withal, that Christ died not in vain, but he will see the fruit of his sufferings to the satisfaction of his soul; and the God of mercy, who is a lover of mankind, will have a multitude innumerable of his saved ones in the earth.

But your strongest probabilities are from the consideration of the work of God upon your souls, and the present frame and inclination of your soul to God. You dare not give up your hopes of heaven for all the world. You would not part with Christ, and say, 'Let him go,' for all the pleasures of sin, or treasures of the earth. If you had, (as you have) an offer of God, Christ, grace, and glory on one side, and worldly prosperity in sin on the other side, you would choose God, and let go the other. You dare not, you would not give over praying, hearing, reading, and Christian company, and give up yourself to worldly, fleshly pleasures; yet you are not assured of salvation, because you find not that delight and life in duty, and that witness of the Spirit, and that communion with God, nor that tenderness of heart as you desire. It is well that you desire them; but though you be not certain of salvation, do you not see a great likelihood, a probability, in all this? Is not your heart raised to a hope, that yet God is merciful to you, and means you good?

The second thing that I am to show you, is, that there may much spiritual comfort and peace of conscience be enjoyed without any certainty of salvation. Your horse or dog know not how you will use them certainly; yet will they lovingly follow you, and put their heads to your hand, and trust you with their lives without fear, and love to be in your company, because they have found you kind to them, and have tried that you do them no hurt, but good: yea, though you do strike them sometimes, yet they find that they have their food from you, and your favor doth sustain them. Yea, your little children have no certainty how you will use them, and yet finding that you have always used them kindly, and expressed love to them, though you whip them sometimes, yet are glad of your company, and desire to be in your lap, and can trust themselves in your hands, without tormenting themselves with such doubts as these, ' I am uncertain how my mother will use me, whether she will wound me, or kill me, or turn me out of doors, and let me perish.' Nature persuades us not to be too distrustful of those that have always befriended us, and especially whose nature is merciful and compassionate; nor to be too suspicious of evil from them that have always done us good. Every man knows that the good will do good, and the evil will do you evil; and accordingly we expect that they should do to us. Naturally, we all fear a toad, a serpent, an adder, a mad dog, a wicked man, a madman, a cruel, blood-thirsty tyrant, and the devil. But no one fears a dove, a lamb, a good man, a merciful, compassionate governor, except only the rebels or notorious offenders, that know he is bound in justice to destroy or punish them. And none should fear distrustfully the wrath of a gracious God, but they who will not submit to his mercy, and will not have Christ to reign over them, and therefore may know that he is bound in justice, if they come not in, to destroy them. But for you that would be obedient and reformed, and are troubled that you are no better, and beg of God to make you better, and have no sin but what you would be glad to be rid of, may not you, at least, see a strong probability that it shall go well with you? Oh! make use therefore of this probability; and if you have but hopes that God will do you good, rejoice in those hopes till you can come to rejoice in assurance.

Direct. XVII. My next advice to you is this, 'For the strengthening your apprehensions of the probability of your salvation, gather up, and improve all your choicest experiences of God's will and mercy to you; and observe also the experiments of others in the same kind.'

We do God and ourselves a great deal of wrong

by forgetting, neglecting, and not improving our experiences. I would this truth were well learned by believers. You are in sickness, and troubles, and dangers, and pinching straits, in fears and anguish of mind: in this case you cry to God for help, and he doth in such a manner deliver you as silenceth your distrust, and convinceth you of his love; at least, of his readiness to do you good. What a wrong is it now to God and yourself, to forget this presently, and in the next temptation to receive no strengthening by the consideration of it. Hath it not been thus oft with you? Have not mercies come so seasonably, so unexpectedly, either by small means, or the means themselves unexpectedly raised up; without your designing or effecting; and plainly in answer to prayers, that they have brought conviction along with them; and you have seen the name of God engraven on them?

And you may make great use also of the experiences of others. Is it not a great satisfaction to hear twenty, or forty, or a hundred Christians, of the most godly lives, to make the very same complaints as you do yourself? The very same complaints have I heard from as many. By this you may see your case is not singular, but the ordinary case of the tenderest consciences, and of many that walk uprightly with God. And also is it not a great he.p to you to hear other Christians tell how they have come into those troubles, and how they have got out of them? What hurt them? And what helped them? And how God dealt with them, while they lay under them? 'How desirous are diseased persons to talk with others that have had the same disease? And to hear them tell how it took them, and how it held them, and especially what cured them? Beside, it will give you much stronger hopes of cure and recovery to peace of conscience, when you hear of so many that have been cured of the same disease. Moreover, is it not a reviving thing, to hear Christians open the goodness of the Lord? And that in particular, as upon experience they have found him to their own souls? To hear them tell you of such notable discoveries of God's special providence and care of his people, as may repel all temptations to atheism and unbelief? To hear them give you their frequent and full experiences of God's hearing, and answering their prayers, and helping them in their distresses?

For my own part, I do soberly and seriously profess to you, that the experiences I have had of God's special providences, and fatherly care, and especially of his hearing prayers, have been so strange and great, and exceeding numerous, that they have done very much to the quieting of my spirit, and the persuading of my soul of God's love to me, and the silencing and shaming of my unbelieving heart, and especially for the conquering of all temptations that lead to atheism or infidelity, to the denying of special providence, or of the verity of the gospel, or of the necessity of holy prayer and worshiping of God. I often pity the poor seduced infidels of this age, that deny Scripture and Christ himself, and doubt of the usefulness of prayer and holy worship; and I wish that they had but the experiences that I have had. Truly I have once or twice had motions in my mind to have publicly and freely communicated my experiences in a relation of the more observable passages of my life; but I found that I was not able to do it to God's praise, as was meet, without a show of ostentation or vanity, and therefore I forbore.

Direct. XVIII. Next, that you may yet further understand the true nature of assurance, faith, doubting and desperation, I would have you observe this, 'That God doth not command every man, nor properly any man, ordinarily, by his word, to believe that his sins are forgiven, and himself is justified, adopted, and shall be saved. But he hath prescribed a way by which they may attain to assurance of these, in which way it is men's duty to seek it.'

Indeed all men are bound to apply Christ and the promise to themselves. But that application consisteth in a belief that this promise is true, as belonging to all, and so to me, and then in acceptance of Christ and his benefits as an offered gift; and after this, in trusting on him for the full performance of this promise. Hence, therefore, you may best see what unbelief and desperation are, and how far men may charge themselves with them. When you doubt whether the promise be true, or when you refuse to accept Christ and his benefits offered in it, and consequently to trust him as one that is able and willing to save you, if you do assent to his truth, and accept him, this is unbelief. But if you do believe the truth of the Gospel, and are heartily willing to accept Christ as offered in it, and only doubt whether your belief and acceptance of him be sincere, and so whether you shall be saved; this is not unbelief, but ignorance of your own sincerity and its consequents. If a friend do promise to give you a hundred pounds, on condition that you thankfully accept it; if you now do believe him, and do thankfully accept it; but yet through some vain scruple shall think, my thankfulness is so small, that it is not sincere, and therefore I doubt I do not perform his condition, and so shall never have the gift; in this case now you do believe your friend, and you do not distrust him properly; but you distrust yourself that you perform the condition; and this hindereth the exercise of that confidence in your friend which is habitually and virtually in you.

Now if you begin to distrust whether God will make good his promise or no, either thinking that it is not true, or he is not able, or hath changed his mind since the making of it, and on these grounds you let go your hopes, this is despair. If because that Christ seems to delay his coming, we should say, I have waited in hope till now, but now I am out of hope that ever Christ will come to judge the world, and glorify believers, I will expect it no longer; this is despair. If you do continue to believe the truth of the Gospel, and particularly of Christ's coming and glorifying his saints, and yet you think he will not glorify you, because you think that you are not a true believer or saint; this is not desperation in the proper sense. In the forementioned example, if your friend promise to give you a hundred pounds on condition of your thankful acceptance, and promiseth to come at such an hour and bring it you: if now you stay till the hour be almost come, and then say, 'I am out of hope of his coming now; he hath broken his word;' this is properly a despair in your friend. But if you only think that you have overstaid the time, and that it is past, and therefore you shall not have the gift, this may be called a despair of the event, and a despair in yourself, but not properly a despair of your friend; only the act of hoping in God is hindered, as is said. So it is in our present case.

And for my part, I am persuaded that it is only

this proper despair in God, which is the damnable desperation, which is threatened in the Scripture, and not the former. And that if a poor soul should go out of this world without any actual hope of his own salvation, merely because he thinks that he is no true believer, that this soul may be saved, and prove a true believer for all this. Alas! the great sin that God threateneth is our distrust of his faithfulness, and not the doubting of our own sincerity and distrust of ourselves. We have great reason to be very jealous of our own hearts, as knowing them to be deceitful above all things, and desperately wicked, who can know them? But we have no reason to be jealous of God. Where find you in Scripture that any is condemned for hard thoughts of themselves, or for not knowing themselves to have true grace, and for thinking they had none?

Do not put the name of unbelief upon all your fears of God's displeasure. Much less should you presently conclude that you have no faith, and that you cannot believe, because of these fears. You may have much faith in the midst of these fears; and God may make them preservers of your faith, by quickening you up to those means that must maintain it, and by keeping you from those evils that would be as a worm at the root of it, and eat out its precious strength and life. Security is no friend to faith, but a more deadly enemy than fear itself.

Direct. XIX. Further understand, 'That those few who do attain to assurance, have it not either perfectly or constantly (for the most part) but mixed with imperfection, and oft clouded and interrupted.'

That measure of assurance which godly men

do partake of, hath here its many sad interruptions, in the most. Upon the prevalency of temptations and the hidings of God's face, their souls are oft left in a state of sadness, that were but lately in the arms of Christ. How fully might this be proved from the examples of Job, David, Jeremy, and others in Scripture? And much more abundantly by the daily complaints and examples of the best of God's people now living among us. Seeing then that best have such storms and sad interruptions, do not you wonder or think your case strange if it be so with you? Would you speed better than the best? Long for heaven then, where only is joy without sorrow, and everlasting rest without interruption.

Direct. XX. Let me also give you this warning, 'That you must never expect so much assurance on earth, as shall set you above the possibility of the loss of heaven; or above all apprehensions of real danger of your miscarrying.'

I entreat you never to expect such an assurance as shall extinguish all your apprehensions of danger. He that sees not the danger is nearest it, and likely to fall into it. Only he that seeth and apprehendeth it, is likely to avoid it. He that seeth no danger of falling away, is in greatest danger of it. Only see that you apprehend not your danger to be greater than it is; nor so apprehend it as to increase it, by driving you from Christ, but as to prevent it by driving you to him. Entertain not fancies and dreams of danger, instead of right apprehensions. Apprehend your happiness and grounds of hope and comfort, and safety in Christ, and let these quite exceed your apprehensions of the danger.

A king having many subjects and sons, which

are all beyond sea, or beyond some river, they must needs be brought over to him before they can live or reign with him. The river is frozen over at the sides, till it come almost to the middle. The foolish children are all playing on the ice, where a deceiving enemy enticeth them to play on till they come to the deep, where they drop in one by one and perish. The eldest son, who is with the father on the other side, undertaketh to cast himself into the water, and swim to the further side, and break the ice, and swim back with them all that will come with him and hold him. The father bids him, 'Bring all my subjects with you, if they will come and hold by you; but be sure you fail not to bring my sons.' This is resolved on; the prince casteth himself into the water, and swimmeth to the further side. He maketh a way through the ice, and offereth all of them his safe carriage, if they will accept him to be their bearer and helper, and will trust themselves on him, and hold fast by him till they come to the further side. Some refuse his help, and think he would deceive them, and lead them into the deep, and there leave them to perish. Some had rather play on the ice, and will not hearken to him. Some dare not venture through the streams, or will not endure the coldness of the water. Some waveringly agree to him, and hold faintly by his skirt, and when they feel the cold water, or are near the deep, or are weary of holding, they lose him; either turning back, or perishing suddenly in the gulf. The children are of the same mind with the rest; but he is resolved to lose none of them, and therefore he chargeth them to come with him, and tells them fully what a welcome they shall have with their father; and ceaseth not his importunity till he persuade them to consent.

Some of them say, 'How shall we ever get over the river? we shall be drowned by the way.' He tells them, 'I will carry you safe over, so you will but hold fast by me. Never fear, I warrant you.' They all lay hold on him, and venture in with him. When they are in the midst some are afraid, and cry out, 'We shall be drowned.' These he encourageth, and bids them trust him; hold fast and fear not. Others, when they hear these words, that they need not fear, grow so bold and utterly secure, as to lose their hold. To these he speaketh in other language, and chargeth them to hold fast by him; for if they lose their hold, they will fall into the bottom, and if they stick not to him they will be drowned. Some of them upon this warning hold fast; others are so boldly confident of his skill, and good-will, and promise, that they forget or value not his warning and threatening, but lose their hold. Some through laziness and weariness do the like. Whereupon he lets them sink till they are almost drowned, and cry out for help, 'Save us or we perish,' and think they are all lost; and then he layeth hold of them and fetcheth them up again, and chideth them for their bold folly, and biddeth them look better to themselves, and hold faster by him hereafter, if they love themselves. Some at last through mere weariness and weakness before they can reach the bank, cry out, 'Oh! I am tired, I faint, I shall never hold fast till I reach the shore, I shall be drowned.' These he comforteth, and gives them cordials, and holdeth them by the hand, and bids them, Despair not: Do your best: Hold fast, and I will help you. And so he brings them all safe to the haven.

This king is God; heaven is his habitation; the subjects are all men; the river or sea is the passage of this life. The further side is all men's natural, sinful distance and separation from God and happiness; the ice that bears them, is this frail life of pleasures, profits, and honors, which delight the flesh; the depth unfrozen is hell; he that enticeth them thither is the devil. The eldest son that is sent to bring them over is Jesus Christ; his commission and undertaking is, to help all over that refuse not his help.

Direct. XXI. The next advice which I must give you, is this, 'Be thankful if you can but reach to a settled peace, and composure of your mind, and lay not too much on the high raptures and feelings of comfort which some do possess; and if ever you enjoy such feeling joys, expect not that they should be either long or often.'

It is the cause of miserable languishing to many a poor soul, to have such importunate expectations of such passionate joys, that they think without these they have no true comfort at all; no witness of the Spirit, no spirit of adoption, no joy in the Holy Ghost. Some think that others have much of this, though they have not, and therefore they torment themselves because it is not with them as with others; when, alas, they little know how it goes with others. Yet I doubt not but solid men have oft high joys; and more we might all have, if we did our duty. And I would have no Christian content himself with a dull quietness of spirit, but by all means possible to be much in laboring to rejoice in God and raising their souls to heavenly delights. Look at these joys and delights as duties and as mercies, but look not at them as marks of trial, so as to place more necessity in them than God hath done, or to think them to be ordinary things. If you do but feel such a high estimation of Christ and heaven, that you would not leave him for all the world, take this for your surest sign. And if you have but so much probability or hope of your interest in him, that you can think of God as one that loveth you, and can be thankful to Christ for redeeming you, and are more glad in these hopes of your interest in Christ and glory, than if you were owner of all the world; take this for a happy mercy and a high consolation.

And let me add this: commonly those that have the highest passionate joys, have the saddest lives; for they have withal, the most passionate fears and sorrows. Mark the same people that usually have the highest joys, and see whether at other times they have not the greatest troubles. This week they are as at the gates of heaven, and the next as at the doors of hell: I am sure with many it is so. Yet it need not be so, if Christians would but look at these high joys as duties to be endeavored, and mercies to be valued; but when they will needs judge of their state by them, and think that God is gone from them or forsaken them, when they have not such joys, then it leaves them in terror and amazement. Live therefore on your peace of conscience as your ordinary diet; when this is wanting, know that God appointeth you a fast for your health; and when you have a feast of high joys, feed on it and be thankful; but when they are taken from you, gape not after them as the disciples did after Christ at his ascension; but return thankfully to your ordinary diet of peace. And remember that these joys, which are now taken from you, may so return again. However there is a place preparing for you, where your joys shall be full.

Direct. XXII. My next direction is this, 'Spend

more of your time and care about your duty than about your comforts: and for the exercise and increase of your graces, than for the discovery of them: and when you have done all that you can for assurance and comfort, you shall find that it will very much depend on your actual obedience.''

Consideration, frequent serious consideration, is God's great instrument to convert the soul, and to confirm it; to get grace, and to keep it, and increase it. If any soul perish for want of grace, it is ten to one it is mainly for want of frequent and serious consideration. That the most of us do languish under such weaknesses, and attain to small degrees of grace, is for want of sober, frequent consideration. We know not how great things this would do, if it were but faithfully managed. This then is my advice, when you feel so great a want of faith and love, (for those be the main graces for trial and use,) that you doubt whether you have any or none, lay by those doubting thoughts awhile, and presently go and set yourself to consider of God's truth, goodness, amiableness, and kindheartedness to miserable, unworthy sinners; think what he is in himself, and what he is to you, and what he hath done for you, and what he will do for you if you will but consent. And then think of the vanity of all the childish pleasures of this world; how soon, and in how sad a case they will leave us; and what silly, contemptible things they are, in comparison of the everlasting glory of the saints! By that time you have warmed your soul a little with such serious thoughts, you will find your faith and love revive, and begin to stir and work within you; and then you will feel that you have faith and love. Use, therefore, instead of doubting of your faith, to believe till you put it out of doubt. And if yet you doubt, study God and Christ, and glory yet better, and keep those objects by consideration close to your heart, whose nature is to work the heart to faith and love.

Let me ask: have you not darkened, buried, or weakened your graces, instead of exercising and increasing them, even when you complained for want of assurance of them? When you found a want of faith and love, have not you weakened them more, and so made them less discernible? Have you not fed your unbelief, and taken Satan's part against yourself; and (which is far worse) have you never, through these doubtings, entertained hard thoughts of God, and presented him to your soul, as unwilling to show you mercy, and in unlovely, dreadful, hideous shape, fitter to affright you from him, than to draw you to him, and likelier to provoke your hatred than your love? If you have not done thus, I know too many troubled souls that have. And if you have, you have taken a very unlikely way to get assurance. If you would have been certain that you loved God in sincerity, you should have labored to love him more, till you had been certain; and that you might do so, you should have kept better thoughts of God in your mind. You will hardly love him while you think of him as evil, or at least as hurtful to you. Never forget this rule which I lay you down in the beginning, that He that will ever love God, must apprehend him to be good. And the more large and deep are our apprehensions of his goodness, the more will be our love. And when you confer with ministers, or others, that may teach you, see that you ask ten times at least, 'How should I get or increase my faith, my love to Christ, and to his people?" for once that you ask, 'How shall I know that I believe or love?' Yet so contrary hath been and still is the practice of most Christians among us in this point, that I have heard it twenty times asked, 'How shall I know that I truly love the brethren?' for once that I have heard it demanded, 'How should I bring my heart to love them better? And the like I may say of love to Christ himself.

Direct. XXIII. My next advice is this, 'Think not those doubts and troubles of mind, which are caused and continued by willful disobedience, will ever be well healed but by the healing of that disobedience; or that the same means must be used, and will suffice to the cure of such troubles; which must be used and will suffice to cure the troubles of a tender conscience, and of an obedient Christian, whose trouble is merely through mistakes of their condition.'

A true Christian would love God more perfectly and delight in him more abundantly, and bring every thought in subjection to his will, and subdue the very remnants of carnal concupiscence, that there should be no stirrings of lust or unjust anger, or worldly desires, or pride within him; and that no vain word might pass his lips: all this he would do, but he cannot. Striving against these unavoidable infirmities, is conquering.

But though we cannot keep under every motion of concupiscence, we can forbear the execution. Anger will stir up provocations; but we may restrain it in degree, that it set us not in a flame, and do not much distemper or discompose our minds. And we can forbid our tongues all raging, furious or abusive words in our anger; all cursing, swearing, or reproachful speaking. If an envious thought against one brother do arise in our hearts, because he is preferred before us, we may hate it, and repress it, and chide our hearts for it, and command our tongues to speak well of him, and no evil. Some pride and self-esteem will remain and be stirring in us, do what we can; it is a sin so deeply rooted in our corrupt natures. But yet we can detest it, and resist it, and meet it with abhorrence of our self-conceited thoughts, and rejoicings in our own reputations and fame, and inward heart-risings against those that undervalue us, and stand in the way of our repute; and we may forbear our boasting language, and our contestings for our credit, and our excuses of our sins, and our backbitings and secret defaming of those that cross us in the way of credit. We may forbear our quarrels, and estrangements, and dividings from our brethren, and stiff insisting on our own conceits, and expecting that others should make our judgments their rule, and say and do as we would have them, and all dance after our pipe; all which are the effects of inward pride. We cannot, while we are on earth, be free from all inordinate love of the world, and the riches and honors of it; but we may so watch against it, and repress it, as that it shall neither be preferred before God, nor draw us to unlawful ways of gain, by lying, deceit, and overreaching our brethren; by stealing, unjust or unmerciful dealings, oppressing the poor, and insulting over those that are in the way of our thriving, and crushing them that would hinder our aspiring designs, and treading them down that will not bow to us, and taken revenge of them that have crossed or disparaged us, or cruelly exacting all our rights and debts of the poor, and squeezing the purses of subjects or tenants, or those that we bargain with, like a sponge, as long as anything will come out. Yea, we may so far subdue our love of the world, as that it shall not hinder us from being merciful to the poor, compassionate to our servants and laborers, and bountiful to our power in doing good works; nor yet shut out God's service from our families and closets; nor rob him of our frequent, affectionate thoughts, especially on the Lord's day. So for sensuality, or the pleasing of our flesh more immediately; we shall never on earth be wholly freed from inordinate motions, and temptations, and fleshly desires, and urgent inclinations and solicitations to forbidden things. But yet we may restrain our appetite by reason, so far that it brings us not to gluttony and drunkenness and a studying for our bellies, and pampering of our flesh, or a taking care for it, and making provision to satisfy its lusts: Rom. xiii, 14. We may forbear the obeying it, in excess of apparel, in indecent, scandalous, or time-wasting recreations, in uncleanness, or unchaste speeches or behavior, or the reading of amorous books and sonnets, or feeding our eyes or thoughts on filthy or enticing objects, or otherwise willfully blowing the fire of lust. So also for the performance of duty. We shall never in this life be able to hear or read so diligently, and understandingly, or affectionately, as we would do; nor to remember or profit by what we hear, as we desire. But yet we can bring ourselves to the congregation, and not prefer our ease, or business, or any vain thing before God's word and worship, or loathe or despise it, because of some weakness in the speaker. And we may in a great measure restrain our thoughts from wandering, and force ourselves to attend; and labor when we come home to recall it to mind. We cannot call on God so fervently believingly, or delightfully, as we would; but yet we may do it as sincerely as we can, and do it constantly. We cannot instruct our children and servants, and reprove or exhort our neighbors, with that boldness, or love, and compassion, and discretion, and meet expressions, as we would; but yet we may do it faithfully and frequently, as we are able.

I advise you, if your soul remain in doubts and troubles, and you cannot enjoy God in any way of peace and comfort, nor see any clear evidence of the sincerity of your faith, take a serious view of your obedience, and faithfully survey your heart and life, and your daily carriage to God in both. See whether there be nothing that provokes God to an unusual jealousy; if there be, it is only the increase of some carnal interest in your heart, or else the willful or negligent falling into some actual sin, of commission or of omission. And here let me tell you, when you are making this search, what particulars they be which I would have you to be most jealous of.

Inquire carefully into your humility. It is not for nothing that Christ hath said so much of the excellency and necessity of this grace, when he bids us learn of him to be meek and lowly; when he blesseth the meek and poor in spirit: when he setteth a little child in the midst of them, and telleth them, except they become as that child, they could not enter into the kingdom of heaven: when he stoopeth to wash and wipe his disciples' feet, requiring them to do so by one another. For though pride may not be so predominant and raging as to damn you, yet may it cause God to afflict you, and hide his face from you, and humble you by the sense of his displeasure, and the concealment of his love. And though one would think that doubting, troubled souls should be always the most humble and freest from pride, yet sad experience hath certified me, that much pride may dwell with great doubtings and distress of mind. Even some of the same souls that cry out of their own unworthiness, and fear lest they shall be firebrands of hell, yet cannot endure a close reproof, especially for any disgraceful sin, nor bear a disparaging word, nor love those, nor speak well of them, who do not value them, nor endure to be crossed or contradicted in word or deed, but must have all go their way, and follow their judgment, and say as they say, and dance after their pipe, and their hearts rise against those that will not do it; much more against those that speak or do any thing to the diminishing of their reputation: they cannot endure to be low, and passed by, and overlooked, when others are preferred before them, or to be slighted and disrespected, or their words, or parts, or works, or judgments to be contemned or disparaged. Nay, some are scarce able to live in the same house, or church or town, in love and peace, with any but those that will humor and please them, and speak them fair, and give them smooth and stroking language, and forbear crossing, reproving, and disparaging them. Every one of these singly is an evident mark and fruit of pride; how much more all jointly. I seriously profess it amazeth me to consider how heinously most professors are guilty of this sin! even when they know it to be the devil's own sin, and the great abomination hated of God.

The next sin that I would have you be specially jealous of, is covetousness, or love of the profits or riches of the world. This is not the sin of the rich only, but also of the poor: and more heinous is it in them, to love the world inordinately, that have so little of it, than in rich men, that have more to tempt them, though dangerous in both.

The third great heart-sin which I would have you jealous of, is sensuality or voluptuousness, or pleasing the senses inordinately. When a man cannot deny his appetite what it would have; or at least, covetousness can do more in restraining it than conscience; when a man cannot make a covenant with his eyes, but must gaze on every alluring object; when the flesh draws to forbidden pleasures, in meats, drinks, apparel, recreations, lasciviousness, and all the considerations of reason cannot restrain it; this is a sad case, and God may well give over such to sadness of heart. If we walk so pleasingly to the flesh, God will walk more displeasingly to us. The cure lieth in break-off sin, to the utmost of your power. This is the Achan that disquieteth all. It is God's great mercy that he disquieteth you in sinning, and gives you not over to so deep a slumber and peace in sin, as might hinder your repentance and reformation.

Direct. XXIV. My next advice for the obtaining of a settled peace of comfort, is this, ' Take heed that you content not yourself with a cheap course of religion, and such a serving of God, as costeth you little or nothing. But in your abstaining from sin, in your rising out of sin, and in your discharge of duty, incline most to that way which is most self-denying, and displeasing to the flesh, (so you be sure it be a lawful way). And when you are called out to any work which will stand you in extraordinary labor and cost, you must be so far from shrinking and drawing your neck out of the yoke, that you must look upon it as a special price that is put into your hand, and singular advantage and opportunity for the increase of your comforts.'

Let the experience of the world of Christians be produced, and all will attest the same truth. That it is God's usual course to give men larger comforts in dearer duties, than in cheap: nay, seldom doth he give large comforts in cheap duties, and seldom doth he deny them in dearer; so be it they are not made dear by our own sin and foolish indiscretion, but by his command, and our faithfulness in obeying him. Who knows not that the consolation of martyrs is usually above other men's, who hath read of their sufferings and strange sustentations? Christian, do but try this by thy own experiences, and tell me, when thou hast most resolutely followed Christ in a good cause; when thou hast stood against the faces of the greatest for God; when thou hast cast thy life, thy family and estate upon Christ, and run thyself into the most apparent hazards for his sake; hast thou not come off with more inward peace and comfort, than the cheaper part of thy religion hath afforded thee? When thou hast stood to the truth and Gospel, and hast done good through the greatest opposition, and lost thy greatest and dearest friends, because thou wouldst not forsake Christ and his service, or deal falsely in some cause that he hath trusted thee in; hast thou not come off with the blessing of peace of conscience? Nay, when thou hast denied thy most importunate appetite, and most crossed thy lusts, and most humbled and abase thyself for God, and denied thy credit, and taken shame to thyself in a free confessing of thy faults, or patiently put up with the greatest abuses, or humbled and tamed thy flesh by necessary abstinence, or any way most displeasing it, by crossing its interest, by bountiful giving, laborious duty, dangers or sufferings, for the sake of the Lord Jesus, his truth and people; hath it not been far better with thee in thy peace and comforts than before? I know some will be ready to say, that may be from carnal pride in our own doing or suffering. I answer, it may be so; and therefore let all watch against that. But I am certain that this is God's ordinary dealing with his people, and therefore we may ordinarily expect it. It is for their encouragement in faithful duty; and I may truly say, for their reward, when himself calls that a reward which he gives for a cup of water.

For my part I think, that if Christians took God's word before them, and spared the flesh less, and trusted themselves and all to Christ alone, and did not balk all the troublesome and costly part of religion, and that which most crosseth the interest of the flesh, it would be more ordinary with them to be filled with the joys of the Holy Ghost, and walk in that peace of conscience which is a continual feast; and to have such full and frequent views both of the sincerity of their evidencing graces, and of God's reconciled face, as would banish their doubts and fears and be a greater help to their certainty of salvation, than much other labor doth prove. If you flinch not the fiery furnace, you shall have the company of the Son of God in it. If you flinch not the prison and stocks, you may be able to sing as Paul and Silas did. If you refuse not to be stoned with Stephen, you may perhaps see heaven opened as he did. If you think these comforts so dear bought, that you will rather venture without them; let me tell you, you may take your course, but the end will convince you to the very heart, of the folly of your choice.

Direct. XXV. My next advice shall be somewhat near of kin to the former. If you would learn the most expeditious way to peace and settled comfort, 'Study well the art of doing good; and let it be your every day's contrivance, care, and business, how you may lay out all that God hath trusted you with, to the greatest pleasing of God, and to your most comfortable account.'

Doing good is a high part of a Christian's obedience, and must be the chief part of his life. The heathen could tell him that asked him, how men might be like to God; that one way was, To do good to all. Now it is not enough to make this your care now and then, or do good when it falls in your way; but you must study which are good works, and which are they that you are called to.

This therefore is the thing that I would persuade you to: take yourself for God's steward; remember the time when it will be said to you, "Give account of thy stewardship; thou shalt be no longer steward." Let it be your every day's contrivance, how to lay out your gifts, time, strength, riches, or interest, to your Master's use. Think which way you may do most, first to promote the Gospel and the public good of the church; and then, which way you may help toward the saving of particular men's souls; and then, which way you may better the commonwealth, and how you may do good to men's bodies, beginning with your own and those of your family, but extending your help as much further as you are able. Ask yourself every morning, "Which way may I this day most further my Master's business, and the good of men?" Ask yourself every night, "What good have I done to-day?" Oh the easiness of man's heart to be deluded! Do rich men never think to lie rotting in the dust? Do they never think that they must be accountable for all their riches, and for all their time, and power, and interests? Do they not know that it will comfort them at death and judgment, to hear in their reckoning, Item, so much given to such and such poor; so much to promote the Gospel; so much to maintain poor scholars, while they study to prepare themselves for the ministry? etc. Than to hear, So much in such a feast; to entertain such gallants; to please such noble friends; so much at dice, at cards, at horse-races, at cock-fights; so much in excess of apparel; and the rest to leave my posterity in the like pomp? Do they not know that it will comfort them more to hear then of their time spent in reading Scripture, secret and open prayer, instructing and examining their children and servants; going to their poor neighbors' houses to see what they want, and to persuade them to godliness; and in being examples of eminent holiness to all; and in suppressing vice, and doing justice, than to hear of so much time spent in vain recreations, visits, luxuries, and idleness?

Direct. XXVI. Having led you thus far toward a settled peace, my next Direction shall contain a necessary caution, lest you run as far into the contrary extreme, viz: 'Take heed that you neither trouble your own soul with needless scruples, about matters of doctrine, of duty, or of sin, or about your own condition. Nor yet that you do not make yourself more work than God hath made you, by feigning things unlawful, which God hath not forbidden; or by placing your religion in will-worship, or in an over-curious insisting on circumstantials, or an over-rigorous dealing with your body.'

It hath ever been the devil's policy to begin in persuading men to worldliness, flesh-pleasing, security, and presumption, and utter neglect of God and their souls, or at least preferring their bodies and worldly things, and by this means he destroyeth the world. But where this will not take, but God awaketh men effectually, and casteth out the sleepy devil, usually he fills men's heads with needless scruples, and next setteth them on a religion not commanded, and would make poor souls believe they do nothing, if they do not more than God hath commanded them. When the devil hath no other way left to destroy religion and godliness, he will pretend to be religious and godly himself, and then he is always over-religious and over-godly in his materials. All overdoing in God's work is undoing; and whoever you meet with that would overdo, suspect him to be either a subtle, destroying enemy, or one deluded by the destroyer.

When he could not persuade the world to persecute Christ, and to refuse him and his worship, the serpent will be the most zealous worshiper, and saith, as Herod, and with the same mind, "Come and tell me, that I may worship him." He persuades men to do and overdo. He sets them on laying out their revenues in sumptuous fabrics, in fighting to be masters of the holy land and sepulcher of Christ; on going pilgrimages; worshiping saints, angels, shrines, relics, adoring the very bread of the sacrament as God, excessive fastings, choice of meats, numbered prayers on beads, repetitions of words, so may Ave Maries, Pater Nosters, the name Jesus so oft repeated in a breath, so many holidays to saints, canonical hours, even at midnight to pray, and that in Latin for greater reverence, crossings, holy garments, variety of prescribed gestures, kneeling and worshiping before images, sacrificing Christ again to his Father in the mass; forswearing marriage; living retiredly, as separate from the world; multitudes of new, prescribed rules and orders of life; vowing poverty; begging without need; creeping to the cross, holy water, and holy bread, carrying palms, kneeling at altars, bearing candles, ashes; in baptism, crossing, conjuring out the devil, salting, spittle, oil; taking pardons, indulgences, and dispensations of the pope; praying for the dead, perambulations, serving God to merit heaven, or to ease souls in purgatory; doing works of supererogation, with multitudes the like. All these hath the devil added to God's worship, so zealous a worshiper of Christ is he, when he takes that way.

If he can but get you by excessive fastings, watchings, labors, studies, or other austerities, especially sadness and perplexities of mind, to have a sick body, a crazed brain, or a short life, you will be able to do him but little hurt, and God but little service, beside the pleasure that he takes in your own vexation. Nay, he will hope to make a further advantage of your weakness, and to keep many a soul in the snares of sensuality, by telling them of your miseries, and saying to them, "Dost thou not see in such a man or woman, what it is to be so holy and precise? They will all run mad at last. If once thou grow so strict, and deny thyself thy pleasures, and take this precise course, thou wilt but make thy life a misery, and never have a merry day again." Such examples as yours the devil will make use of that he may terrify poor souls from godliness, and represent the word and ways of Christ to them in an odious, and unpleasing, and discouraging shape. You are commanded to love your neighbors but as yourself; and there

fore by cruelty and unmerciful dealing with your
own body, you will go about to justify the like
dealings with others. You durst not deny to feed,
to clothe, to comfort, and refresh the poor, lest
Christ should say, "You did it not to me." And
how should you dare to deny the same to
yourself? How will you answer God for the
neglect of all that service which you should have
done him, and might, if you had not disabled your
bodies and mind? He requireth that you delight
yourself in him. And how can you do that when
you habituate both mind and body to a sad,
dejected, mournful garb?

The next part of my Direction is, That you
avoid causeless scruples, about doctrines, duties,
sins, or your own state. If you send a man on
a journey, would you like him better that would
stand questioning and scrupling every step he
goes, whether he set the right foot before? Or
whether he should go in the footpath or in the
road? Or him that would cheerfully go on, not
thinking which foot goeth forward; and rather step
a little beside the path, and in again, than to stand
scrupling when he should be going? If you send
reapers into your harvest, which would you like
better, him that would stand scrupling how many
straws he should cut down at once, and at what
height; and with fears of cutting them too high or
too low, too many at once or too few, should do
you but little work? Or him that should do his
work cheerfully, as well as he can? Would you
not be angry at such childish, unprofitable diligence or curiosity, as is a hinderance to your work?

Satan will make you believe that everything is a
sin, that he may disquiet you, if he cannot get you
to believe that nothing at all is sin, that he may

destroy you. You shall not put a bit in your mouth, but he will move a scruple, whether it were not too good, or too much. You shall not clothe yourself, but he will move you to scruple the lawfulness of it. You shall not come into any company, but he will afterward vex you about every word you spoke, lest you sinned.

Direct. XXVII. 'When God hath once showed you a certainty, or but a strong probability of your sincerity and his especial love, labor to fix this so deep in your apprehension and memory, that it may serve for the time to come, and not only for the present. And leave not your soul too open to changes, upon every new apprehension, nor to question all that is past upon every jealousy; except when some notable declining to the world, and the flesh, or a committing of gross sins, or a willfulness or carelessness in other sins that you may avoid, do give you just cause of questioning your sincerity, and bringing your soul again to the bar, and your estate to a more exact review.'

If when God hath given you assurance, or strong probabilities of your sincerity, you will make use of it but only for that present time, you will never then have a settled peace in your soul: beside, the great wrong you do to God, by necessitating him to be so often renewing such discoveries, and repeating the same words to you so often over. If your child offend you, would you have him when he is pardoned, no longer to believe it, than you are telling him? Should he be still asking you over and over every day, 'Father, am I forgiven, or no?' Should not one answer serve his turn? Will you not believe that your money is in your purse or chest any longer than you are looking on it? Or that your corn is growing on your land, or your cattle in your grounds, any longer than you are looking on them? By this course a rich man should have no more content than a beggar, longer than he is looking on his money, or goods, or lands; and when he is looking on one, he should again lose the comfort of all the rest. What hath God given you a memory for, but to lay up former apprehensions, and discoveries, and experiences, and make use of them on all meet occasions afterward? When God hath once resolved your doubts, and showed you the truth of your faith, love, or obedience, write it deep in your memory; and do not suffer any fancies, or fears, or light surmises, to cause you to question this again, as long as you fall not from the obedience or faith which you then discovered. Alas! man's apprehension is a most mutable thing! If you leave your soul open to every new apprehension, you will never be settled: you may think two contrary things of yourself in an hour. You will never want some occasion of jealousy and fears as long as you have corruption in your heart, and sin in your life, and a tempter to be troubling you; but if you will suffer any such wind to shake your peace and comforts, you will be always shaking and fluctuating, as a wave of the sea.

Oh that you could well observe this Direction! How much it would help you to escape extremes, and conduce to the settling of a well-grounded peace, and at once to the well ordering of your whole conversation!

Direct. XXVIII. 'Be very careful that you create not perplexities and terrors in your own soul, by rash misinterpretations of any passages either of Scripture, of God's providence, or of the sermons or private speeches of ministers: but resolve with patience, yea, with gladness, to suffer preachers to deal with their congregations in the most searching, serious, and awakening manner, lest your weakness should be a wrong to the whole assembly, and possibly the undoing of many a sensual, drowsy, or obstinate soul, who will not be convinced and awakened by a comforting way of preaching, or by any smoother or gentler means.'

Some weak-headed, troubled Christians can scarce read a chapter, or hear one read, but they will find something which they think doth condemn them. If they read of God's wrath and judgment, they think it is meant against them. If they read, "Our God is a consuming fire," they think presently it is themselves that must be the fuel; whereas justice and mercy have each their proper objects; the burning fire will not waste the gold, nor is water the fuel of it; but combustible matter it will presently consume. A humble soul that lies prostrate at Christ's feet, confessing its unworthiness, and bewailing its sinfulness, this is not the object of revenging justice. Another reads in Psalm l, "I will set thy sins in order before thee;" and he thinks, certainly God will deal thus by him, not considering that God chargeth only their sins upon them that charge them not by true repentance on themselves, and accept not of Christ who hath discharged them by his blood. He makes not a poor sinner's burden more heavy by hitting him in the teeth with his sins, but makes it the office of his Son to ease him by disburdening him.

Nothing more common with troubled souls, than upon every new cross and affliction that befalls them, presently to think, God takes them for hypocrites; and to question their sincerity! As if David and Job had not left them a full warning against this temptation. Do you lose your goods? So did Job. Do you lose your children? So did Job; and that in no very comfortable way. Do you lose your health? So did Job. What if your godly friends should come about you in this case, and bend all their wits and speeches to persuade you that you are but a hypocrite, as Job's friends did by him, would not this put you harder to it? Yet could Job resolve, "I will not let go mine integrity till I die." How many a soul have I known that, by misinterpreting providences, have in a blind jealousy, been turned quite from truth and duty, supposing it had been error and sin; and all because of their afflictions.

The third enemy to your peace is: Misinterpreting or misapplying the passages of preachers in their sermons, writings, or private speeches. A minister cannot deal thoroughly or seriously with any sort of sinners, but some fearful, troubled souls apply all to themselves. I must entreat you to avoid this fault, or else you will turn God's ordinances and the daily food of your souls, into bitterness and wormwood, and all through your mistakes. I confess it is a better sign of an honest heart and self-judging conscience, to say, 'He speaks now to me, this is my case;' than to say, 'He speaks now to such or such a one, this is their case.' For it is the property of hypocrites to have their eye most abroad, and in every duty to be minding most the faults of others: and you may much discern such in their prayers, in that they will fill their confessions most with other men's sins, and you may feel them all the while in the bosom of their neighbors, when you may even feel a sincere man speaking his own heart, and most opening his own bosom to God.

Let me now desire you hereafter, to be glad to hear ministers awaken the profane and dead-hearted hearers, and search all to the quick, and misapply nothing to yourself; but if you think any passage doth nearly concern you, open your mind to the minister privately, when he may satisfy you more fully, and that without doing hurt to others: and consider what a straight ministers are in, that have so many of so different conditions, inclinations, and conversations to preach to.

Direct. XXIX. 'Be sure you forget not to distinguish between causes of doubting of your sincerity, and causes of mere humiliation, repentance, and amendment; and do not raise doubtings and fears, where God calleth you but to humiliation, amendment, and fresh recourse to Christ.'

What more common than for poor Christians to pour out a multitude of complaints of their weaknesses, and wants, and miscarriages; and never consider all the while that there may be cause of sorrow in these, when yet there is no cause of doubting of their sincerity. God dealeth very variously with his chosen in their conversion, as to the accidentals and circumstantials of the work. Some he calleth not home till they have run a long race in the way of rebellion, in open drunkenness, swearing, worldliness, and derision of holiness: these he usually humbleth more deeply, and they can better observe the several steps of the Spirit in the work; (and yet not always neither). Others he so restraineth in their youth, that though they have not saving grace, yet they are not guilty of any gross sins, but have a liking to the people and ways of God: and yet he doth not savingly convert them till long after. It is much harder for these to discern the time or manner of their conversion; yet usually some conjectures they may make: and usually their humiliation is not so deep. Others, as is said, have the saving workings of the Spirit in their very childhood, and these can least of all discern the certain time or order. The ordinary way of God's dealing with those that are children of godly parents, and have good education, is, by giving them some liking of godly persons and ways, some conscience of sin, some repentance and recourse by prayer to God in Christ for mercy; yet youthful lusts and folly, and ill company, do usually much stifle it, till at last, by some affliction, or sermon, or book, or good company, God setteth home the work, and maketh them more resolute and victorious Christians. These persons now can remember that they had convictions, and stirring consciences when they were young, and the other forementioned works, perhaps they can remember some more notable rousings and awakenings long after, and perhaps they have had many such fits and steps, and the work hath stood at this pass for a long time, even many years together. But at which of all these changes it was that the soul began to be savingly sincere, I think is next to an impossibility to discern. According to that experience which I have had of the state of Christians, I am forced to judge the most of the children of the godly that ever are renewed, are renewed in their childhood, or much toward it then done, and that among forty Christians there is not one that can certainly name the month in which his soul first began to be sincere; and among a thousand Christians, I think not one can name the hour. The sermon which awakened them, they may name, but not the hour when they first arrived at a saving sincerity.

My advice to all Christians, is this: Find Christ by his Spirit dwelling in your hearts, and then never trouble yourselves, though you know not the time or manner of his entrance. Do you value Christ above the world, and resolve to choose him before the world, and perform these resolutions? Then need you not doubt but the Spirit of Jesus is victorious in you.

Direct. XXX. 'Whatsoever new doubtings do arise in your soul, see that you carefully discern whether they are such as must be resolved from the consideration of general grace, or of special grace. And especially be sure of this, that when you want or lose your certainty of sincerity and salvation, you have presently recourse to the probability of it, and lose not the comforts of that. Or if you should lose the sight of a probability of special grace, yet see that you have recourse at the utmost to general grace, and never let go the comforts of that at the worst.'

Let the first thing which you do upon every doubt, be this: To consider, whether it come from the unbelieving or low apprehensions of the general grounds of comfort, or from the want of evidence of special grace. For that which is a fit remedy for one of these, will do little for the cure of the other. If your doubting be only, Whether you be sincere in believing, loving, hoping, repenting, and obeying, then it will not answer this doubt, though you discern never so much of God's merciful nature, or Christ's gracious office, or the universal sufficiency of his death and satisfaction, or the freeness and extent of the promise of pardon. It will be no saving plea at the day of judgment to say, Though I repented not, and believed not, yet Christ died for me. or God is merciful, or Christ repented and believed for me, or God made me a free promise and gift of salvation, if I would repent and believe. What comfort would such an answer give them? And therefore, doubtless it will not serve now to quiet any knowing Christian against those doubts that arise from the want of particular evidence of special grace, though in their own place, the general grounds of comfort are of absolute necessity thereto.

Now I would ask you this question in your greatest fears that you are out of Christ: Are you willing to have Christ to pardon, sanctify, guide, and save you, or not? If you are, then you are a true believer, and did not know it. If you are not, if you will but wait on God's word in hearing, and reading, and consider frequently and seriously of the necessity and excellency of Christ and glory, and the evil of sin, and the vanity of the world, and will but beg earnestly of God to make you willing, you shall find that God hath not appointed you this means in vain, and that this way will be more profitable to you than all your complainings.

Direct. XXXI. 'If God do bless you with an able, faithful, prudent, judicious pastor, take him for your guide under Christ in the way to salvation; and open to him your case, and desire his advice in all your extraordinary, pressing necessities, where you have found the advice of other godly friends to be insufficient; and this not once or twice only, but as often as such pressing necessities shall return. Or if your own pastor be more defective for such a work, make use of some other minister of Christ, who is more meet.'

The devil hath great advantage while you keep his counsel; two are better than one; for if one of them fall, he hath another to help him. It is dangerous, resisting such an enemy alone. A uniting of forces oft procureth victory. God giveth others knowledge, prudence, and other gifts for our good; that so every member of the body may have need of another, and each be useful to the other. An independency of Christian upon Christian, is most unchristian; much more of people on their guides. It ceaseth to be a member, which is separated from the body; and to make no use of the body or fellow members, is next to separation from them. Sometimes bashfulness is the cause, sometimes self-confidence (a far worse cause); but whatever is the cause of Christians smothering their doubts, the effects are oft sad. The disease is oft gone so far, that the cure is very difficult, before some bashful, or proud, or tender patients will open their disease. The very opening of a man's grief to a faithful friend, doth oft ease the heart of itself.

But you must understand well when this is your duty. Not in every small infirmity, which accompanies Christians in their daily most watchful conversation. Nor yet in every lesser doubt, which may be otherwise resolved. It is a folly and a wrong to physicians to run to them for every cut finger or prick with a pin. But first study the case yourself, and seek God's direction: if that will not serve, open your case to your nearest bosom friend that is godly and judicious. If you either fall into any grievous sin, or any terrible pangs of conscience, or any great straits and difficulties about matters of doctrine or practice, go presently to your pastor for advice. The devil, and pride, and bashfulness, will do their utmost to hinder you; but see that they prevail not.

But I know some will say, That is near to Popish auricular confession, which I here persuade Christians to, and it is to bring Christians under the tyranny of the priests again, and make them acquainted with all men's secrets, and masters of their consciences.

Answ. 1. To the last, I say to the railing devil of this age, no more but "The Lord rebuke thee." If any minister have wicked ends, let the God of heaven convert him, or root him out of his church, and cast him among the weeds and briers. But is it not the known voice of sensuality, and hell, to cast reproaches upon the way and ordinances of God? Who knoweth not that it is the very office of the ministry, to be teachers and guides to men in matters of salvation, and overseers of them? and that they watch for their souls, as those that must give an account. A disease unknown is unlike to be cured; and a disease well known is half cured. Not that every man is bound to open all his sins to his pastor; but those that cannot well be otherwise cured, he must; either if the sense of the guilt cannot be removed, and true assurance of pardon obtained: or else, if power against the sin be not otherwise obtained, but that it still prevaileth; in both these cases we must go to those that God hath made our directors and guides. I am confident many a thousand souls do long strive against anger, lust, flesh-pleasing, worldliness, and trouble of conscience to little purpose, who if they would but have taken God's way, and sought for help, and opened all their case to their minister, they might have been delivered in a good measure long ago. *Answ.* 2. And for Popish confession, I detest it. We would not persuade men that there is a necessity of confessing every sin to a minister, before it can be pardoned. Nor do we do it in a perplexed formality only at one time of the year; nor in order to Popish pardons or satisfactions; but we would have men go for physic to their souls, as they do for their bodies, when they feel they have need. And let me advise all Christian congregations to practice this excellent duty more. See that you knock oftener at your pastor's door, and ask his advice in all your pressing necessities; do not let him sit quietly in his study for you; make him know by experience, that the tenth part of a minister's labor is not in the pulpit. If your sins are strong, and you have wounded conscience deep, go for his advice for a safe cure; many a man's sore festers to damnation for want of this; and poor, ignorant, and scandalous sinners have far more need to do this than troubled consciences.

Direct. XXXII. 'As ever you would live in peace and comfort, and well pleasing unto God, be sure that you understand and deeply consider wherein the height of a Christian life, and the greatest part of our duty doth consist; to wit: In a loving delight in God, and a thankful and cheerful obedience to his will; and then make this your constant aim, and be still aspiring after it, and let all other affections and endeavors be subservient unto this.'

This one rule well practiced, would do wonders on the souls of poor Christians, in dispelling all their fears and troubles, and helping not only to a settled peace, but to live in the most comfortable state that can be expected upon earth. Write, therefore, these two or three words deep in your understandings and memory; that the life which God is best pleased with, and we should be always

endeavoring, is, a loving delight in God through
Christ; and a thankful and cheerful obedience to
him. I do not say, that godly sorrows, and fears,
and jealousies are no duties; but these are the
great duties, to which the rest should all subserve.
Many Christians look upon brokenheartedness,
and much grieving, and weeping for sin, as if it
were the great thing that God delighteth in, and
requireth of them; and therefore, they bend all
their endeavors this way; and are still striving
with their hearts to break them more, and wring-
ing their consciences to squeeze out some tears;
and they think no sermon, no prayer, no meditation, speeds so well with them, as that which can
help them to grieve or weep. I am far from persuading men against humiliation and godly sorrow,
and tenderness of heart. But yet I must tell you,
that this is a sore error that you lay so much upon
it, and so much overlook that great and noble work
and state to which it tendeth. Do you think that
God hath any pleasure in your sorrows as such?
Doth it do him good to see you dejected, afflicted,
and tormented? Alas, it is only as your sorrows
do kill your sins, and mortify your fleshly lusts,
and prepare for your peace and joys, that God regards them. Because God doth speak comfortably
to troubled, drooping spirits, and tells them that he
delighteth in the contrite, and loveth the humble,
and bindeth up the brokenhearted; therefore men
misunderstanding him, do think they should do
nothing, but be still breaking their own hearts.
Whereas God speaks it but partly to show his
hatred to the proud, and partly to show his tender
compassions to the humbled, that they might not
be overwhelmed or despair. But, O Christians,
understand and consider, that all your sorrows are

but preparatives to your joys; and that it is a higher and sweeter work that God calls you to, and would have you spend your time and strength in. The first part of it is love: a work that is wages to itself. He that knows what it is to live in the love of God, doth know that Christianity is no tormenting and discontented life. The next part is, "Delight in God, and in the hopes and forethoughts of everlasting glory." Psal. xxxvii, 4, "Delight thyself in the Lord, and he shall give thee the desires of thy heart." This is it that you should be bending your studies and endeavors for, that your soul might be able to delight itself in God. The third part is thankfulness and praise. The fourth part of the Christian life is cheerful obedience.

Will you now lay all this together, and make it for the time to come your business, and try whether it will not be the truest way to comfort, and make your life a blessed life? Will you make it your end in hearing, reading, praying, and meditation, to raise your soul to delight in God?

Oh how the subtle enemy disadvantageth the Gospel, by the misapprehensions and dejected spirits of believers! It is the very design of the ever blessed God, to glorify love and mercy as highly in the work of redemption, as ever he glorified omnipotency in the work of creation. So that he hath laid the foundation of the kingdom of grace in love and mercy; and in love and mercy hath he framed the whole structure of the edifice; and love and mercy are written in legible, indelible characters upon every piece. And the whole frame of his work and temple-service, hath he so composed, that all might be the resounding echoes of love, and the praise and glorious commemoration of love and mercy might be the great business of our solemn assemblies. And the new creation within us, and without us, is so ordered, that love, thankfulness, and delight, might be both the way and the end. And the serpent who most opposeth God where he seeketh most glory, especially the glory of his grace, doth labor so successfully to obscure this glory, that he hath brought multitudes of poor Christians to have poor, low thoughts of the riches of his grace; and to set every sin of theirs against it, which should but advance it; and even to question the very foundation of the whole building, whether Christ hath redeemed the world by his sacrifice. Yea, he puts such a vail over the glory of the Gospel, that men can hardly be brought to receive it as glad tidings, till they first have assurance of their own sanctification! And the very nature of God's kingdom is so unknown, that some men think it to be unrighteousness, and libertinism, and others to be pensive dejections, and tormenting scruples and fears; and but few know it to be righteousness and peace, and joy in the Holy Ghost. And the very business of a Christian's life and God's service, is rather taken to be scrupling, quarreling, and vexing ourselves and the church of God, than to be love and gratitude, and a delighting our souls in God, and cheerfully obeying him. And thus when Christianity seems a thraldom and torment; and the service of the world, the flesh, and the devil, seems the only freedom, and quiet, and delight, no wonder if the devil have more unfeigned servants than Christ; and if men tremble at the name of holiness, and fly away from religion as a mischief. What can be more contrary to its nature, and to God's design in forming it, than for the professors to live such dejected and dolorous lives? God calls men from vexation and vanity, to high delights and peace; and men come to God as from peace and pleasure to vexation. All our preaching will do little to win souls from sensuality to holiness, while they look upon the sad lives of the professors of holiness; as it will more deter a sick man from meddling with a physician, to see all he hath in hand to lie languishing in continual pains to their death, than all his words and promises will encourage them. Oh what blessed lives might God's people live, if they understood the love of God in the mystery of man's redemption, and did addict themselves to the consideration and improvement of it, and did believingly eye the promised glory, and hereupon did make it the business of their lives to delight their souls in him that hath loved them!

DIRECTIONS

TO

PERSONS JUST COMMENCING A RELIGIOUS LIFE.

1. REMEMBER that the commencement of the Christian life is to be like the "dawning light, which increaseth more and more to the perfect day." Therefore when the hope of peace and pardon dawns in the heart, do not consider the great business of life as *accomplished*, but only as *begun*.

2. Do not expect so sudden and remarkable a change, as to leave no doubt of its reality. Did religion enter the soul in perfection, and to the entire exclusion of sin, the change would be so marked and obvious as to leave no room for doubt. But usually the Christian character is full of contrarieties. There is a perpetual struggle between good and evil, and thus a continual competition of evidence for and against, according as the good or evil prevails.

3. Evidence of piety is not so much to be sought in *high emotions* of any kind, as in real humility, self-distrust, hungering and thirsting after righteousness, sorrow for sin, and a *continual effort*, in every-day life, to regulate our thoughts, feelings, and conduct by the word of God. It is the *nature* and not the *degree* of our affections which are to

be regarded in the examination of our evidences Some persons are so *constituted*, that they are not susceptible of very strong emotions, and ought not to expect them, in reference to religion, any more than other subjects that interest the mind. The best way to know our feelings is, to see how they influence the *conduct*. "By their fruit ye shall know them."

4. Do not expect to find in your own case, everything you have heard or read of in the experience of others. For it may be many things we hear and read of, are not correct feelings, and do not afford just grounds of confidence to any one; and if they are *correct* experience, it may be the experience of a *mature* Christian, and not to be expected in the beginning of a religious life. It must be remembered that as no two countenances are formed alike, so no two hearts are fashioned alike, or placed in exactly the same circumstances; and it would be as vain to seek all the varieties of Christian experience in one person, as to seek all the varieties of human features in one face.

5. Do not expect that the evidence desired will all come immediately and at once. It must come *progressively*, as the result of continued effort in obedience to the will of God.

6. Do not suppose that religion is a principle of such self-persevering energy, as that when once implanted in the soul it will continue to thrive and increase without effort. The plant of divine grace can no more thrive without care and diligent and patient cultivation, than can those rare and valued plants, that demand the physical efforts and culture of man.

God will not sustain and bring to maturity the work of grace, without your own voluntary concurrence in the diligent use of means. He will not do it any more than he would cause the harvest to whiten in the field of the sluggard. Indulge, therefore, no such ideas of inability and dependence on God, as shall impair a full sense of perfect obligation to do whatever *can be done* in working out your own salvation. God never assists any but those who make efforts to aid and advance themselves.

7. Entertain no such ideas of the sovereignty of God in the bestowment of his grace, as would awaken any doubt of his affording needful aid, where he sees sincere endeavors to grow in grace. If some Christians are more eminent than others, it is simply because they make *more efforts* to be so, and God aids these efforts. So that all worldly minded and indifferent Christians continue in this state, because they do not choose to make efforts to get out of it. Any person can be an eminent Christian that chooses to be so. Christians are too apt to feel as if eminence in piety was a distinction made by the sovereignty of God, and to suppose that high attainments are not within the reach of all, and that languid and inefficient piety is the result of divine sovereignty rather than negligence and sloth. A more false or more pernicious opinion cannot easily be adopted by Christians. The truth is, that the road to eminence in gifts and graces, and the means of obtaining them are open to all who seek them, and if any do not obtain them, it is owing to their own sloth and inefficiency, and not to any deficiency on the part of God in blessing diligent efforts. It always pleases him to crown with success the hand of the *diligent* instead of the hand of the slothful, not only in temporal but in spiritual things. This thought cannot

be too strongly impressed upon the minds of those who are just commencing a Christian life. To them *peculiarly*, are such promises as these directed: "Ask, and ye shall receive, seek and ye shall find, knock, and it shall be opened unto you. *Every one* that asketh receiveth," etc.

Do not be afraid of indulging in feelings which may seem to be right, from the fear of deception. On the contrary, cherish such feelings, and try to recall them often. Go forward and *do your duty*, and God will save you from deception while thus employed.

8. There is one caution which is peculiarly needful to those who have been greatly interested in the subject of religion, and that is, *to take particular care of the health.*

There is such a mysterious and intimate connection between the mind and the body, that one cannot be wearied or suffer, without affecting the other. When the mind is fatigued or exhausted, it affects the body, and this again reacts on the mind.

Every person ought to be aware, that the more anxiously and intensely the mind is interested on any subject, the greater is the need of *exercise, sleep, and frequent relaxation.* Attention to religion, does not demand that *all* lawful business be suspended, and forbids the neglect of all needful rest and exercise.

9. Do not expect to be made happy by religion, unless you become *eminent Christians.* A *halfway* Christian can neither enjoy the pleasures of the world nor the pleasures of religion; for his conscience will not let him seek the one, and he is too indolent to obtain the other. The Christian may be the happiest man on earth, but he must be

a faithful, active, and devoted Christian. None are disappointed in finding religion a source of unfailing peace and joy, but those who refuse to drink deep of the wells of salvation; unless we except those who from some derangement of the nervous system, or failure of health, do not enjoy the clear and undisturbed exercise of their faculties. A healthy mind in a healthy body, may always be made happy by religion.

10. Do not look at the practice and example of *other* Christians in forming the standard of piety at which you aim. The allowance of this thing, has probably had a more disastrous influence on the church and on the world, than all other causes that could be named. Generally, when persons commence a Christian life, their consciences are susceptible and tender. They are strict and watchful in the performance of duty, and are pained even by a slight neglect. They have been wont to feel that becoming religious implies a *great change;* that "old things must pass away and *all things* become new." But when they begin to look around among their Christian friends, and turn to them for aid, as those who have had experience and have made advances in Christian life, they find that *they* seem to look upon duties and deficiencies in a very different manner. *They* seem to neglect many things which the young Christian has felt to be very important; and to practice many things which he had supposed to be inconsistent with religion. *Then commences the disastrous effect.* The young Christian begins to feel that he need not be more particular than those to whom he has ever looked up with deference and respect. He begins to imagine that he has been rather *too strict* and particular. He begins to

take a retrograde course, and though his conscience and the Bible often check and reprove, yet after a few inefficient struggles, he lowers his standard and walks as others do.

Look into your Bible and see how Christians ought to live. See how the Bible says those who are Christians *must* live, and then if you find your Christian friends living in a *different* way, instead of having cause for feeling that you may do so too; you have only cause to fear that they are deceiving themselves with the belief that they are Christians, when they are not. Remember that the farther your Christian friends depart from the standard of Christian character laid down in the Bible, the less reason have you to hope that they *are* Christians. And do not hesitate on this subject because you find *many* professed Christians, who are indifferent and lax in their practice and example. Remember that Christ has said: "*Many* shall say unto me in that day, Lord, Lord," thus claiming to be his disciples, to whom he will say, "I never knew you." Do not let *professed* Christians tempt you to fall into the society of such unhappy *castaways*.

11. Do not be *periodical* Christians. There are some who profess religion, who never seem to feel any interest on the subject except when every one else does. It is true, there are special seasons of revived religion in the hearts of all Christians, but if it is only at such times that progress is made in divine life, and interest is manifested in the salvation of souls, there is great reason to fear that what is called religion is nothing but sympathy with the feelings of others.

12 Be sure that there exists a *marked differ ence* between your appearance and conduct, and

that of those who are not Christians. Remember that Christ has required this of you, and that even *the world* expects it.

Do not suppose you can recommend religion, by appearing interested in everything that interests those who have no better portion than this world. Remember that your deportment, your conversation: your interest in dress, in company and amusements; the manner in which you perform your religious duties, are all carefully noted and weighed by those around you, who do not love religion; and if they do not see a *marked difference* between you and themselves, they either conclude there is nothing in religion, or else, that you are a hypocrite. The world *expect* that you will be *very* different from them, and *despise* you in their hearts if you are not. If you wish to recommend religion let the world see it acted out according to the beautiful pattern laid down in the Bible, and do not suppose that you can improve this pattern by any addition or subtraction of your own. On one subject there are some who need instruction.

There is a class of Christians who appear taciturn, unsocial and even sad. This appearance is altogether inconsistent with the spirit of religion. Christians ought to appear cheerful and happy; to appear to receive with pleasure and gratitude all the lawful enjoyments bestowed by their heavenly Father. Such a gloomy deportment as has been described, does not do honor to religion, and causes those whom we wish to win to the ways of pleasantness and peace, to feel that religion is a melancholy, unsocial, and forbidding subject.

All professors of religion should endeavor to have such views of God, his love, his providence, his care; and should so live, as to *be* cheerful and happy, and to *appear* so.

On the contrary, there is a class of professed Christians, who indulge in frequent trifling and levity. This is quite as inconsistent and injurious as the former, and if anything it is more so. Let the *Christian* at least, learn to make a distinction between *cheerfulness* and *levity*. Remember we are commanded to avoid *foolish talking and jesting*, and that it is possible to be happy, cheerful, affable, and kind, without any trifling or levity.

13. Remember that your evidence of possessing religion ceases, when anything else has the first place in your thoughts and interests.

Religion should not lessen our love for our friends, or our enjoyment of rational pleasures, but the *desire to please God in all our ways* should be the prevailing feeling of the mind. Our Saviour says, we cannot have two masters; God and his service must be first in our thoughts and affections, or else the world and its pleasures, are first. If then we would find whose servants we are, we must find who has the first place in our thoughts and affections.

14. Never for one day omit to read the Bible with prayer. This is a most important direction. It is of the utmost importance that you should never for once break over this habit. Prayer and the Bible are your anchor and your shield; what will hold you firmly in the path of duty, and protect you from temptation. You had better give up one meal every day, if it is necessary, in order to secure time for this duty. You had better give up anything else. *Nothing is a duty*, if the performance of it will interfere with this duty.

Remember this is the bread of your life, and the water of your salvation; and that you cannot live in health a single day without their strengthening and invigorating influence.

15. Be regulated by a principle of duty in *little things*. This is the way that common Christians are to cause their light to shine. Few Christians can expect to do any *great* things to show their love for the Saviour, but all can "deny themselves, and thus daily take the cross and follow him." Religion should govern the temper and the tongue; should save us from indolence, from vanity, from pride, from foolishness, from levity, from moroseness, from selfishness, and all the little every-day foibles to which we are exposed. Religion should exemplify its gentleness in your kind and affable manners; its purity and propriety, in your conversation; its benevolence in your conduct, and its consistency and heavenly tendency, in all your ways.

It is a most excellent method to go to some sincere and candid friend, and inquire what are your own defects in temper, character, and every-day deportment, and when you have discovered these, make it the object of your prayers and efforts to correct them.

One thing ought to be strictly regulated by principle, and that is the *employment of time*. Always feel that you are doing wrong when your time is passing unprofitably. Have some regularity and method on this subject. Endeavor to ascertain how much time should be devoted to your friends and to relaxation, and to let the remainder be all of it employed in the most useful manner you can devise. Never be satisfied with the manner in which you are spending your time, if you can think of any possible way in which it might be more usefully employed.

Remember that time is the precious talent for which you must account to God, and if you find yourself indulging in listless inactivity, or tempted to engage in employments of no practical use, *remember your account to God. Be in a habit* of inquiring when you commence any employment, " Is there anything I can do, more useful than this?" And do not be satisfied till you have settled the question, that you are doing all the good you can.

16. Attempt by your efforts and example, to raise the standard of piety and activity. If all who are now commencing Christian life, should make this an object, and not fall into temptation which professed Christians so often set before the lambs of the flock, the church would indeed soon rise before the world, " fair as the moon, clear as the sun, and terrible as an army with banners."

Resolve to be an example to those who ought to be an example to you, and take the Bible, and the Bible only, for your guide in forming Christian character.

Be active in promoting all benevolent objects. Make it an object to prepare to lead with propriety in all social devotional duties. At this period, when prayer and effort must unite in hastening the great day of the Lord, let every young Christian learn to guide the devotions of others, as well as to lift up his own private supplication. There is nothing which so much promotes the " brotherly love " required in the Bible, and nothing which so much promotes union of effort and interest, as social prayer, and every one who commences religious life, should aim to be prepared to perform such duties with propriety; and should stimulate others to engage in them.

17 Do not hesitate in the performance of all the *external* duties of a Christian, because you do not find satisfactory evidence that your *feelings* are right.

Religious duty consists of two parts — feeling and action — and because we find great deficiency in one respect, we surely ought not to neglect the whole. It is as unreasonable, as it would be not to attempt to *feel right* till every *external* duty was perfectly performed.

If we are dissatisfied with our evidence, let us go on and *do* everything that a Christian should do, as the most hopeful way to *produce* right *feelings*. We surely cannot hope to bring our hearts right by neglecting our outward duties.

Go forward then, and take a stand as an active Christian, and if your hearts are not right with God, you may be sure you are in less danger in taking this course than in neglecting it.

18. Remember that the principal duty of a Christian, as it respects others, is to excite them to the *immediate performance* of their religious duty.

Jesus Christ has instituted his church in the world, that through their instrumentality the perishing may be saved. There is no Christian but can find some *one* mind at least, over which he can have some influence, and if we can do *anything* to save others from eternal death, nothing should, for a moment, prevent our attempting it.

But to perform our duty faithfully in this respect, requires both discretion, and some knowledge derived from the experience of others. The following hints, therefore, are added as the result of long experience and observation, and as a sort of guide to those who may be anxious to save a soul from death.

Let your *first* object be to persuade your friend to give an earnest and immediate attention to the subject. Serious remarks upon religion, do not produce much effect, unless some *direct object* is had in view. Endeavor to persuade your friends to *commence the daily reading of the Bible with prayer*. Show them that the Holy Spirit operates by means of the truths which we find in the Bible, and which are most forcibly presented to the mind in the solitude and solemnity of closet devotion. The character of the God we are commanded to love, can no more be perceived by a mind that is engrossed by other subjects and turned away from this, than the human eye can perceive the beauties of a picture, when it is not directed toward it. And as it is not only needful in beholding a picture, that light should shine upon it, but that the eye should be turned to it, so in order that the heart may be sanctified by the truth, is as needful that the mind should be turned toward it, as that the Holy Spirit should enlighten by his illuminating influences. Always then, in all your efforts, have this definite end in view, to persuade your friends to spend much time in studying the Bible with prayer.

When this object is secured, then urge the immediate duty of giving the affections of the heart to God. Show them that if they will only love God, they will then feel their guilt in refusing to obey him, and will greatly desire to live for his glory. If they will only love their God and

Saviour, they will feel that they can trust in the merits of his atoning blood. Do not, for a moment, allow them to feel that performing the outward duties of religion, is doing anything to recommend them to God, but is only a *means* of making them feel more deeply their immediate obligation to give the affections of their hearts to him, and of realizing the reasonableness of his holy law which requires it. Speak to them as if you really *felt* that there was no need of any delay, but that they could immediately perform what God requires; and in order to do this, endeavor to have a deep and realizing sense of this truth yourself. If they complain of their inability, or of the difficulty they find in performing their duty, show them that it is because they have so long forgotten and neglected these things, and formed such bad habits, that though it has really become difficult, it is a difficulty they have made for themselves, and which is an addition to their guilt. Show them that whatever the difficulty is, they can overcome it; for God never requires of his creatures what they cannot perform, and his standing, unalterable law is, "Thou shalt love the Lord thy God with all thy heart." Remember always that the more clearly, constantly, and forcibly the truth is presented to any mind that will attend to it, the more hope there is that it will be obeyed.

One caution, however, needs to be added, and that is, that when it becomes apparent that the mind *will not* be brought to attend to the subject; when you find that the efforts become wearisome and unpleasant, always *cease for a while*, and wait for another time, or else you will do more harm than good. Persevering after this, will only affect their minds with disgust and aversion toward a subject to which they have resolved they will not attend.

Another caution is also important. Always *speak kindly and affectionately* to friends upon this subject, and if you find all your efforts vain, though you cease to urge neglected duty, still continue to express the same kindness and interest for them. Do not give them occasion to feel that because they will not take your advice, you have cast them off as reprobates, and no longer desire their society. We may still continue to love the amiable natural traits of our friends, even though we find that they refuse to have them crowned and beautified by religion. Let all your efforts for the good of others be accompanied by earnest and constant prayer.

Lastly, do not be discouraged because you find that you are *very deficient in every one of the particulars specified.*

Remember that Christian life is a *warfare*, and that it is only at the *end* that we are to come off conquerors and more than conquerors. Remember that He whom you are striving to serve and please, is not a hard master. Though you have been inexcusable in forming such inveterate habits of sin, and all the difficulties you find are of your own making, yet he can be "touched with the feeling of your infirmities." When He sees that you really are afflicted because you so constantly abuse and forget him, he pities you as a father pitieth his children; and so long as you use the means he has appointed to keep you from sin, and wait upon him for strength and guidance, he will never leave nor forsake you. When you feel your own strength and resolution failing, go to him who hath said, "my grace is sufficient for thee, and my strength shall be made perfect in weakness." Call upon him, "and he will be very gracious unto the voice of thy cry; when he shall hear it, he will answer thee. And thine ears shall hear a word behind thee, saying, this is the way, walk ye therein, when ye turn to the right and when ye turn to the left." Remember, also, that the conflict is short; the race will speedily be accomplished—soon your deficiencies and guilt shall pain you no more—soon you shall "see him as he is," and "awake in his likeness and be satisfied therewith."

RESOLUTIONS OF REV. JONATHAN EDWARDS, D. D.

BEING sensible that I am unable to do anything without God's help, I do humbly entreat him by his grace to enable me to keep these resolutions, so far as they are agreeable to his will, for Christ's sake.

REMEMBER TO READ OVER THESE RESOLUTIONS ONCE A WEEK.

1st. That I will do whatsoever I think to be most to God's glory, and my own good, profit, and pleasure, in the whole of my duration, without any consideration of the time, whether now or never so many myriads of ages hence. Resolved to do whatever I think to be my duty, and most for the good advantage of mankind in general. Resolved to do this, whatever difficulties I meet with, how many and how great soever. 2d. To be continually endeavoring to find out some new invention and contrivance to promote the fore-mentioned things. 3d. Never to do any manner of thing, whether in soul or body, less or more, but what tends to the glory of God; nor be, nor suffer it, if I can avoid it. 4th. Never to lose one moment of time; but improve it the most profitable way I possibly can. 5th. To live with all my might, while I do live. 6th. Never to do anything which I should be afraid to do, if it were the last hour of my life. 7th. To think much on all occasions, of my own dying, and of the common circumstances which attend death. 8th. When I think of any theorem in divinity to be solved, immediately to do what I can toward solving it, if circumstances do not hinder. 9th. To be endeavoring to find out fit objects of charity and liberality.

10th. Never to do anything out of revenge. 11th. Never to suffer the least motions of anger to irrational beings. 12th. That I will live so as I shall wish I had done when I come to die. 13th. To live so at all times, as I think is best in my devout frames, and when I have clearest notions of things of the Gospel, and another world. 14th. To maintain the strictest temperance in eating and drinking. 15th. Never to do anything, which, if I should see in another, I should count a just occasion to despise him for, or to think any way the more meanly of him. 16th. Whenever I can do any conspicuously evil action, to trace it back, till I come to the original cause; and then both carefully endeavor to do so no more, and to fight and pray with all my might against the original of it. 17th. To study the Scriptures so steadily, constantly, and frequently, as that I may find, and plainly perceive myself to grow in the knowledge of the same. 18th. To strive to my utmost every week to be brought higher in religion, and to a higher exercise of grace, than I was the week before. 19th. To be strictly and firmly faithful to my trust, that that in Prov. xx, 6, *a faithful man who can find?* may not be partly fulfilled in me.

20th. Always to do what I can toward making, maintaining, and establishing peace, when it can be without over-balancing detriment in other respects. 21st. In narrations never to speak anything but the pure and simple verity. 22d. Never to speak evil of any, except I have some particular good call for it. 23d. To inquire every night, as I am going to bed, wherein I have been negligent, what sin I have committed, and wherein I have denied myself; also at the end of every week, month, and year. 24th. Never to speak anything that is ridiculous, or matter of laughter on the Lord's day. 25th. Never to do anything that I so much question the lawfulness of, as that I intend, at the same time, to consider and examine afterward, whether it be lawful or no: except I as much question the lawfulness of the omission. 26th. To ask myself at the end of every day, week, month, and year, wherein I could possibly in any respect have done better. 27th. Frequently to renew the dedication of myself to God, which was made at my baptism; which I solemnly renewed when I was received into the communion of the Church; and which I have solemnly re-made this 12th day of January, 1722-3. 28th. Never henceforward, till I die, to act as if I were any way my own, but entirely and altogether God's; agreeable to what is to be found in Saturday, January 12. 29th. Never to allow the least measure of any fretting uneasiness at my father or mother. Resolved to suffer no effects of it, so much as in the least alteration of speech, or motion of my eye: and to be especially careful of it, with respect to any of our family.

30th. Constantly, with the utmost niceness and diligence, and the strictest scrutiny, to be looking into the state of my soul, that I may know whether I have truly an interest in Christ or no; that when I come to die, I may not have any negligence respecting this to repent of. 31st. I will act so as I think I shall judge would have been best and most prudent, when I come into the future world. 32d. I frequently hear persons in old age say how they would live, if they were to live their lives over again: Resolved, that I will live just so as I can think I shall wish I had done, supposing I live to old age. 33d. Whenever I hear anything spoken in conversation of any person, if I think it would be praiseworthy in me, Resolved to endeavor to imitate it. 34th. To endeavor to my utmost, to act as I can think I should do, if I had already seen the happiness of heaven, and hell torments. 35th. Never to give over, nor in the least to slacken my fight with my corruptions, however unsuccessful I may be. 36th. When I fear misfortunes and adversities, to examine whether I have done my duty, and resolve to do it; and let it be just as Providence orders it, I will, as far as I can, be concerned about nothing but my duty, and my sin. 37th. Never to do anything but duty; and then, according to Eph. vi, 6, 7, 8, do it willingly and cheerfully, as unto the Lord, and not to man; knowing that whatever good thing any man doth, the same shall he receive of the Lord. 38th. Very much to exercise myself in this all my life long, viz: with the greatest openness I am capable of, to declare my ways to God, and lay open my soul to him: all my sins, temptations, difficulties, sorrows, fears, hopes, desires, and everything, and every circumstance, according to Dr. Manton's 27th sermon on the 119th Psalm. 39th. After afflictions, to inquire, what I am the better for them, what good I have got by them, and what I might have got by them.

www.ingramcontent.com/pod-product-compliance
Lightning Source LLC
Chambersburg PA
CBHW030601300426
44111CB00009B/1064